enVision™ Algebra 2
Student Companion

Pearson
Boston, Massachusetts

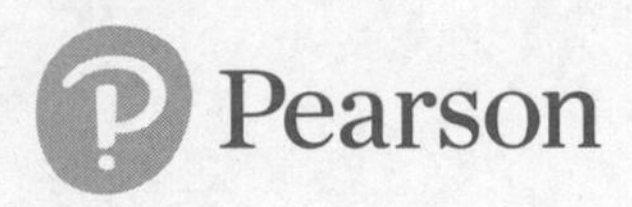

ISBN-13: 978-0-328-9
ISBN-10: 0-328-9

Contents

enVision™ Algebra 2

About the Authors

Authors

Dan Kennedy, Ph.D

- Classroom teacher and the Lupton Distinguished Professor of Mathematics at the Baylor School in Chattanooga, TN
- Co-author of textbooks *Precalculus: Graphical, Numerical, Algebraic* and *Calculus: Graphical, Numerical, Algebraic, AP Edition*
- Past chair of the College Board's AP Calculus Development Committee.
- Previous Tandy Technology Scholar and Presidential Award winner

Eric Milou, Ed.D

- Professor of Mathematics, Rowan University, Glassboro, NJ
- Member of the author team for Pearson's **enVision**math**2.0** 6-8
- Member of National Council of Teachers of Mathematics (NCTM) feedback/advisory team for the Common Core State Standards
- Author of *Teaching Mathematics to Middle School Students*

Christine D. Thomas, Ph.D

- Professor of Mathematics Education at Georgia State University, Atlanta, GA
- Past-President of the Association of Mathematics Teacher Educators (AMTE)
- Past NCTM Board of Directors Member
- Past member of the editorial panel of the NCTM journal *Mathematics Teacher*
- Past co-chair of the steering committee of the North American chapter of the International Group of the Psychology of Mathematics Education

Rose Mary Zbiek, Ph.D

- Professor of Mathematics Education, Pennsylvania State University, College Park, PA
- Series editor for the NCTM *Essential Understanding* project

Contributing Author

Al Cuoco, Ph.D

- Lead author of CME Project, a National Science Foundation (NSF)-funded high school curriculum
- Team member to revise the Conference Board of the Mathematical Sciences (CBMS) recommendations for teacher preparation and professional development
- Co-author of several books published by the Mathematical Association of America and the American Mathematical Society
- Consultant to the writers of the Common Core State Standards for Mathematics and the PARCC Content Frameworks for high school mathematics

EXPLORE & REASON

A diver is doing ocean search-and-rescue training. The graph shows the relationship between her depth and the time in seconds since starting her dive.

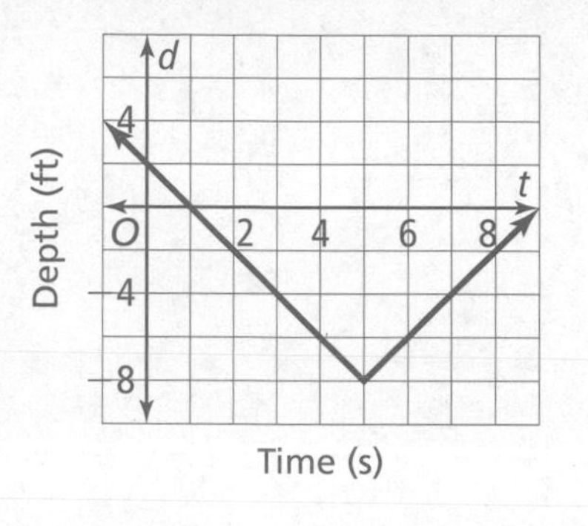

A. Which point on the graph shows the starting location of the diver? Explain.

B. What details can you determine about the dive from the coordinates of the point (5, −8)?

C. What is the average speed of the diver's descent? How can you tell from the graph?

D. Communicate Precisely What does the V-shape of the graph tell you about the dive? What information does it not tell you about the dive?

HABITS OF MIND

Reason What do the points where the graph intersects the *x*-axis tell you about the dive?

Notes

Assess

EXAMPLE 1

Try It! Understand Domain and Range

1. What are the domain and range of each function? Write the domain and range in set-builder notation and interval notation.

   a. $y = |x - 4|$

   b. $y = 6x - 2x^2$

EXAMPLE 2

Try It! Find x- and y-intercepts

2. What are the x- and y-intercepts of $g(x) = 4 - x^2$?

HABITS OF MIND

Make Sense and Persevere A function does not have any x-intercepts. What might be true about its domain and range?

EXAMPLE 3

Try It! Identify Positive or Negative Intervals

3. a. For what interval(s) is the function $h(x) = 2x + 10$ positive?

   b. For what interval(s) is the function negative?

Notes

Assess

EXAMPLE 4

Try It! Identify Where a Function Increases or Decreases

4. For what values of x is each function increasing? For what values of x is each function decreasing?

   a. $f(x) = x^2 - 4x$

   b. $f(x) = -2x - 3$

HABITS OF MIND

Use Structure Can a function be increasing and negative on the same interval? Explain.

EXAMPLE 5

Try It! Understand Average Rate of Change Over an Interval

5. What do the average rates of change of the function $y = |x| + 2$ over the intervals $[-2, 0]$, $[0, 3]$, and $[-2, 3]$ indicate about the function?

HABITS OF MIND

Construct Arguments If a function has a positive average rate of change over an interval, does that mean that the function must be increasing over that interval? Explain.

Do You UNDERSTAND?

1. **ESSENTIAL QUESTION** How do graphs and equations reveal information about a relationship between two quantities?

2. **Vocabulary** Define the term *zero of a function* in your own words.

3. **Error Analysis** Lonzell said the function shown in the graph is positive on the interval (–1, 5) and negative on the interval (–5, –1).

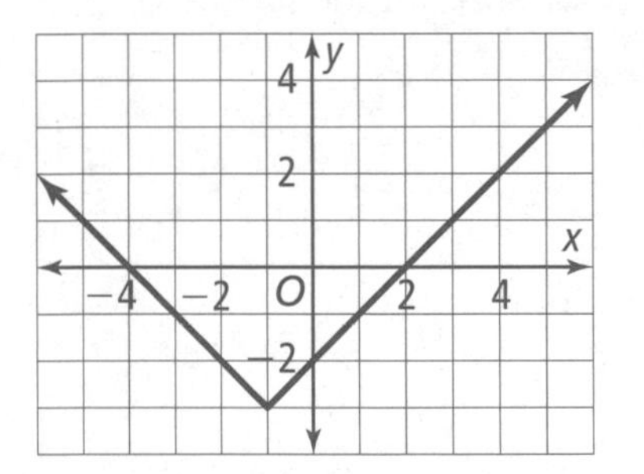

Identify and correct Lonzell's error.

Do You KNOW HOW?

Find each key feature.

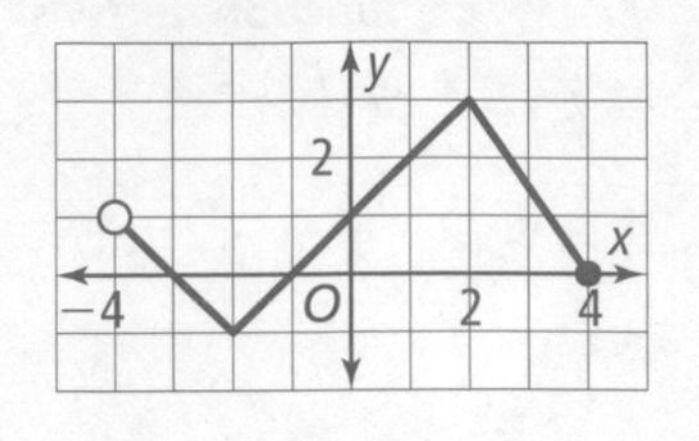

4. domain

5. range

6. *x*-intercept(s)

7. *y*-intercept(s)

8. interval(s) where the graph is positive

9. interval(s) where the graph is decreasing

10. interval(s) where the graph is increasing

11. rate of change on [–1, 4]

Activity

1-2 Transformations of Functions

PearsonRealize.com

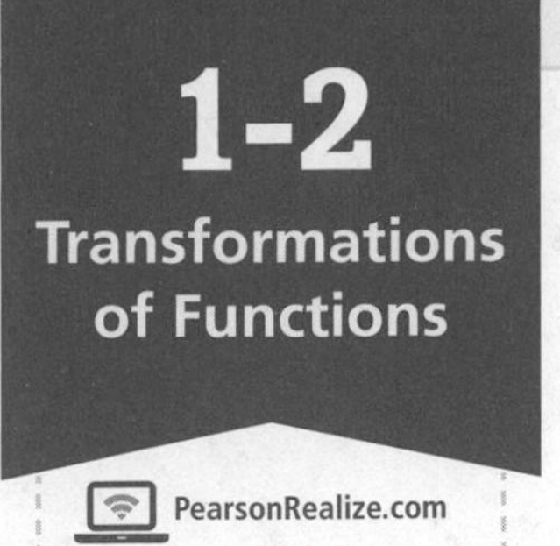

EXPLORE & REASON

The graph of the function $f(x) = |x|$ is shown.

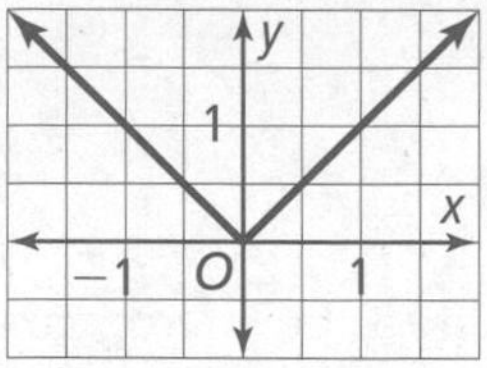

A. Graph the function $g(x) = |x + c|$ for each of several different values of c between −5 and 5.

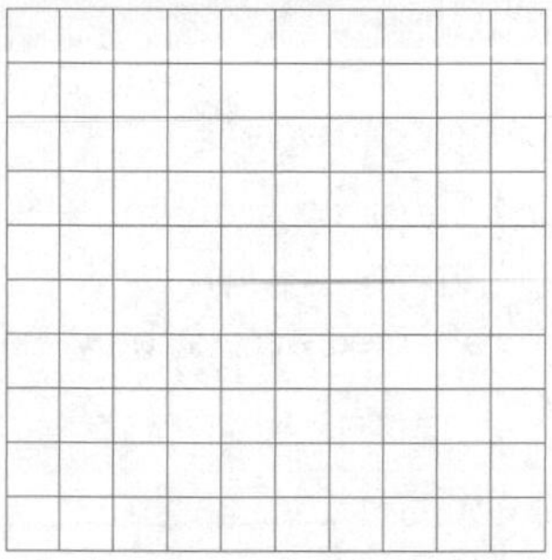

B. **Look for Relationships** Predict what will happen to the graph if c is a number greater than 100. What if c is a number between 0 and $\frac{1}{2}$?

HABITS OF MIND

Reason What happens to the graph if c is a negative number?

Notes

Assess

EXAMPLE 1

Try It! Translate a Function

1. a. How did the transformation of f to g in part (a) affect the intercepts?

   b. How did the transformation of f to g in part (b) affect the intercepts?

EXAMPLE 2

Try It! Reflect a Function Across the x- or y-Axis

2. What is an equation for the reflected graph? Check by graphing.

   a. the graph of $f(x) = x^2 - 2$ reflected across the x-axis.

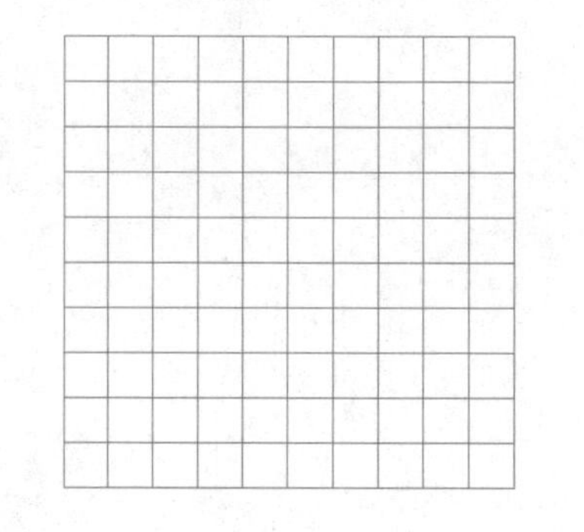

   b. the graph of $f(x) = x^2 - 2$ reflected across the y-axis.

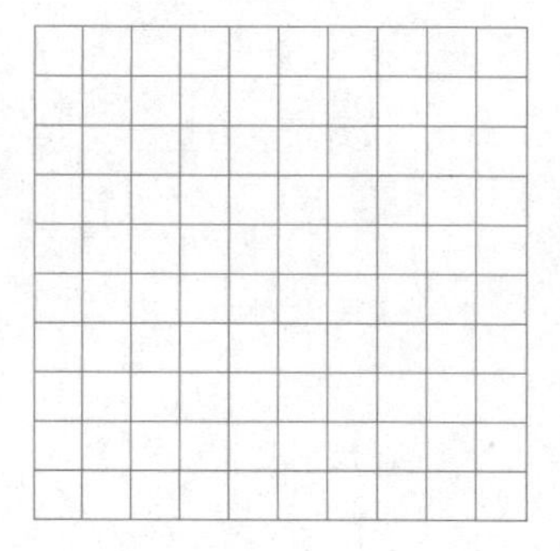

HABITS OF MIND

Look for Relationships How are the intercepts of a graph affected by reflection across the x-axis? Explain.

EXAMPLE 3

Try It! Understand Stretches and Compressions

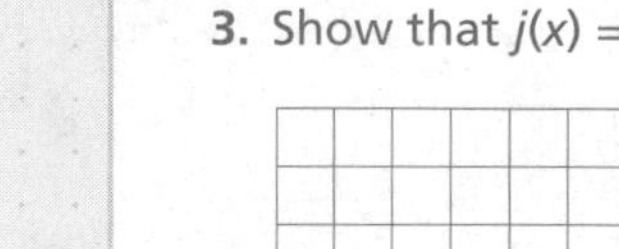

3. Show that $j(x) = f\left(\frac{1}{2}x\right)$ is a horizontal stretch of the graph of f.

Assess

EXAMPLE 4

Try It! Graph a Combination of Transformations

4. Using the graph of f in Example 4, graph each equation.

   a. $y = f(2x) - 4$

   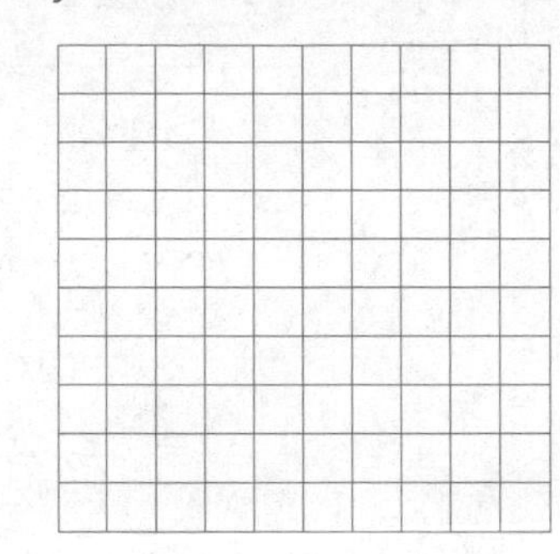

   b. $y = f(2x - 3) - 2$

   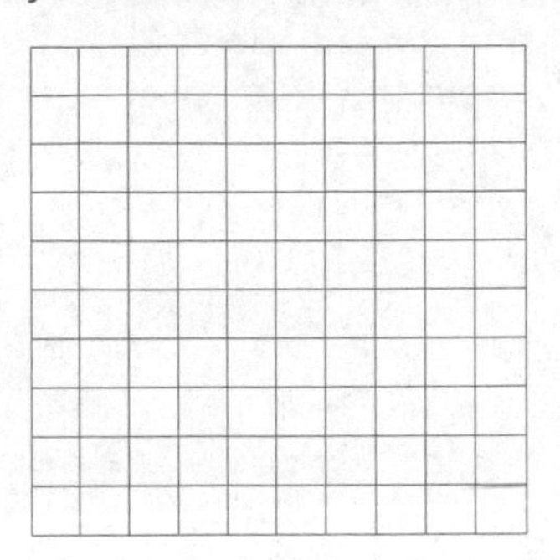

HABITS OF MIND

Model With Mathematics If the graph of a parent function is vertically stretched by a factor of 2 and then translated 3 units down, would you get the same graph if you translated the parent graph 3 units down first and then vertically stretched it by a factor of 2? Explain.

EXAMPLE 5

Try It! Identify Transformations From an Equation

5. What transformations of the graph of $f(x) = |x|$ are applied to graph the function g?

   a. $g(x) = \frac{1}{2}|x + 3|$

   b. $g(x) = -|x| + 2$

EXAMPLE 6

Try It! Write an Equation From a Graph

6. How would the graph and equation be affected if the train traveled twice as far in the same amount of time?

HABITS OF MIND

Make Sense and Persevere The function $f(x) = |x|$ is translated 3 units right and 2 units down, and then stretched by a factor of 4. What is an equation for the transformed function g?

Do You UNDERSTAND?

1. ESSENTIAL QUESTION What do the differences between the equation of a function and the equation of its parent function tell you about the differences in the graphs of the two functions?

2. **Reason** Do k and h affect the input or output for $g(x) = f(x) + k$ and $g(x) = f(x - h)$? Explain.

3. **Error Analysis** Margo is comparing the functions $f(x) = |x|$ and $g(x) = |x + 1| - 5$. She said the graph of g is a vertical translation of the graph of f 5 units down and a horizontal translation of the graph of f 1 unit right. What is Margo's error?

Do You KNOW HOW?

Graph each function and its parent function.

4. $g(x) = |x| - 1$

5. $g(x) = (x - 3)^2$

6. $g(x) = -|x|$

7. $g(x) = -x$

8. $g(x) = x^2 - 2$

9. $g(x) = \frac{1}{2}|x|$

10. $g(x) = 4x$

11. $g(x) = |5x|$

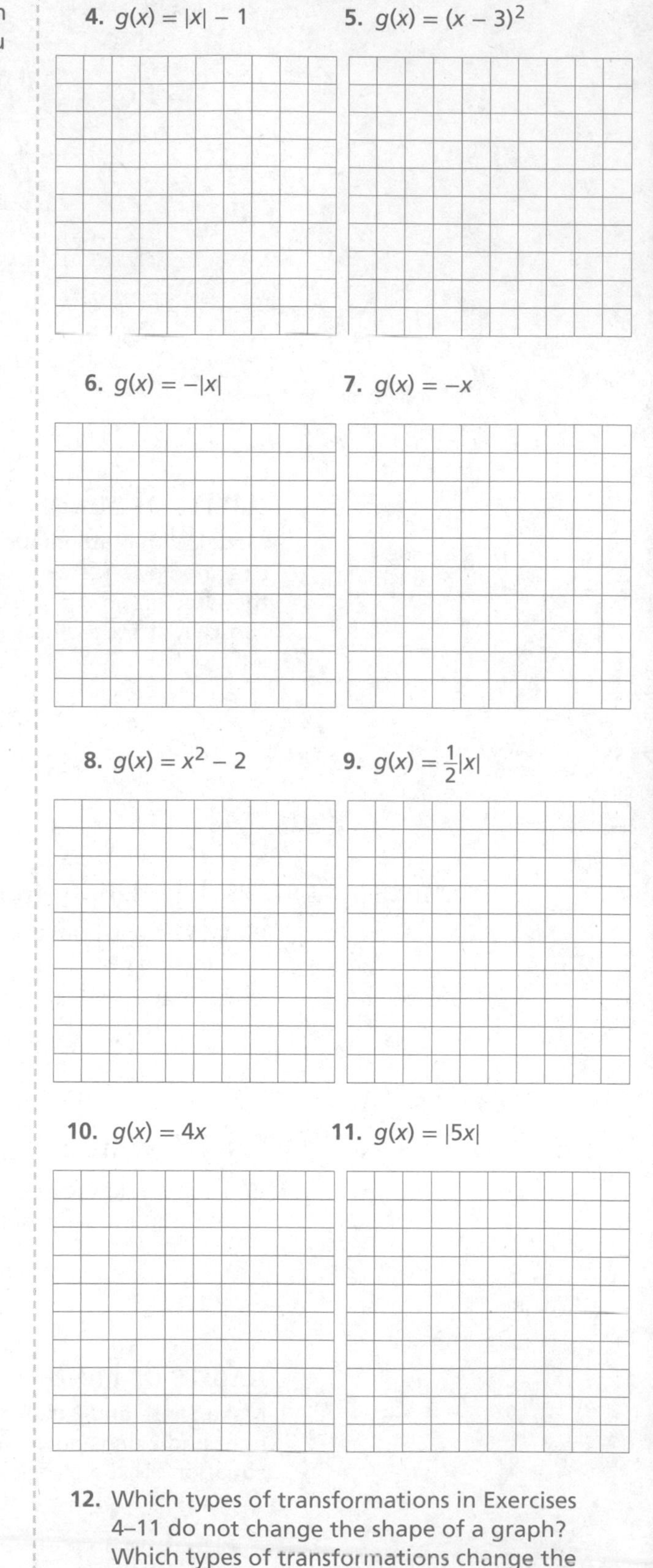

12. Which types of transformations in Exercises 4–11 do not change the shape of a graph? Which types of transformations change the shape of a graph? Explain.

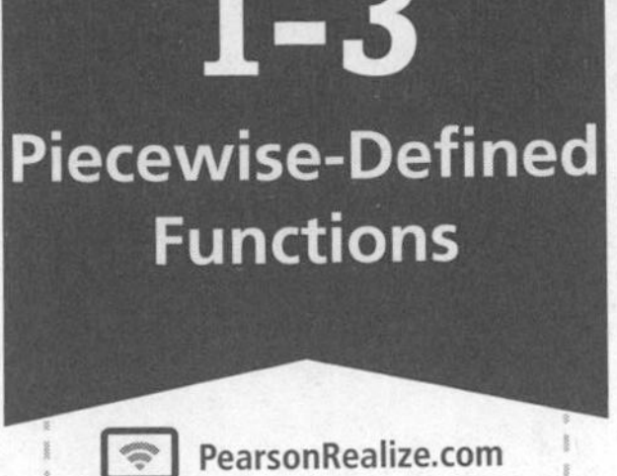

MODEL & DISCUSS

A music teacher needs to buy guitar strings for her class. At store A, the guitar strings cost $6 each. At store B, the guitar strings are $20 for a pack of 4.

A. Make graphs that show the income each store receives if the teacher needs 1–20 guitar strings.

B. Describe the shape of the graph for store A. Describe the shape of the graph for store B. Why are the graphs different?

C. Communicate Precisely Compare the graphs for stores A and B. For what numbers of guitar strings is it cheaper to buy from store B? Explain how you know.

HABITS OF MIND

Communicate Precisely Why do you use dots rather than line segments to graph these two functions?

Assess

EXAMPLE 1

Try It! Model With a Piecewise-Defined Function

1. How much will Alani earn if she works:

   a. 37 hours?

   b. 43 hours?

EXAMPLE 2

Try It! Graph a Piecewise-Defined Function

2. Graph the piecewise-defined function. What are the domain and range? Over what intervals is the function increasing or decreasing?

   a. $f(x) = \begin{cases} 2x + 5, & -6 \le x \le -2 \\ 2x^2 - 7, & -2 < x < 1 \\ -4 - x, & 1 \le x \le 3 \end{cases}$

   b. $f(x) = \begin{cases} 3, & -4 < x \le 0 \\ -x, & 0 \le x \le 2 \\ 3 - x, & 2 < x < 4 \end{cases}$

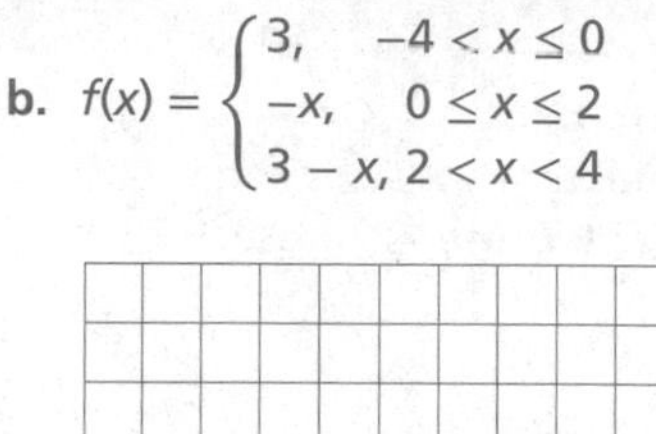

HABITS OF MIND

Reason Why is the interval for the domain of the second piece of the function in Try It! 2(a) defined using the < symbol rather than the ≤ symbol?

EXAMPLE 3

Try It! Write a Piecewise-Defined Rule From a Graph

3. What rule defines the function in each of the following graphs?

   a.

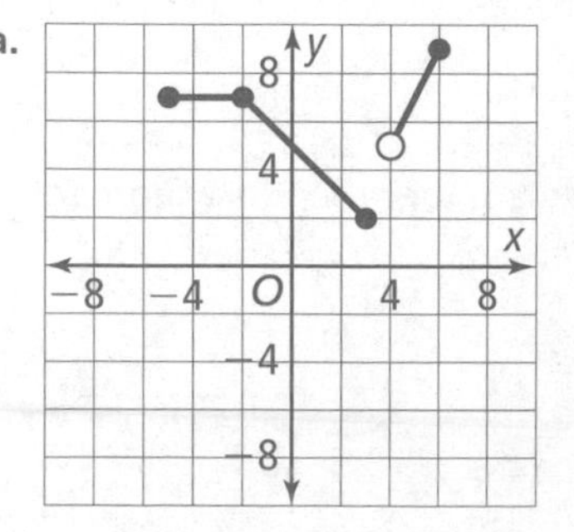

   b.

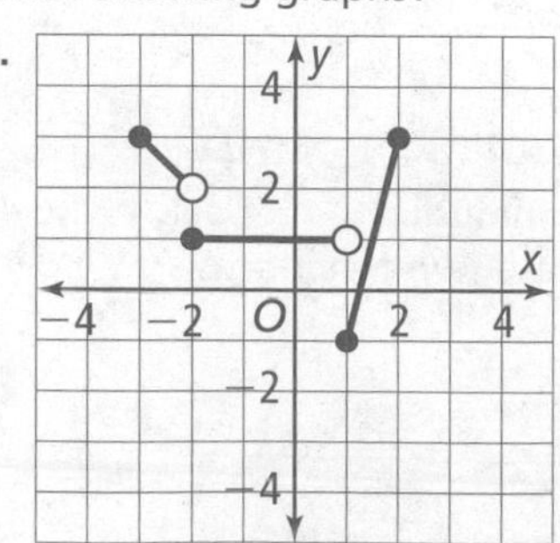

Notes

Assess

EXAMPLE 4

Try It! Write a Rule for an Absolute Value Function

4. How can you rewrite each function as a piecewise-defined function?

a. $f(x) = |-5x - 10|$

b. $f(x) = -|x| + 3$

HABITS OF MIND

Use Structure Why can the graph of an absolute value function also be defined as a piecewise-defined function?

EXAMPLE 5

Try It! Graph a Step Function

5. The table below represents fees for a parking lot. Graph the function. What are the domain and range of the function? What are the maximum and minimum values?

Time	$0 < t \leq 3$h	$3 < t \leq 6$h	$6 < t \leq 9$h	$9 < t \leq 12$h
Cost	\$10	\$15	\$20	\$25

HABITS OF MIND

Make Sense and Persevere How would a piecewise-defined rule for the function in the Try It! show that the graph is a step function?

Do You UNDERSTAND?

1. ESSENTIAL QUESTION How do you model a situation in which a function behaves differently over different parts of its domain?

2. **Vocabulary** How do piecewise-defined functions differ from step functions?

3. **Error Analysis** Given the function

$$f(x) = \begin{cases} 2x + 5, & -2 < x \leq 4 \\ -4x - 7, & 4 < x \leq 9 \end{cases},$$

Rebecca says there is an open circle at $x = 4$ for both pieces of the function. Explain her error.

4. **Communicate Precisely** What steps do you follow when graphing a piecewise-defined function?

5. **Make Sense and Persevere** Is the relation defined by the following piecewise rule a function? Explain.

$$y = \begin{cases} 7x - 4, & x < 2 \\ -x + 5, & x \geq -2 \end{cases}$$

Do You KNOW HOW?

Graph the function.

6. $f(x) = \begin{cases} -x + 1, & -10 \leq x < -3 \\ x^2 - 9, & -3 \leq x \leq 3 \\ 2x + 1, & 3 < x < 5 \end{cases}$

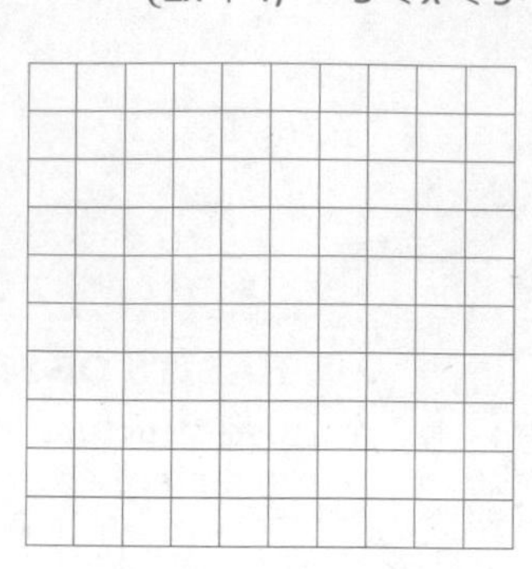

7. $g(x) = \begin{cases} 1, & 0 \leq x < 2 \\ 3, & 2 \leq x < 4 \\ 5, & 4 \leq x < 6 \\ 7, & 6 \leq x < 8 \end{cases}$

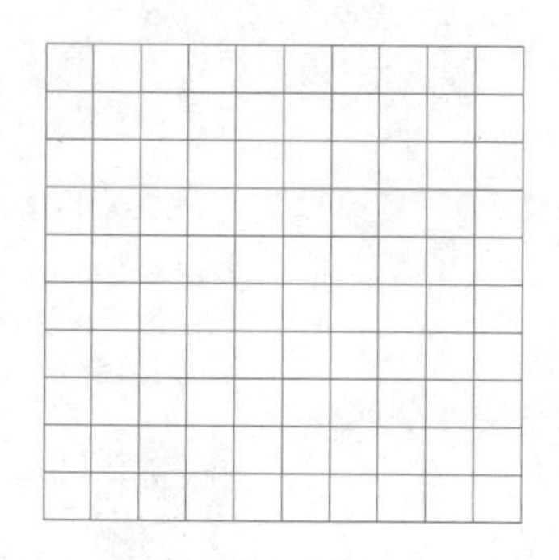

8. Given the function

$$f(x) = \begin{cases} -2x + 4, & 0 \leq x < 8 \\ -5x + 11, & x \geq 8 \end{cases}$$

is the function increasing or decreasing over the interval [2, 7]? Find the rate of change over this interval.

9. What is the rule that defines the function shown in the graph?

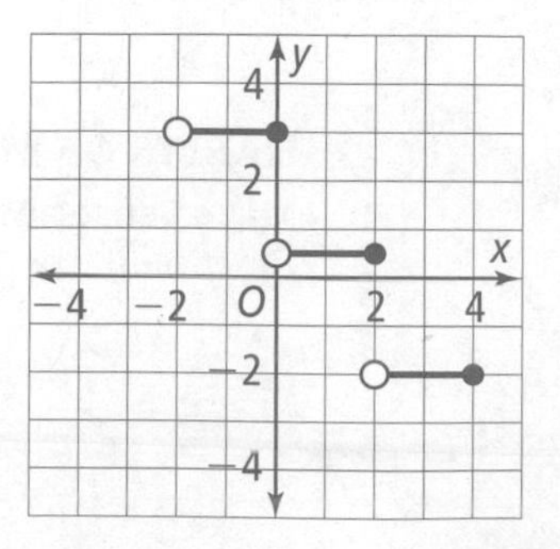

Activity

1-4 Arithmetic Sequences and Series

PearsonRealize.com

CRITIQUE & EXPLAIN

Yumiko and Hugo are looking at the table of data.

Yumiko writes

$f(1) = 1 + 4 = 5,$
$f(2) = f(1) + 4 = 5 + 4 = 9,$
$f(3) = f(2) + 4 = 9 + 4 = 13,$
$f(4) = f(3) + 4 = 13 + 4 = 17.$

Hugo writes $g(x) = 1 + 4x$.

Input	Output
0	1
1	5
2	9
3	13
4	17

A. Describe the pattern Yumiko found for finding an output value.

B. Describe the pattern Hugo found for finding an output value.

C. **Use Structure** Compare the two methods. Which method would be more useful in finding the 100th number in the list? Why?

HABITS OF MIND

Use Structure Find the average rate of change between a few pairs of points. What can you conclude about the function represented in the table?

Assess

EXAMPLE 1

Try It! Understand Arithmetic Sequences

1. Are the following sequences arithmetic? If so, what is the recursive definition, and what is the next term in the sequence?
   a. 25, 20, 15, 10, . . .

   b. 2, 4, 7, 12, 13, . . .

EXAMPLE 2

Try It! Translate Between Recursive and Explicit Forms

2. a. For the recursive definition $a_n = \begin{cases} 45, & n = 1 \\ a_{n-1} - 2, & n > 1 \end{cases}$, what is the explicit definition?

   b. For the explicit definition $a_n = 1 + 7(n - 1)$, what is the recursive definition?

EXAMPLE 3

Try It! Solve Problems With Arithmetic Sequences

3. Samantha is training for a race. The distances of her training runs form an arithmetic sequence. She runs 1 mi the first day and 2 mi the seventh day.
   a. What is the explicit definition for this sequence?

   b. How far does she run on day 19?

HABITS OF MIND

Use Appropriate Tools How can you use the recursive definition for an arithmetic sequence to find the 120th term?

Notes

Assess

EXAMPLE 4

Try It! Find the Sum of an Arithmetic Series

4. Find the sum of each arithmetic series.

a. series with 12 terms, $a_1 = 3$ and $a_{12} = 25$

b. $5 + 11 + 17 + 23 + 29 + 35 + 41$

EXAMPLE 5

Try It! Use Sigma Notation

5. a. What is the sum of the series $\sum_{i=1}^{13} 3i + 2$?

b. How can you write the series $8 + 13 + 18 + \ldots + 43$ using sigma notation? What is the sum?

EXAMPLE 6

Try It! Use a Finite Arithmetic Series

6. A flight of stairs gets wider as it descends. The top stair is 15 bricks across, the second stair is 17 bricks across, and the third stair is 19 bricks across. What is the total number of bricks used in all 16 stairs?

HABITS OF MIND

Make Sense and Persevere What is the sum of the first 50 odd whole numbers? Explain how you found your answer.

Do You UNDERSTAND?

1. ESSENTIAL QUESTION What is an arithmetic sequence, and how do you represent and find its terms and their sums?

2. **Vocabulary** How do arithmetic sequences differ from arithmetic series?

3. **Error Analysis** A student claims the sequence 0, 1, 3, 6, . . . is an arithmetic sequence, and the next number is 10. What error did the student make?

4. **Communicate Precisely** How would you tell someone how to calculate $\sum_{n=1}^{5}(2n+1)$?

Do You KNOW HOW?

Find the common difference and the next three terms of each arithmetic sequence.

5. $\frac{1}{4}, \frac{1}{2}, \frac{3}{4}, 1, \frac{5}{4}, \ldots$

6. 6, 1, −4, −9, −14, . . .

7. 215, 227, 239, 251, . . .

8. −4, −5, −6, −7, . . .

9. 4.1, 6.3, 8.5, 10.7, . . .

10. −17, −9, −1, 7, 15, . . .

11. In June, you start a holiday savings account with a deposit of $30. You increase each monthly deposit by $4 until the end of the year. How much money will you have saved by the end of December?

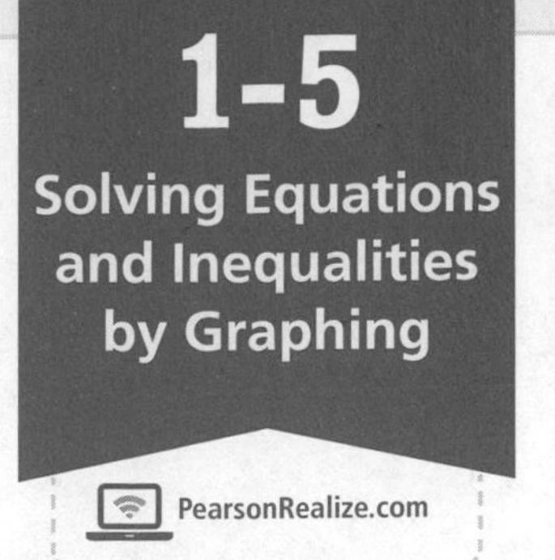

MODEL & DISCUSS

A homeowner has 32 feet of fencing to build three sides of a rectangular chicken run.

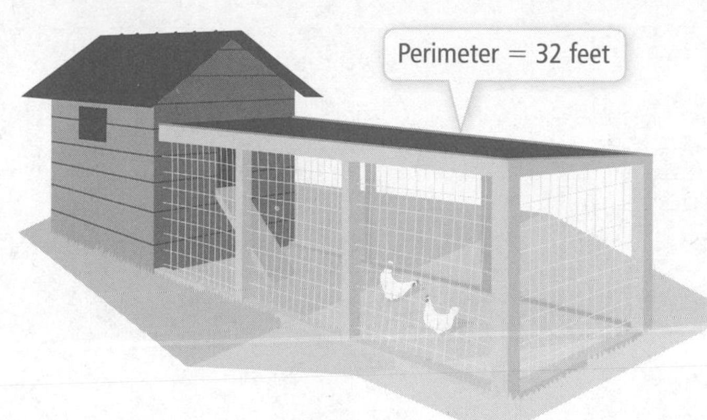

A. Make a table of values for the length, width, and area of different rectangles that will utilize 32 feet of fencing. Then write a function for the area, in terms of width, of a rectangular run using this much fencing.

B. Graph your function.

C. Reason Explain what happens where the graph intersects the *x*-axis.

HABITS OF MIND

Make Sense and Persevere For what widths will the area of the chicken run be at least 55 ft^2?

Notes

Assess

EXAMPLE 1 **Try It! Use a Graph to Solve an Equation**

1. Use a graph to solve the equation.

a. $5x - 12 = 3$

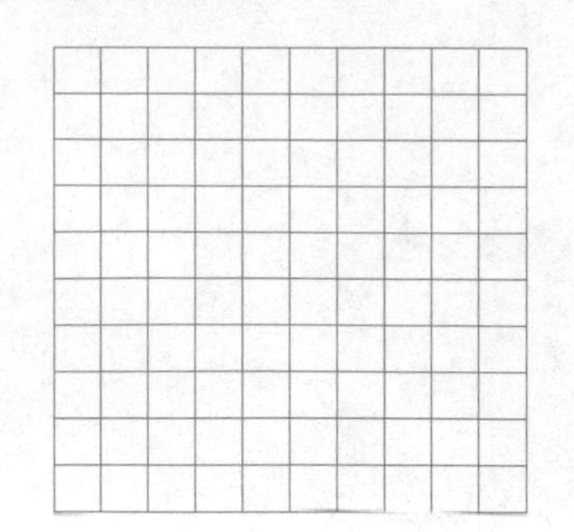

b. $-|x - 2| = -\frac{1}{2}x - 2$

EXAMPLE 2 **Try It! Solve a One-Variable Inequality by Graphing**

2. Use a graph to solve each inequality.

a. $x^2 + 6x + 5 \geq 0$

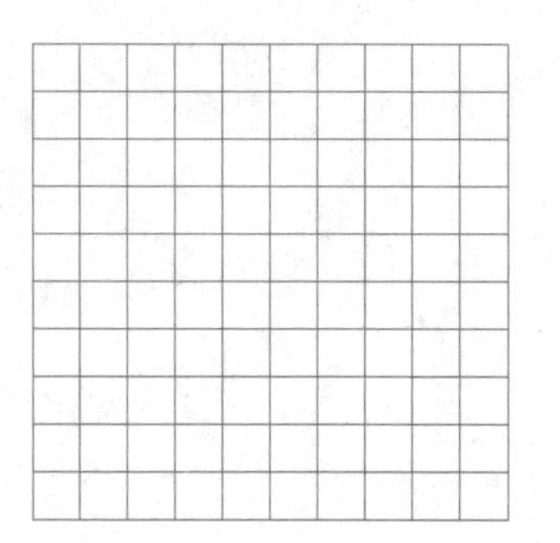

b. $x + 3 > 7 - 3x$

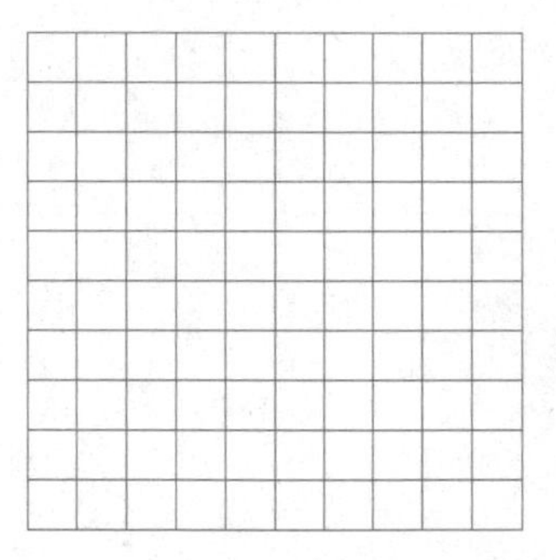

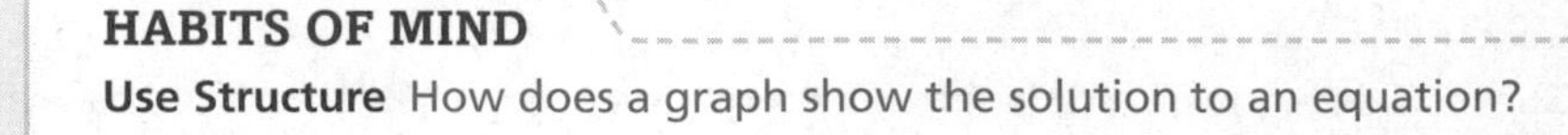

HABITS OF MIND

Use Structure How does a graph show the solution to an equation?

Notes

Assess

EXAMPLE 3

Try It! Use a Table to Solve an Equation

3. The equation $x^2 - 4x + 1 = x - 2$ has a second solution in the interval $4 < x < 5$. Use a spreadsheet to approximate this solution to the nearest thousandth.

EXAMPLE 4

Try It! Use Graphing Technology to Solve Equations

4. Use graphing technology to approximate the solutions of the equation $x^2 + 2x - 1 = |x + 2| + 2$ to the nearest tenth.

HABITS OF MIND

Use Appropriate Tools What are the advantages and disadvantages of using spreadsheets and graphing technology?

Do You UNDERSTAND?

1. ESSENTIAL QUESTION How can you solve an equation or inequality by graphing?

2. **Communicate Precisely** What is an advantage of solving an equation graphically by finding the points of intersection?

3. **Error Analysis** Ben said the graph of the inequality $-x^2 + 9 > 0$ shows the solution is $x < -3$ or $x > 3$. Is Ben correct? Explain.

Do You KNOW HOW?

4. Using the graph below, what is the solution to $-2x + 4 = -2$? How can you tell?

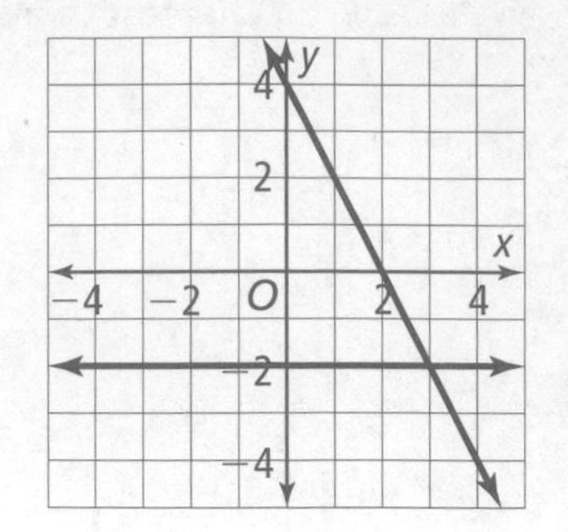

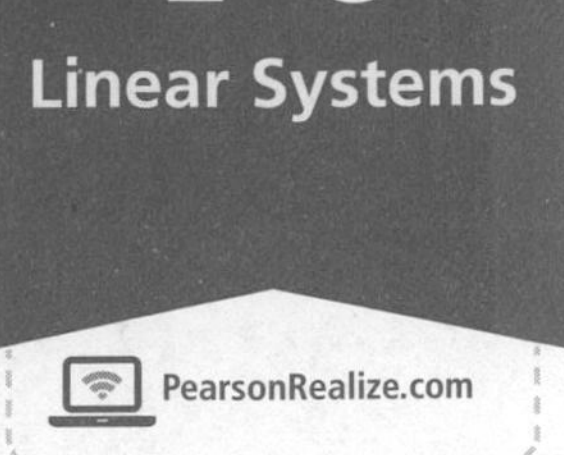

EXPLORE & REASON

The graph shows two lines that intersect at one point.

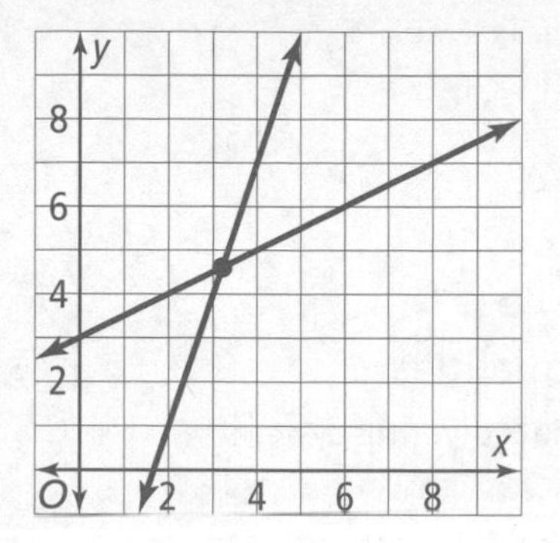

A. What are the approximate coordinates of the point of intersection?

B. How could you verify whether the coordinates you estimated are, in fact, the solution? Is the point the solution to the equations of both lines?

C. Make Sense and Persevere Use your result to refine your approximation, and try again. Can you find the point of intersection this way? Is there a more efficient way?

HABITS OF MIND

Communicate Precisely The graphs of two equations appear to intersect at the point (2, 3). Does that guarantee that $x = 2$ and $y = 3$ is a solution to both equations? Explain.

Notes

Assess

EXAMPLE 1

Try It! Solve a System of Linear Equations

1. Solve each system of equations.

a. $\begin{cases} 2x + y = -1 \\ 5y - 6x = 7 \end{cases}$

b. $\begin{cases} 3x + 2y = 5 \\ 6x + 4y = 3 \end{cases}$

EXAMPLE 2

Try It! Solve a System of Linear Inequalities

2. Sketch the graph of the set of all points that solve this system of linear inequalities.

$$\begin{cases} 2x + y \leq 14 \\ x + 2y \leq 10 \\ x \geq 0 \\ y \geq 0 \end{cases}$$

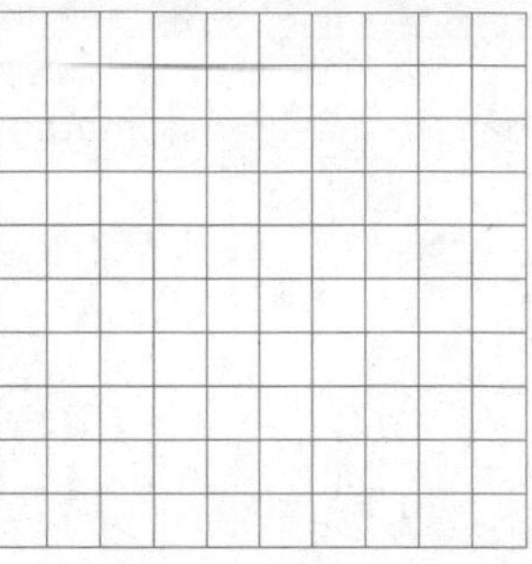

HABITS OF MIND

Make Sense and Persevere Is it possible to solve a system of linear inequalities using the same methods you used to solve a system of linear equations?

EXAMPLE 3

Try It! Solve a System of Equations in Three Variables

3. Solve the following systems of equations.

a. $\begin{cases} x + y + z = 3 \\ x - y + z = 1 \\ x + y - z = 2 \end{cases}$

b. $\begin{cases} 2x + y - 2z = 3 \\ x - 2y + 7z = 12 \\ 3x - y + 5z = 10 \end{cases}$

HABITS OF MIND

Generalize What is the goal of the substitution and elimination methods?

Assess

EXAMPLE 4

Try It! Write a System of Equations as a Matrix

4. Write the matrix for the system of equations or the system of equations for the matrix.

a. $\begin{cases} 3x - y = 4 \\ -2x + 7y = 20 \end{cases}$

b. $\left[\begin{array}{ccc|c} 0 & 2 & 3 & 4 \\ 8 & -1 & -2 & 5 \\ 2 & 0 & 1 & 9 \end{array}\right]$

EXAMPLE 5

Try It! Relate Systems of Equations and Matrices

5. a. Write the system of equations described by the augmented matrix. Describe a real-world situation that could be modeled by the system.

$$\left[\begin{array}{cc|c} 1 & 1 & 10 \\ 3 & 2 & 80 \end{array}\right]$$

b. What would the matrix $\left[\begin{array}{cc|c} 1 & 0 & 20 \\ 0 & 1 & 10 \end{array}\right]$ represent in terms of your real-world situation?

HABITS OF MIND

Communicate Precisely What characteristics must a system of equations have for it to be appropriate to rewrite it in matrix form?

Do You UNDERSTAND?

1. ESSENTIAL QUESTION How can you find and represent solutions of systems of linear equations and inequalities?

2. **Error Analysis** Shandra said the solution of the system of equations $\begin{cases} 2x + y = 3 \\ -x + 4y = -6 \end{cases}$ is $(-1, 2)$. Is she correct? Explain.

3. **Communicate Precisely** Why is a system of linear inequalities often solved graphically?

4. **Make Sense and Persevere** How does knowing how to solve a system of two equations in two variables help you to solve a system of three equations in three variables?

5. **Vocabulary** What is the difference between a coefficient matrix and an augmented matrix?

Do You KNOW HOW?

6. Solve the following system of equations.

$$\begin{cases} 2x + 2y = 10 \\ x + 5y = 13 \end{cases}$$

7. Graph the following system of inequalities.

$$\begin{cases} -x + 2y < 1 \\ x \geq 0 \\ y \geq 0 \end{cases}$$

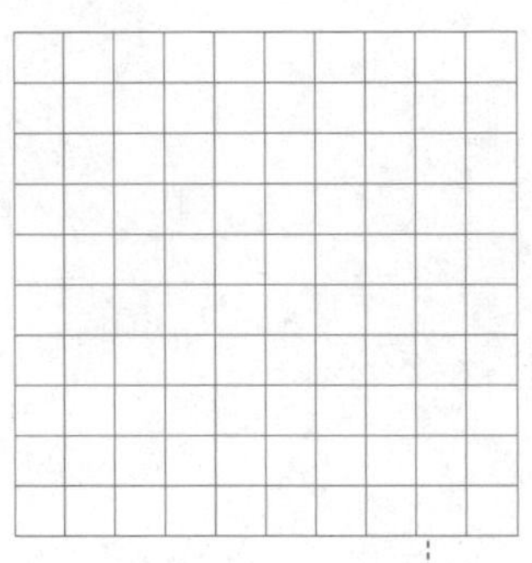

8. Write the system of equations represented by the matrix $\begin{bmatrix} 1 & -2 & 2 \\ -4 & 3 & -5 \end{bmatrix}$.

9. Equations with two variables that are raised only to the first power represent lines. There are three possible outcomes for the intersections of two lines. Describe the outcomes.

Current Events

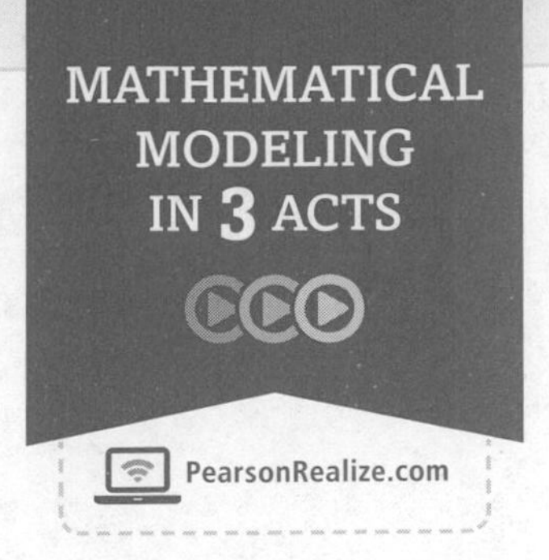

You might say that someone who loses their temper has "blown a fuse." However, it's rare to hear about electrical fuses blowing these days. That's because most fuses have been replaced by circuit breakers. A fuse must be replaced once it's blown, but a circuit breaker can be reset.

Ask for permission to look at the electrical panel in your home. If there is a series of switches inside, each of those is a circuit breaker, designed to interrupt the circuit when the electrical current inside is too dangerous. How much electricity does it take to trip a circuit breaker? Think about this question during the Mathematical Modeling in 3-Acts lesson.

ACT 1 Identify the Problem

1. What is the first question that comes to mind after watching the video?

2. Write down the Main Question you will answer.

3. Make an initial conjecture that answers this Main Question.

4. Explain how you arrived at your conjecture.

5. What information will be useful to know to answer the main question? How can you get it? How will you use that information?

Video

ACT 2 Develop a Model

6. Use the math that you have learned in the topic to refine your conjecture.

ACT 3 Interpret the Results

7. Did your refined conjecture match the actual answer exactly? If not, what might explain the difference?

Activity

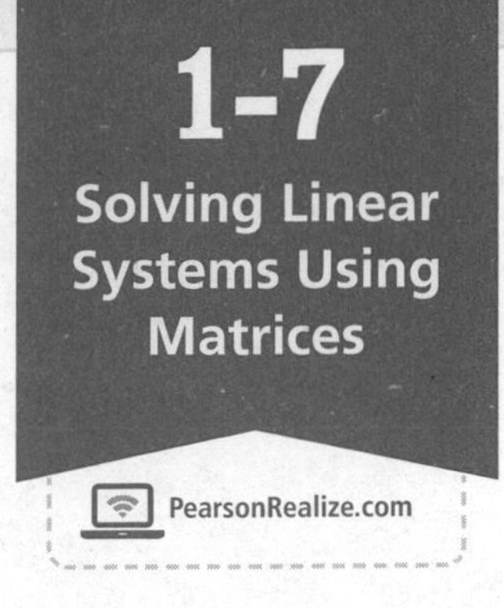

CRITIQUE & EXPLAIN

Alejandro and Emaan each set up a matrix to represent a system of equations.

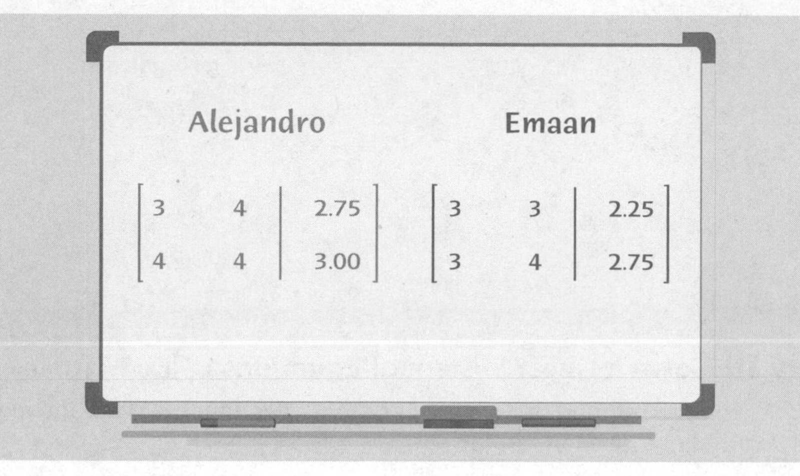

A. Write a system of equations that represents each student's matrix.

B. How are Alejandro's and Emaan's matrices alike? How are they different?

C. Use Structure Simplify the equation in each system in which the coefficients for x and y are the same. How does this change your understanding of the two systems of equations?

HABITS OF MIND

Construct Arguments Write a new matrix by switching the position of the rows in Emaan's matrix. Will the system of equations represented by this new matrix have the same solution as Emaan's original matrix? Explain.

EXAMPLE 1

Try It! Understand Row Operations on a Matrix

1. What is the solution of each system of linear equations?

a. $\begin{cases} 2x - 5y = 11 \\ 4x + 3y = 9 \end{cases}$

b. $\begin{cases} 3x - 4y = -18 \\ -4x + 8y = 32 \end{cases}$

EXAMPLE 2

Try It! Solve a Linear System of Equations Using Matrices

2. What is the solution to each linear system of equations? Write the matrix in reduced row echelon form to solve.

a. $\begin{cases} x + y + z = 13 \\ y - z = 3 \\ z = 2x \end{cases}$

b. $\begin{cases} x - y + z = 5 \\ 4x - z = 3 \\ y = -1 \end{cases}$

HABITS OF MIND

Use Structure What do the zeros in a matrix represent in the system of equations?

EXAMPLE 3

Try It! Use Technology With Matrices

3. What is solution of the linear system of equations?

a. $\begin{cases} x + y + z = 55 \\ 2x - y - z = -7 \\ x + 2y - 2z = 10 \end{cases}$

b. $\begin{cases} x + y + z = 1.8 \\ z = 2x + 0.1 \\ 3x + y - z = 0.8 \end{cases}$

Notes

Assess

EXAMPLE 4

Try It! Interpret the Reduced Row Echelon Form

4. What is the solution of each system of equations?

a. $\begin{cases} x - 2y + z = 8 \\ -2x + 4y - 2z = 16 \\ x + 2y - z = -8 \end{cases}$

b. $\begin{cases} 0.9x - 0.3y + 0.6z = 4.2 \\ 2y + 28 = 6x + 4z \\ 3x - y + 2z = 14 \end{cases}$

EXAMPLE 5

Try It! Apply a Linear System in Three Variables

5. A student has \$128 in a savings account. If she were to withdraw the money and was only given one, five, and twenty-dollar bills, how many bills of each denomination would she have? Assume she has a total of 28 bills, and she has 3 times as many one-dollar bills as she does five-dollar bills.

HABITS OF MIND

Reason How can you tell when a system of equations has no solutions?

Do You UNDERSTAND?

1. ESSENTIAL QUESTION How can matrix row operations be used to solve a system of linear equations?

2. **Vocabulary** The number of rows in a matrix representing a system of equations will be equal to the number of unique variables in the system of equations. True or False? Explain.

3. **Error Analysis** Dwayne was reducing a matrix into reduced row echelon form. He used row operations to get a matrix with a bottom row that was all zeros. He then added the first row to the bottom row to get a 1 in the bottom row. What error did Dwayne make?

4. **Use Appropriate Tools** Explain how to use technology to find the solution to a system of equations with three variables.

Do You KNOW HOW?

Solve each system of equations using a matrix.

5. $\begin{cases} -x + 2y = -2 \\ x = 6y \end{cases}$

6. $\begin{cases} 2x + 2y = 50 \\ x + y - z = 0 \\ z = 2y - 5 \end{cases}$

Find the reduced row echelon form of each matrix.

7. $\left[\begin{array}{cc|c} -3 & 2 & 10 \\ 1 & -3 & -22 \end{array}\right]$

8. $\left[\begin{array}{ccc|c} 0 & 2 & 5 & 5 \\ 2 & 2 & 1 & -1 \\ -1 & 0 & 3 & 2 \end{array}\right]$

9. Find the reduced row echelon form of $\begin{bmatrix} 0 & -1 \\ 1 & 2 \\ 0 & 3 \end{bmatrix}$.

Activity

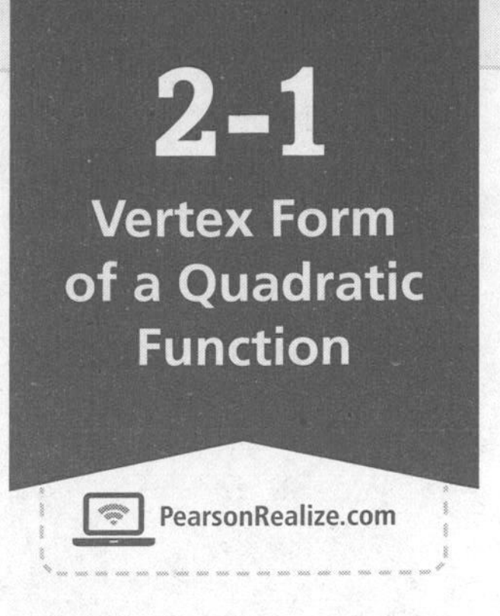

EXPLORE & REASON

The table represents $A(x)$, the area of a square as a function of side length x units, where x is a positive real number.

Side Length (units)	x	1	2	3	4
Model	x by x square	1×1 square	2×2 grid	3×3 grid	
Area (sq. units)	$A(x)$	1	4	9	

A. Consider the function where the areas in the table are doubled. Write the equation of a function that represents this.

B. Look for Relationships Graph the ordered pairs for both A(x) and your new function. How would you describe the differences in the locations of these points?

C. Find the equation for a function whose x-values are the same as A(x) but whose y-values are 2 units greater than each y-value in A(x).

HABITS OF MIND

Communicate Precisely Do you think the effect of altering A(x) in the two ways you did would work for any function you start with? Explain.

Notes

Assess

EXAMPLE 1

Try It! Transform a Quadratic Function

1. Describe the transformations of the parent function $f(x) = x^2$. Then graph the function.

a. $g(x) = -(x + 2)^2$

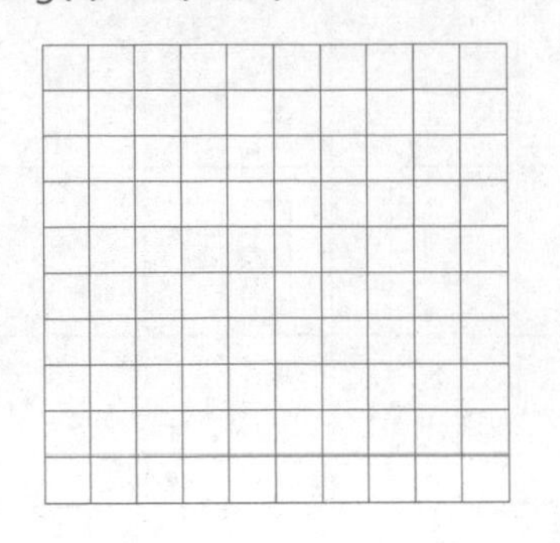

b. $g(x) = (x - 1)^2 + 2$

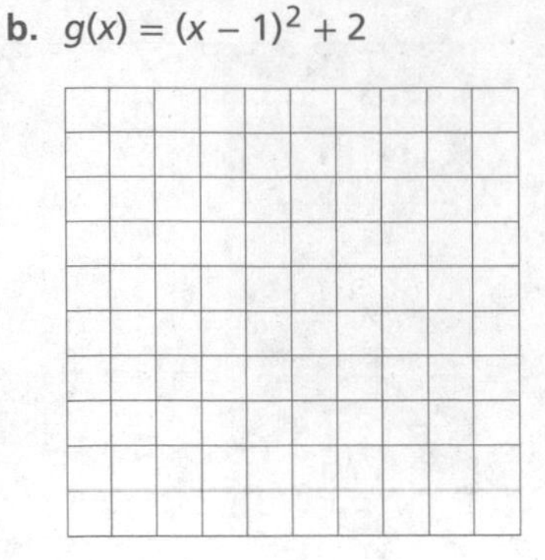

EXAMPLE 2

Try It! Determine Key Features of a Quadratic Function

2. Identify the vertex, axis of symmetry, minimum or maximum, domain, and range of the function $f(x) = -(x + 4)^2 - 5$.

HABITS OF MIND

Make Sense and Persevere In what order should you apply the transformations shown in the Try It! for Example 2?

EXAMPLE 3

Try It! Write an Equation of a Parabola

3. What is the equation of a parabola with a vertex of (1, −4) and which passes through (−2, −1)?

EXAMPLE 4 Try It! Write an Equation of a Parabola Given the Graph

4. The graph shows the height of the flying disk with respect to time. What is the equation of the function? Write the equation in vertex form. Then write the equation in the form $y = ax^2 + bx + c$.

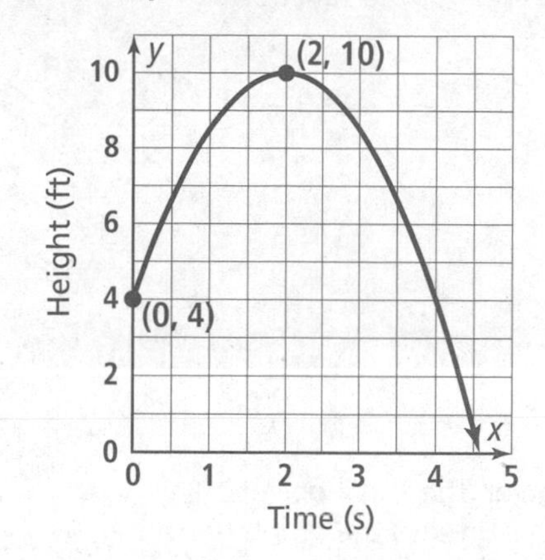

EXAMPLE 5 Try It! Write an Equation of a Transformed Function

5. What is the equation of j? Write the equation in vertex form and in the form $y = ax^2 + bx + c$.

a. Let j be a quadratic function whose graph is a translation 2 units right and 5 units down of the graph of f.

b. Let j be a function whose graph is a reflection of the graph of f in the x-axis followed by a translation 1 unit down.

HABITS OF MIND

Generalize What information do you need to write the equation of a transformed quadratic function in vertex form?

Do You UNDERSTAND?

1. ESSENTIAL QUESTION How does the equation of a quadratic function in vertex form highlight key features of the function's graph?

2. Error Analysis Given the function $g(x) = (x + 3)^2$, Martin says the graph should be translated right 3 units from the parent graph $f(x) = x^2$. Explain his error.

3. **Vocabulary** What shape does a quadratic function have when graphed?

4. Communicate Precisely How are the graphs of $f(x) = x^2$ and $g(x) = -(x + 2)^2 - 4$ related?

Do You KNOW HOW?

Describe the transformation of the parent function $f(x) = x^2$.

5. $g(x) = -(x + 5)^2 + 2$

6. $h(x) = (x + 2)^2 - 7$

Write the equation of each parabola in vertex form.

7. Vertex: (−3, 7); Point: (−2, −5)

8. Vertex: (1, 3); Point: (2, 5)

9. Vertex: (−4, 6); Point: (−2, −2)

10. Vertex: (7, 4); Point: (5, 16)

CRITIQUE & EXPLAIN

Jordan and Emery are rewriting the vertex form of the quadratic function $y = 2(x - 4)^2 + 5$ in the form $y = ax^2 + bx + c$.

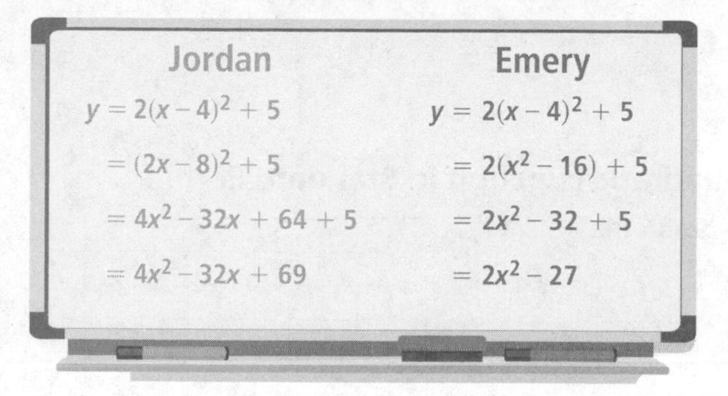

Jordan	Emery
$y = 2(x - 4)^2 + 5$	$y = 2(x - 4)^2 + 5$
$= (2x - 8)^2 + 5$	$= 2(x^2 - 16) + 5$
$= 4x^2 - 32x + 64 + 5$	$= 2x^2 - 32 + 5$
$= 4x^2 - 32x + 69$	$= 2x^2 - 27$

2-2 Standard Form of a Quadratic Function

PearsonRealize.com

A. **Communicate Precisely** Did Jordan rewrite the equation correctly? Did Emery? Explain.

B. Without rewriting the equation, how could you prove that Jordan's or Emery's equation is not equivalent to the original?

HABITS OF MIND

Reason Casey rewrote the vertex form, too.

$$\begin{aligned} y &= 2(x - 4)^2 + 5 \\ &= 2(x + 1)^2 \\ &= 2(x^2 + 2x + 1) \\ &= 2x^2 + 4x + 2 \end{aligned}$$

Is Casey correct? Explain.

Assess

EXAMPLE 1

Try It! Find the Vertex of a Quadratic Function in Standard Form

1. What is the vertex of the graph of the function $f(x) = x^2 - 8x + 5$?

EXAMPLE 2

Try It! Graph a Quadratic Function in Standard Form

2. Use key features to graph the function $f(x) = x^2 - 6x - 1$.

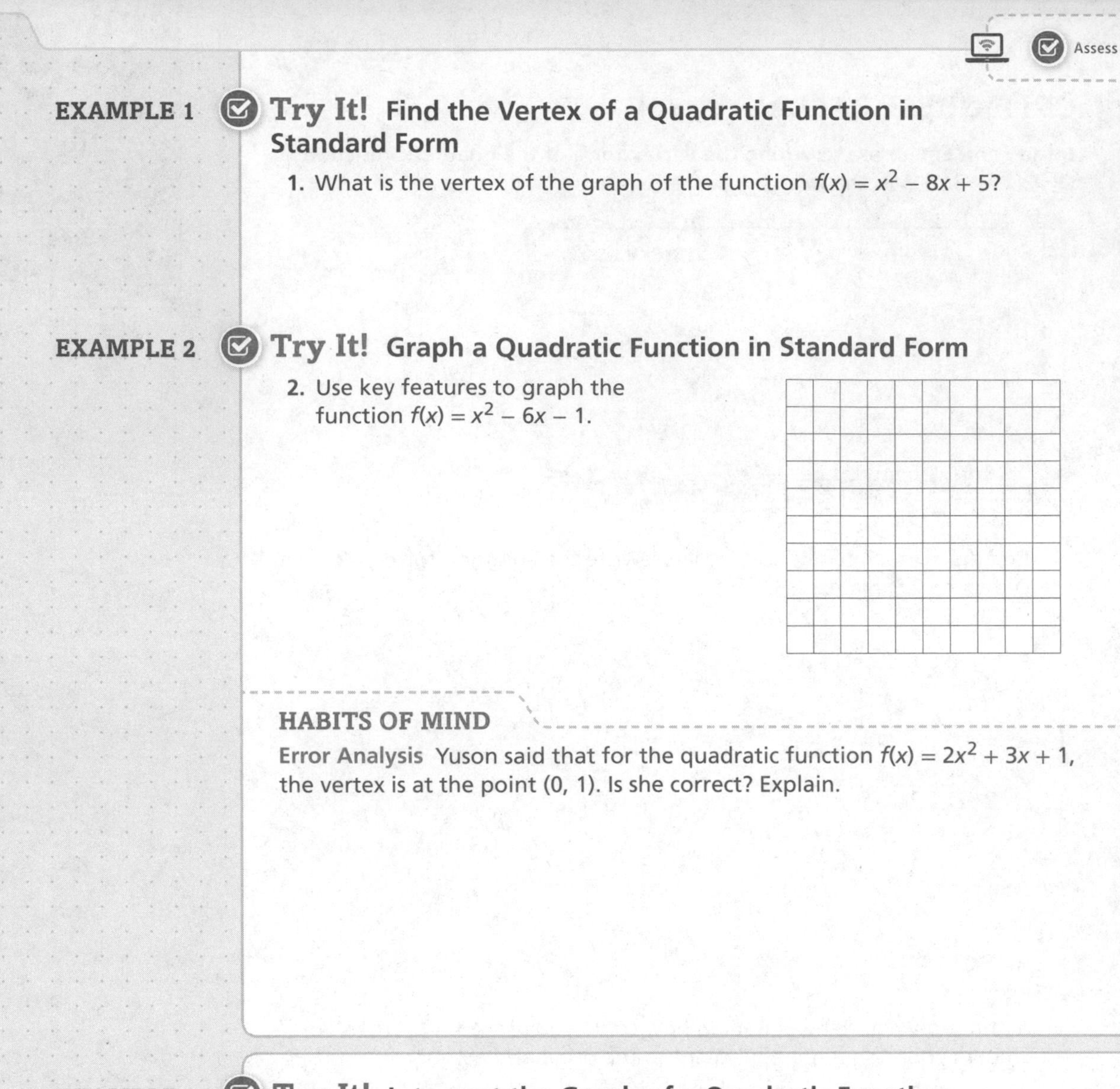

HABITS OF MIND

Error Analysis Yuson said that for the quadratic function $f(x) = 2x^2 + 3x + 1$, the vertex is at the point (0, 1). Is she correct? Explain.

EXAMPLE 3

Try It! Interpret the Graph of a Quadratic Function

3. A water balloon was thrown from a window. The height of the water balloon over time can be modeled by the function $y = -16x^2 + 160x + 50$. What was the maximum height of the water balloon after it was thrown?

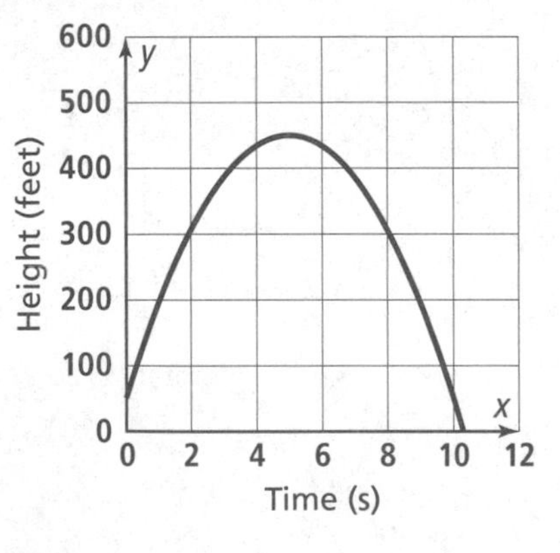

HABITS OF MIND

Make Sense and Persevere How long did it take for the water balloon to reach its maximum height?

Assess

EXAMPLE 4 **Try It! Write the Equation of a Parabola Given Three Points**

4. What is the equation of a parabola that passes through the points (2, −12), (−1, −15), and (−4, −90)?

EXAMPLE 5 **Try It! Use Quadratic Regression**

5. A fan threw a souvenir football into the air from the top of the bleachers toward the bottom of the bleachers. The table shows the height of the football, in feet, above the ground at various times, in seconds. If the football wasn't touched by anyone on its way to the ground, about how long did it take the football to reach the ground after it was thrown?

Time (s)	0	0.2	0.4	0.6	0.8	1.0
Height (ft)	10	11.76	12.24	11.44	9.36	6.0

HABITS OF MIND

Model With Mathematics How many points does it take to determine the equation of a quadratic function? Why are so many more points used in Example 4?

Do You UNDERSTAND?

1. ESSENTIAL QUESTION What key features can you determine about a quadratic function from an equation in standard form?

2. **Error Analysis** Cameron said that the *y*-intercept of a quadratic function always tells the maximum value of that function. Explain Cameron's error.

3. **Vocabulary** Write a quadratic function in standard form.

4. **Make Sense and Persevere** Why do you need at least three points to graph a quadratic function when not given an equation?

Do You KNOW HOW?

Find the vertex and *y*-intercept of the quadratic function.

5. $y = 3x^2 - 12x + 40$

6. $y = -x^2 + 4x + 7$

For 7 and 8, find the maximum or minimum of the parabola.

7. $y = -2x^2 - 16x + 20$

8. $y = -x^2 + 12x - 15$

9. Find the equation in standard form of the parabola that passes through the points (0, 6), (−3, 15), and (−6, 6).

10. $y = 3x^2 + 6x - 2$

11. $y = -2x^2 + 4x + 1$

2-3 Factored Form of a Quadratic Function

PearsonRealize.com

CRITIQUE & EXPLAIN

Corey wrote an equation in factored form, $y = (x + 8)(x - 2)$, to represent a quadratic function. Kimberly wrote the equation $y = x^2 + 6x - 16$, and Joshua wrote the equation $y = (x + 3)^2 - 25$.

A. **Reason** Do all three equations represent the same function? If not, whose is different? Explain algebraically.

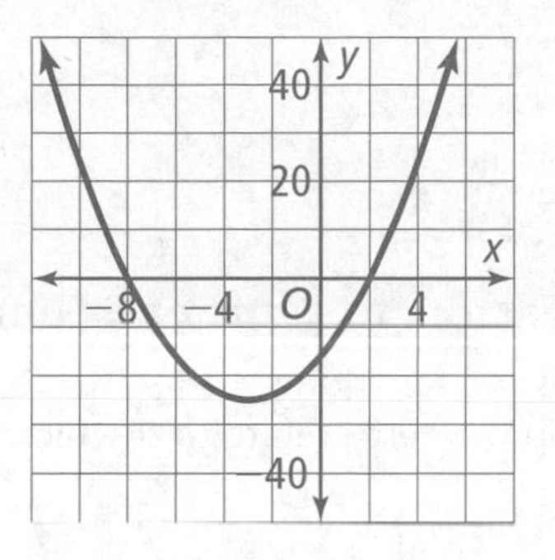

B. How else could you determine if all three equations represent the same function?

C. What information can Corey's form help you find that is more difficult to find using Kimberly's or Joshua's form?

HABITS OF MIND

Use Structure Whose form of the equation is most useful for finding the vertex? The y-intercept? The x-intercepts?

Notes

Assess

EXAMPLE 1

Try It! Factor a Quadratic Expression

1. Factor the expression.

a. $x^2 - 9$

b. $3x^2 - 7x + 2$

EXAMPLE 2

Try It! Relate Factors to Zeros of a Function

2. The graph shows the function $y = x^2 - 9x + 20$. Identify the zeros of the function. How do the zeros relate to the factors of $x^2 - 9x + 20$?

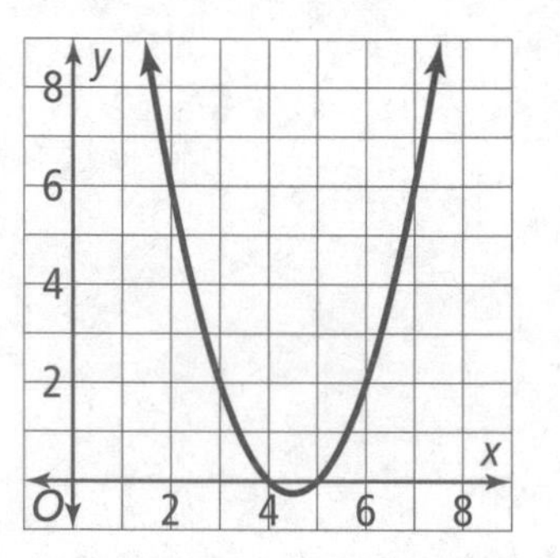

EXAMPLE 3

Try It! Solve Quadratic Equations by Factoring

3. Solve the equation by factoring.

a. $x^2 + 8x = 20$

b. $2x^2 = 3x + 2$

HABITS OF MIND

Error Analysis Anna solved the equation $x^2 + 8x - 20 = 0$ by factoring. She wrote $(x - 10)(x + 2) = 0$ and expected the x-intercepts of the function $y = x^2 + 8x - 20$ to be at -10 and 2. Was she right?

Notes

Assess

EXAMPLE 4

Try It! Find the Zeros of a Quadratic Function

4. A baseball is thrown from the upper deck of a stadium, 128 ft above the ground. The function $h(t) = -16t^2 + 32t + 128$ gives the height of the ball t seconds after it is thrown. How long will it take the ball to reach the ground?

EXAMPLE 5

Try It! Determine Positive or Negative Intervals

5. Identify the interval(s) on which the function $y = x^2 - 4x - 21$ is negative.

HABITS OF MIND

Construct Arguments Is it always true that the y-values of a quadratic function have opposite signs on either side of a zero of the function? Explain why or give a counterexample.

EXAMPLE 6

Try It! Write the Equation of a Parabola in Factored Form

6. Write an equation of a parabola with x-intercepts at (3, 0) and (–3, 0) and which passes through the point (1, 2).

HABITS OF MIND

Model With Mathematics Is there any other parabola with x-intercepts at (–2, 0) and (–1, 0)? Give an equation or explain why there is no such parabola.

Do You UNDERSTAND?

1. ESSENTIAL QUESTION How is the factored form helpful in solving quadratic equations?

2. Error Analysis Amir says the graph of $y = x^2 + 16$ has -4 as a zero. Is Amir correct? Explain.

3. **Vocabulary** How does the factored form of a quadratic equation relate to the Zero Product Property?

4. Generalize How does knowing the zeros of a function help determine where a function is positive?

Do You KNOW HOW?

Factor each expression.

5. $x^2 - 5x - 24$

6. $5x^2 + 3x - 2$

Solve each equation.

7. $x^2 = 12x - 20$

8. $4x^2 - 5x = 6$

9. The height, in feet, of a t-shirt launched from a t-shirt cannon high in the stands at a football stadium is given by $h(x) = -16x^2 + 64x + 80$, where x is the time in seconds after the t-shirt is launched. How long will it take before the t-shirt reaches the ground?

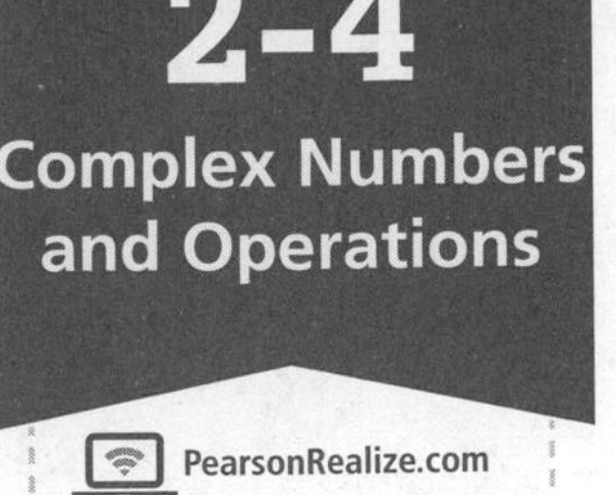

EXPLORE & REASON

A math class played a game called "Solve It, You're Out." At the start of each round, students chose a card from a deck marked with integers from −5 to 5. When an equation is shown, any student whose card states the solution to the equation is eliminated. Five students remain.

Five remaining students with the cards they hold:
Mercedes: −3
Steve: 0
Aubrey: 1
Elijah: −2
Fatima: 3

A. The next equation presented was $x^2 = 9$. Which student(s) was eliminated? Explain.

B. Construct Arguments In the next round, the equation presented was $x^2 = -4$. Darius thought he was eliminated, but this is not the case. Explain why Darius was incorrect.

C. What is true about solutions to $x^2 = a$ when a is a positive number? When a is a negative number? What about when $a = 0$?

HABITS OF MIND

Reason Steve thought that he was a sure winner because he could not be eliminated. Is he correct? Explain. If not, write an equation of the form $x^2 = a$ that would eliminate Steve.

Notes

Assess

EXAMPLE 1

Try It! Solve a Quadratic Equation Using Square Roots

1. Use square roots to solve each equation. Write your solutions using the imaginary unit, *i*.

a. $x^2 = -5$

b. $x^2 = -72$

HABITS OF MIND

Communicate Precisely How do you know that the solution to the equation $x^2 = -5$ must be an imaginary number?

EXAMPLE 2

Try It! Add and Subtract Complex Numbers

2. Find the sum or difference.

a. $(-4 + 6i) + (-2 - 9i)$

b. $(3 - 2i) - (-4 + i)$

HABITS OF MIND

Generalize How is adding and subtracting complex numbers similar to adding and subtracting binomials?

Assess

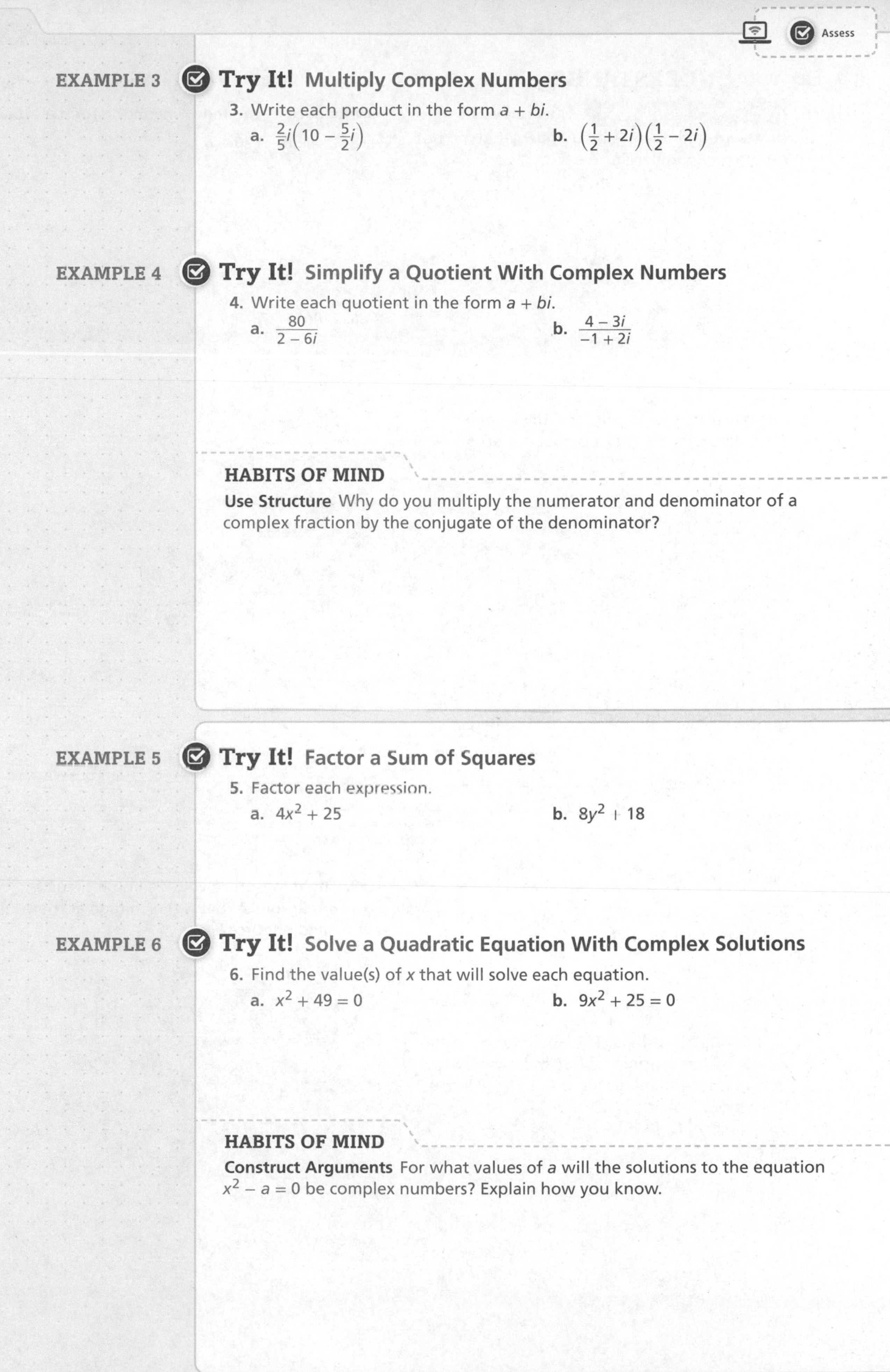

EXAMPLE 3

Try It! Multiply Complex Numbers

3. Write each product in the form $a + bi$.

a. $\frac{2}{5}i\left(10 - \frac{5}{2}i\right)$

b. $\left(\frac{1}{2} + 2i\right)\left(\frac{1}{2} - 2i\right)$

EXAMPLE 4

Try It! Simplify a Quotient With Complex Numbers

4. Write each quotient in the form $a + bi$.

a. $\frac{80}{2 - 6i}$

b. $\frac{4 - 3i}{-1 + 2i}$

HABITS OF MIND

Use Structure Why do you multiply the numerator and denominator of a complex fraction by the conjugate of the denominator?

EXAMPLE 5

Try It! Factor a Sum of Squares

5. Factor each expression.

a. $4x^2 + 25$

b. $8y^2 + 18$

EXAMPLE 6

Try It! Solve a Quadratic Equation With Complex Solutions

6. Find the value(s) of x that will solve each equation.

a. $x^2 + 49 = 0$

b. $9x^2 + 25 = 0$

HABITS OF MIND

Construct Arguments For what values of a will the solutions to the equation $x^2 - a = 0$ be complex numbers? Explain how you know.

Do You UNDERSTAND?

1. ESSENTIAL QUESTION How can you represent and operate on numbers that are not on the real number line?

2. **Vocabulary** How do you form the *complex conjugate* of a complex number $a + bi$?

3. **Error Analysis** Helena was asked to write the quotient $\frac{4}{3-i}$ in the form $a + bi$. She began this way: $\frac{4}{3-i} \times \frac{3-i}{3-i} = \frac{4(3-i)}{3^2+1^2} = \frac{12-4i}{10}$. Explain the error Helena made.

4. **Look for Relationships** The quadratic equation $x^2 + 9 = 0$ has solutions $x - 3i$ and $x = -3i$. How many times will the graph of $f(x) = x^2 + 9$ cross the x-axis? Explain.

Do You KNOW HOW?

Write each of the following in the form $a + bi$.

5. $(2 + 5i) - (-6 + i)$

6. $(2i)(6 + 3i)$

Solve each equation.

7. $x^2 + 16 = 0$

8. $y^2 = -25$

9. The total source voltage in the circuit is $6 - 3i$ volts. What is the voltage at the middle source?

$(2 + 6i)V$ E_1
$(a + bi)V$ E_2
$(2 - 5i)V$ E_3

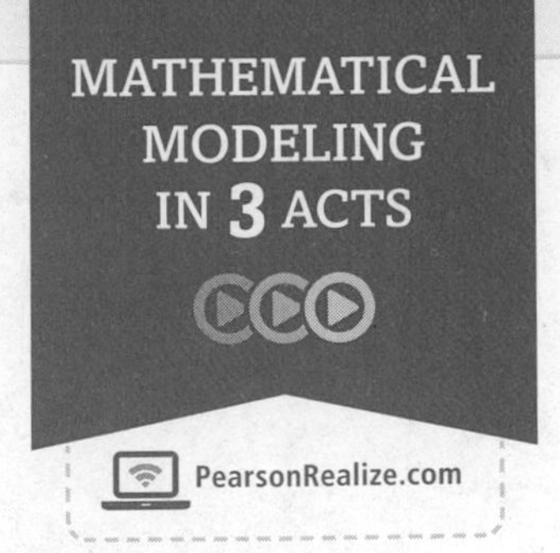

Swift Kick

Whether you call it soccer, football, or fùtbol, it's the most popular sport in the world by far. Even if you don't play soccer, you probably know several people who do.

There are many ways to kick a soccer ball: you can use any part of either foot. If you want the ball to end up in the goal, you also need to try different amounts of spin and power. You'll see one person's effort in the Mathematical Modeling in 3-Acts lesson.

ACT 1 Identify the Problem

1. What is the first question that comes to mind after watching the video?

2. Write down the Main Question you will answer.

3. Make an initial conjecture that answers this Main Question.

4. Explain how you arrived at your conjecture.

5. What information will be useful to know to answer the main question? How can you get it? How will you use that information?

Video

ACT 2 Develop a Model

6. Use the math that you have learned in the topic to refine your conjecture.

ACT 3 Interpret the Results

7. Did your refined conjecture match the actual answer exactly? If not, what might explain the difference?

Activity

2-5 Completing the Square

PearsonRealize.com

CRITIQUE & EXPLAIN

Hana and Enrique used different methods to solve the equation $x^2 - 6x + 9 = 16$.

Hana	Enrique
$x^2 - 6x + 9 = 16$	$x^2 - 6x + 9 = 16$
$x^2 - 6x - 7 = 0$	$(x - 3)^2 = 16$
$(x - 7)(x + 1) = 0$	I can square 4 or −4 to get 16.
$x - 7 = 0$ OR $x + 1 = 0$	$x - 3 = 4$ OR $x - 3 = -4$
$x = 7$ OR $x = -1$	$x = 7$ OR $x = -1$
The solutions are 7 and −1.	The solutions are 7 and −1.

A. Does Hana's method work? If her method is valid, explain the reasoning she used. If her method is not valid, explain why not.

B. Does Enrique's method work? If his method is valid, explain the reasoning he used. If his method is not valid, explain why not.

C. Use Structure Can you use either Hana's or Enrique's method to solve the equation $x^2 + 10x + 25 = 3$? Explain.

HABITS OF MIND

Make Sense and Persevere Why does Hana set her two factors equal to zero, while Enrique sets his factor equal to 4 and −4?

Notes

Assess

EXAMPLE 1

Try It! Use Square Roots to Solve Quadratic Equations

1. Find the solution(s) to the equations.

   a. $81 = x^2 + 12x + 36$?

   b. $9 = x^2 - 16x + 64$

HABITS OF MIND

Use Structure How do you recognize a perfect square trinomial?

EXAMPLE 2

Try It! Understand the Process of Completing the Square

2. How can you write the equation $x^2 - 6x - 11 = 0$ in the form $(x - p)^2 = q$?

EXAMPLE 3

Try It! Solve a Quadratic Equation by Completing the Square

3. Solve the following equations by completing the square.

   a. $0 = x^2 + 4x + 8$

   b. $0 = x^2 - 8x + 17$

HABITS OF MIND

Reason Richard is completing the square to solve the equation $2x^2 + 8x = 19$. He wrote: $2(x^2 + 4x + 4) = 19 +$ ____. What number should Richard write in the blank?

Notes

Assess

EXAMPLE 4 **Try It!** **Complete the Square to Solve a Real-World Problem**

4. The relationship between the time since the ball was thrown and height of the ball can be modeled by the equation $h = 32t - 16t^2 + 4$, where h is the height of the ball after t seconds. Complete the square to find how long it will take the ball to reach a height of 20 ft.

EXAMPLE 5 **Try It!** **Write a Quadratic Equation in Vertex Form**

5. Write each equation in vertex form. Identify the maximum or minimum value of the graph of each equation.

   a. $y = -3x^2 - 9x + 7$

   b. $y = 2x^2 + 12x + 9$

HABITS OF MIND

Make Sense and Persevere A pelican swoops down under the surface of the ocean to catch a fish. An equation that describes the pelican's path is $y = 4x^2 - 16x + 15$. The pelican catches the fish at the deepest point of the dive. How deep was the fish swimming?

Do You UNDERSTAND?

1. **ESSENTIAL QUESTION** How can you solve a quadratic equation by completing the square?

2. Paula said that only quadratic equations with leading coefficients of 1 can be solved by completing the square. Is Paula correct? Explain.

3. **Generalize** Given the expression $x^2 + bx$, describe how to find c so that $x^2 + bx + c$ is a perfect square trinomial.

4. **Make Sense and Persevere** How can you complete the square to find the vertex of a parabola?

Do You KNOW HOW?

Solve each equation by completing the square.

5. $0 = x^2 + 12x + 11$

6. $27 = 3x^2 + 12x$

7. $0 = 2x^2 + 6x - 14$

Write the equation in vertex form, and identify the maximum or minimum point of the graph of the function.

8. $y = x^2 + 6x - 6$

9. $y = -2x^2 + 20x - 42$

10. The daily profit for a company is modeled by the function $p(x) = -0.5x^2 + 40x - 300$, where x is the number of units sold. How many units does the company need to sell each day to maximize profits?

Activity

2-6 The Quadratic Formula

PearsonRealize.com

EXPLORE & REASON

You can complete the square to solve the general quadratic equation, $ax^2 + bx + c = 0$.

$$ax^2 + bx + c = 0$$
$$ax^2 + bx = -c$$
$$x^2 + \left(\frac{b}{a}\right)x = -\frac{c}{a}$$
$$x^2 + \left(\frac{b}{a}\right)x + \left(\frac{b}{2a}\right)^2 = -\frac{c}{a} + \left(\frac{b}{2a}\right)^2$$
$$\left(x + \frac{b}{2a}\right)^2 = \frac{b^2}{4a^2} - \frac{c}{a}$$
$$\left(x + \frac{b}{2a}\right)^2 = \frac{b^2 - 4ac}{4a^2}$$
$$x + \frac{b}{2a} = \pm\sqrt{\frac{b^2 - 4ac}{4a^2}}$$
$$x = \frac{-b \pm \sqrt{b^2 - 4ac}}{2a}$$

A. Construct Arguments Justify each step in this general solution.

B. What must be true of the value of $b^2 - 4ac$ if the equation $ax^2 + bx + c = 0$ has two non-real solutions? If it has just one solution?

HABITS OF MIND

Communicate Precisely Why is there a $\pm$ in the second to last step of the derivation of the Quadratic Formula?

Assess

EXAMPLE 1

Try It! Solve Quadratic Equations

1. Solve using the Quadratic Formula.

   a. $2x^2 + 6x + 3 = 0$

   b. $3x^2 - 2x + 7 = 0$

EXAMPLE 2

Try It! Choose a Solution Method

2. Solve the equation $6x^2 + x - 15 = 0$ using the Quadratic Formula and one other method.

HABITS OF MIND

Construct Arguments Is it possible for a quadratic equation to have one real solution and one complex solution? Explain.

EXAMPLE 3

Try It! Identify the Number of Real-Number Solutions

3. Describe the nature of the solutions for each equation.

   a. $16x^2 + 8x + 1 = 0$

   b. $2x^2 - 5x + 6 = 0$

Notes

Assess

EXAMPLE 4

Try It! Interpret the Discriminant

4. According to the model of Rachel's serve, will the ball reach a height of 3 meters?

HABITS OF MIND

Reason Create a quadratic equation that has two complex solutions.

EXAMPLE 5

Try It! Use the Discriminant to Find a Particular Equation

5. Determine the value(s) of b that ensure $5x^2 + bx + 5 = 0$ has two non-real solutions.

HABITS OF MIND

Use Appropriate Tools Why is the Quadratic Formula helpful?

Do You UNDERSTAND?

1. ESSENTIAL QUESTION How can you use the Quadratic Formula to solve quadratic equations or to predict the nature of their solutions?

2. **Vocabulary** Why is the discriminant a useful tool to use when solving quadratic equations?

3. **Error Analysis** Rick claims that the equation $x^2 + 5x + 9 = 0$ has no solution. Jenny claims that there are two solutions. Explain how Rick could be correct, and explain how Jenny could be correct.

4. **Use Appropriate Tools** What methods can you use to solve quadratic equations?

Do You KNOW HOW?

5. Describe the number and type of solutions of the equation $2x^2 + 7x + 11 = 0$.

6. Use the Quadratic Formula to solve the equation $x^2 + 6x - 10 = 0$.

7. At time t seconds, the height, h, of a ball thrown vertically upward is modeled by the equation $h = -5t^2 + 33t + 4$. About how long will it take for the ball to hit the ground?

8. Use the Quadratic Formula to solve the equation $x^2 - 8x + 16 = 0$. Is this the only way to solve this equation? Explain.

2-7 Linear-Quadratic Systems

PearsonRealize.com

EXPLORE & REASON

Draw a rough sketch of a parabola and a line on the coordinate plane.

A. Count the number of points of intersection between the two graphs.

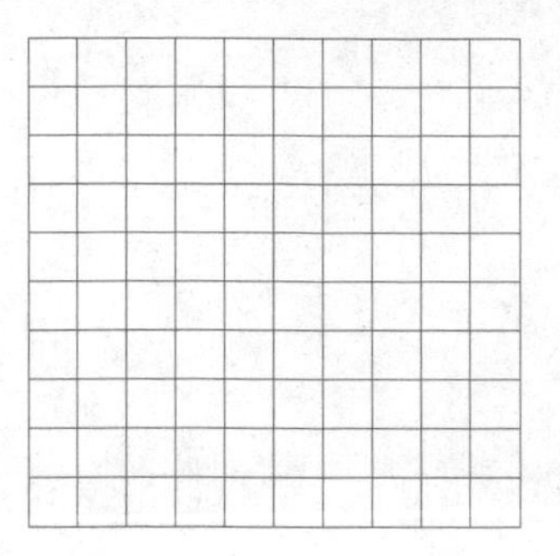

B. Sketch another parabola on a coordinate plane. Use a straightedge to investigate the different ways that a line and a parabola intersect. What conjectures can you make?

C. Construct Arguments How many different numbers of intersection points are possible between a quadratic function and a linear function? Justify that you have found all of the possibilities.

HABITS OF MIND

Reason What must be true about the equation for a horizontal line that has no points of intersection with the parabola with equation $y = x^2$?

Assess

EXAMPLE 1

Try It! Determine the Number of Solutions

1. Determine the number of real solutions of the system $\begin{cases} y = 3x^2 \\ y = 3x - 2 \end{cases}$.

EXAMPLE 2

Try It! Solve a Linear-Quadratic System Using Substitution

2. Solve each system by substitution.

   a. $\begin{cases} y = 2x^2 - 6x - 8 \\ 2x - y = 16 \end{cases}$

   b. $\begin{cases} y = -3x^2 + x + 4 \\ 4x - y = 2 \end{cases}$

EXAMPLE 3

Try It! Applying a Linear-Quadratic System

3. Revenue for the high school band concert is given by the function $y = -30x^2 + 250x$, where x is the ticket price, in dollars. The cost of the concert is given by the function $y = 490 - 30x$. At what ticket price will the band make enough revenue to cover their costs?

HABITS OF MIND

Make Sense and Persevere Why does the substitution method work? How does it change the problem and make it possible for you to solve?

Notes

Assess

EXAMPLE 4

Try It! Solve a Linear-Quadratic System of Inequalities

4. Solve the system of inequalities $\begin{cases} y > x^2 + 6x - 12 \\ 3x - y \geq -8 \end{cases}$ using shading.

EXAMPLE 5

Try It! Using a System to Solve an Equation

5. Solve the equation $3x^2 - 7x + 4 = 9 - 2x$ by writing a linear-quadratic system and solving using the intersection feature of a graphing calculator.

HABITS OF MIND

Look for Relationships How could you solve the inequality $3x + 8 > x^2 + 6x - 2$ graphically?

Do You UNDERSTAND?

1. ESSENTIAL QUESTION How can you solve a system of two equations or inequalities in which one is linear and one is quadratic?

2. **Error Analysis** Dyani was asked to use substitution to solve this system:

$$\begin{cases} y = 2x^2 - 6x + 4 \\ x - y = 7 \end{cases}$$

She began as follows, to find the x-coordinate(s) to the solution(s) of the system:

$x + 2x^2 - 6x + 4 = 7$	Substitute for y.
	Simplify.
$2x^2 - 5x - 3 = 0$	Factor.
$(2x + 1)(x - 3) = 0$	
$x = -\frac{1}{2}, x = 3$	Set each factor equal to 0, solve for x. ✗

But Dyani has already made an error. What was her mistake?

Do You KNOW HOW?

Determine the number of solutions for the system of equations.

3. $\begin{cases} y = \frac{2}{5}x^2 \\ y = x - 2 \end{cases}$

4. $\begin{cases} y = -x - 1 \\ 3x^2 + 2y = 4 \end{cases}$

Use substitution to solve the system of equations.

5. $\begin{cases} y = 3x^2 + 7x - 10 \\ y - 19x = 22 \end{cases}$

6. $\begin{cases} y = 3x^2 \\ y - 3x = -2 \end{cases}$

3-1 Graphing Polynomial Functions

PearsonRealize.com

EXPLORE & REASON

Consider functions of the form $f(x) = x^n$, where n is a positive integer.

A. Graph $f(x) = x^n$ for $n = 1, 3,$ and 5. Look at the graphs in Quadrant I. As the exponent increases, what is happening to the graphs? Which quadrants do the graphs pass through?

B. Look for Relationships Now graph $f(x) = x^n$ for $n = 2, 4,$ and 6. What happens to these graphs in Quadrant I as the exponent increases? Which quadrants do the graphs pass through?

C. Write two equations in the form $f(x) = x^n$ with graphs that you predict are in Quadrants I and II. Write two equations with graphs that you predict are in Quadrants I and III. Use graphing technology to test your predictions.

HABITS OF MIND

Construct Arguments Compare and contrast the end behavior of the graphs of $f(x) = x^n$ when $n = 1, 3,$ & 5 with the graphs of $f(x) = x^n$ when $n = 2, 4,$ & 10. Write a general statement that compares the end behavior of the graphs when the exponents are odd to the end behavior when the exponents are even.

Assess

EXAMPLE 1

Try It! Classify Polynomials

1. What is each polynomial in standard form. What are the leading coefficient, the degree, and the number of terms of each?
   a. $2x - 3x^4 + 6 - 5x^3$
   b. $x^5 + 2x^6 - 3x^4 - 8x + 4x^3$

EXAMPLE 2

Try It! Interpret Leading Coefficients and Degrees

2. Use the leading coefficient and degree of the polynomial function to determine the end behavior of each graph.
   a. $f(x) = 2x^6 - 5x^5 + 6x^4 - x^3 + 4x^2 - x + 1$
   b. $g(x) = -5x^3 + 8x + 4$

HABITS OF MIND

Communicate Precisely How does the leading coefficient help determine the end behavior of an even function?

EXAMPLE 3

Try It! Graph a Polynomial Function

3. Consider the polynomial function $f(x) = x^5 + 18x^2 + 10x + 1$.
   a. Make a table of values to identify key features and sketch a graph of the function.
   b. Find the average rate of change over the interval [0, 2].

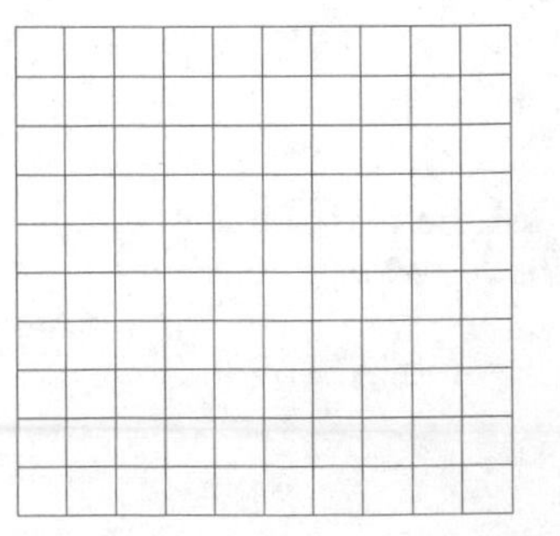

EXAMPLE 4

Try It! Sketch a Graph from a Verbal Description

4. Use the information below to sketch a graph of the polynomial function $y = f(x)$.
   - $f(x)$ is positive on the intervals $(-2, -1)$ and $(1, 2)$.
   - $f(x)$ is negative on the intervals $(-\infty, -2)$, $(-1, 1)$, and $(2, \infty)$.
   - $f(x)$ is increasing on the intervals $(-\infty, -1.5)$ and $(0, 1.5)$.
   - $f(x)$ is decreasing on the intervals $(-1.5, 0)$ and $(1.5, \infty)$.

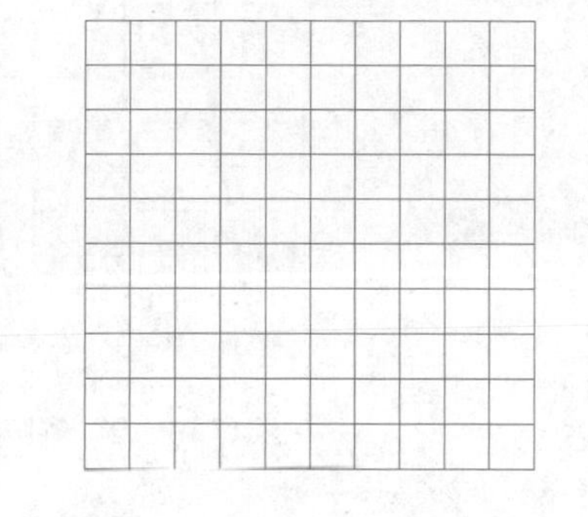

HABITS OF MIND

Generalize What can you tell about the graph of a function if its equation has an odd degree and a negative leading coefficient?

EXAMPLE 5

Try It! Interpret a Polynomial Model

5. Danielle is engineering a new brand of shoes. For x shoes sold, in thousands, a profit of $p(x) = -3x^4 + 4x^3 - 2x^2 + 5x + 10$ dollars, in ten thousands, will be earned.

   a. How much will be earned in profit for selling 1,000 shoes?

   b. What do the x- and y-intercepts of the graph mean in this context? Do those values make sense?

HABITS OF MIND

Use Appropriate Tools Estimate the turning point of the graph of $p(x) = -3x^4 + 4x^3 - 2x^2 + 5x + 10$. What does this point represent in the context of Try It! 5?

Do You UNDERSTAND?

1. ESSENTIAL QUESTION How do the key features of a polynomial function help you sketch its graph?

2. **Error Analysis** Allie said the degree of the polynomial function $f(x) = x^5 + 2x^4 + 3x^3 - 2x^6 - 9x^2 - 6x + 4$ is 5. Explain and correct Allie's error.

3. **Vocabulary** Explain how to determine the **leading coefficient** of a polynomial function.

4. **Look for Relationships** What is the relationship between the degree and leading coefficient of a polynomial function and the end behavior of the polynomial?

Do You KNOW HOW?

The graph shows the function $f(x) = x^4 + 2x^3 - 13x^2 - 14x + 24$. Find the following.

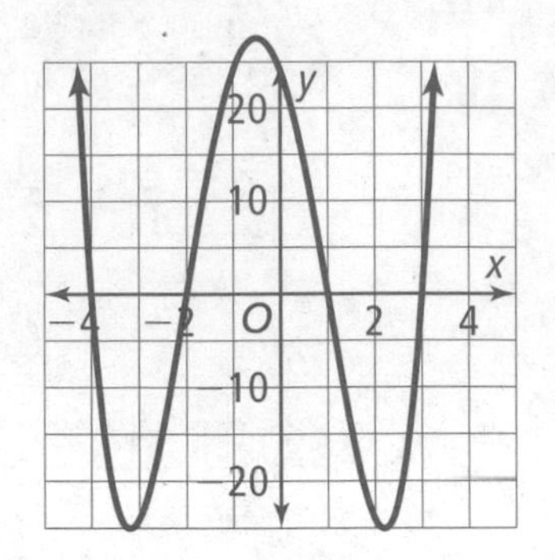

5. number of terms

6. degree

7. leading coefficient

8. end behavior

9. turning point(s)

10. x-intercept(s)

11. relative minimum(s)

12. relative maximum(s)

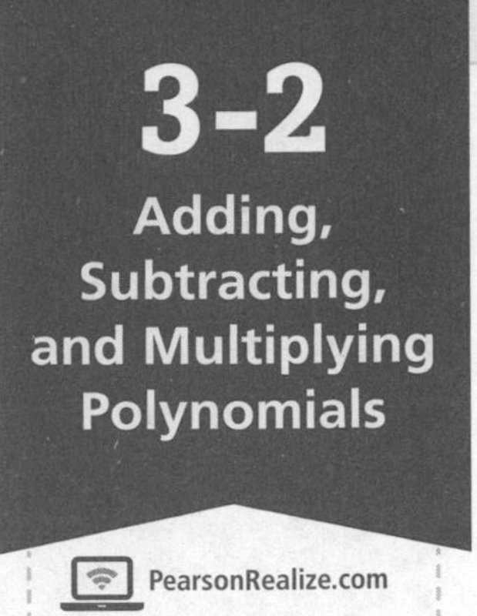

3-2
Adding, Subtracting, and Multiplying Polynomials
PearsonRealize.com

EXPLORE & REASON

Let S be the set of expressions that can be written as $ax + b$, where a and b are real numbers.

A. Describe the Associative Property, the Commutative Property, and the Distributive Property. Then, explain the role of each in simplifying the sum $(3x + 2) + (7x - 4)$ and identify the leading coefficient and the constant term in the result.

B. Is the sum you found in part A a member of S? Explain.

C. Construct Arguments Is the product of two expressions in S also a member of S? Explain why or produce a counterexample.

HABITS OF MIND

Construct Arguments Is the quotient of two expressions in S also a member of S? Explain why or produce a counterexample.

Notes

Assess

EXAMPLE 1

Try It! Add and Subtract Polynomials

1. Add or subtract the polynomials.
   a. $(4a^4 - 6a^3 - 3a^2 + a + 1) + (5a^3 + 7a^2 + 2a - 2)$

   b. $(2a^2b^2 + 3ab^2 - 5a^2b) - (3a^2b^2 - 9a^2b + 7ab^2)$

HABITS OF MIND

Generalize When can you combine two terms using addition or subtraction?

EXAMPLE 2

Try It! Multiply Polynomials

2. Multiply the polynomials.
   a. $(6n^2 - 7)(n^2 + n + 3)$

   b. $(mn + 1)(m^2n - 1)(mn^2 + 2)$

EXAMPLE 3

Try It! Understand Closure

3. Is the set of monomials closed under multiplication? Explain.

HABITS OF MIND

Construct Arguments Is the set of polynomials closed under multiplication? Explain.

Notes

Assess

EXAMPLE 4

Try It! Write a Polynomial Function

4. The cost of Carolina's materials changes so that her new cost function is $c(x) = 4x + 42$. Find the new profit function. Then find the quantity that maximizes profit and calculate the profit.

EXAMPLE 5

Try It! Compare Two Polynomial Functions

5. Compare the profit functions of two additional market sellers modeled by the graph of f and the equation $g(x) = (x + 1)(5 - x)$. Compare and interpret the y-intercepts of these functions and their end behavior.

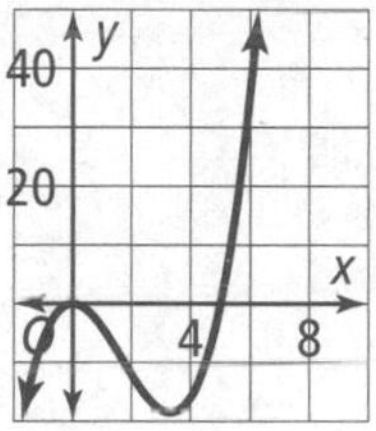

y
40
20
x
O
4
8

HABITS OF MIND

Make Sense and Persevere Find the quantity that maximizes profit for $g(x) = (x + 1)(5 - x)$. Calculate the profit.

Assess

Do You UNDERSTAND?

1. ESSENTIAL QUESTION How do you add, subtract, and multiply polynomials?

2. **Error Analysis** Chen subtracted two polynomials as shown. Explain Chen's error.

$p^2 + 7mp + 4 - (-2p^2 - mp + 1)$

$p^2 + 2p^2 + 7mp - mp + 4 + 1$

$3p^2 + 6mp + 5$ ✗

3. **Communicate Precisely** Why do we often write the results of polynomial calculations in standard form?

4. **Construct Arguments** Is the set of whole numbers closed under subtraction? Explain why you think so, or provide a counterexample.

Do You KNOW HOW?

Add or subtract the polynomials.

5. $(-3a^3 + 2a^2 - 4) + (a^3 - 3a^2 - 5a + 7)$

6. $(7x^2y^2 - 6x^3 + xy) - (5x^2y^2 - x^3 + xy + x)$

Multiply the polynomials.

7. $(7a + 2)(2a^2 - 5a + 3)$

8. $(xy - 1)(xy + 6)(xy - 8)$

9. The length of a rectangular speaker is three times its width, and the height is four more than the width. Write an expression for the volume V of the rectangular prism in terms of its width, w.

3-3 Polynomial Identities

PearsonRealize.com

EXPLORE & REASON

Look at the following triangle. Each number is the sum of the two numbers diagonally above. If there is not a second number, think of it as 0.

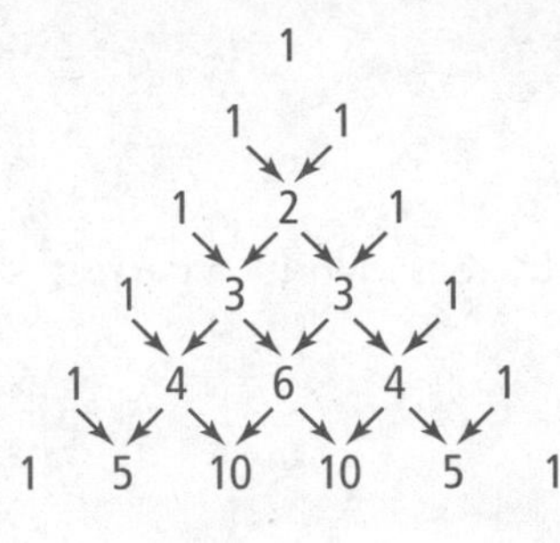

A. Write the numbers in the next 3 rows.

B. Look for Relationships What other patterns do you see?

C. Write a formula for the sum of the numbers in the nth row of the triangle.

HABITS OF MIND

Look for Relationships Create a triangle that starts with 2 instead of 1. How does this new triangle relate to the original triangle?

Notes

Assess

EXAMPLE 1

Try It! Prove a Polynomial Identity

1. Prove the Difference of Cubes Identity.

HABITS OF MIND

Reason Is the trinomial factor in the Difference of Cubes Identity a perfect square trinomial? Explain.

EXAMPLE 2

Try It! Use Polynomial Identities to Multiply Polynomials

2. Use polynomial identities to multiply each expression.

a. $(3x^2 + 5y^3)(3x^2 - 5y^3)$

b. $(12 + 15)^2$

EXAMPLE 3

Try It! Use Polynomial Identities to Factor Polynomials

3. Use polynomial identities to factor each polynomial or simplify each expression.

a. $m^8 - 9n^{10}$

b. $27x^9 - 343y^6$

c. $12^3 + 2^3$

HABITS OF MIND

Look for Relationships What binomial has factors $(a - 3b)$ and $(a^2 + 3ab + 9b^2)$?

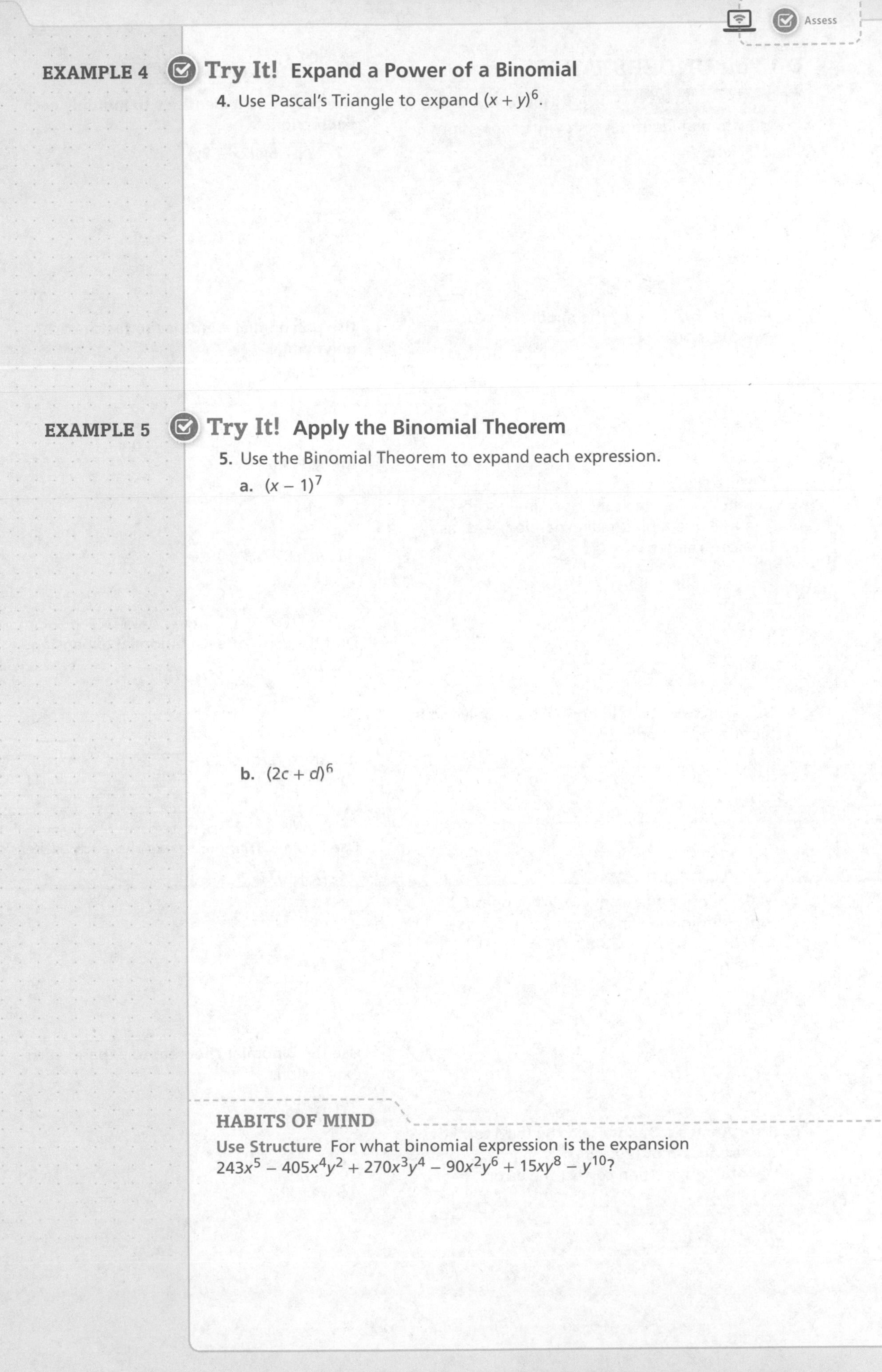

Notes

Assess

EXAMPLE 4

Try It! Expand a Power of a Binomial

4. Use Pascal's Triangle to expand $(x + y)^6$.

EXAMPLE 5

Try It! Apply the Binomial Theorem

5. Use the Binomial Theorem to expand each expression.

a. $(x - 1)^7$

b. $(2c + d)^6$

HABITS OF MIND

Use Structure For what binomial expression is the expansion $243x^5 - 405x^4y^2 + 270x^3y^4 - 90x^2y^6 + 15xy^8 - y^{10}$?

Assess

Do You UNDERSTAND?

1. ESSENTIAL QUESTION How can you use polynomial identities to rewrite expressions efficiently?

2. **Reason** Explain why the middle term of $(x + 5)^2$ is $10x$.

3. **Communicate Precisely** How are Pascal's Triangle and a binomial expansion, such as $(a + b)^5$, related?

4. **Use Structure** Explain how to use a polynomial identity to factor $8x^6 - 27y^3$.

5. **Make Sense and Persevere** What does C_3 represent in the expansion $C_0a^5 + C_1a^4b + C_2a^3b^2 + C_3a^2b^3 + C_4ab^4 + C_5b^5$? Explain.

6. **Error Analysis** Dakota said the third term of the expansion of $(2g + 3h)^4$ is $36g^2h^2$. Explain Dakota's error. Then correct the error.

Do You KNOW HOW?

Use polynomial identities to multiply each expression.

7. $(2x + 8y)(2x - 8y)$

8. $(x + 3y^3)^2$

Use polynomial identities to factor each polynomial.

9. $36a^6 - 4b^2$

10. $8x^6 - y^3$

11. $m^9 + 27n^6$

Find the term of each binomial expansion.

12. fifth term of $(x + y)^5$

13. third term of $(a - 3)^6$

Use Pascal's Triangle to expand each expression.

14. $(x + 1)^5$

15. $(a - b)^6$

Use the Binomial Theorem to expand each expression.

16. $(d - 1)^4$

17. $(x + y)^7$

3-4 Dividing Polynomials

PearsonRealize.com

EXPLORE & REASON

Benson recalls how to divide whole numbers by solving a problem with 6 as the divisor and 83 as the dividend. He determines that the quotient is 13 with remainder 5.

A. Explain the process of long division using Benson's example.

B. How can you express the remainder as a fraction?

C. Use Structure Use the results of the division problem to write two expressions for 83 that include the divisor, quotient, and remainder.

HABITS OF MIND

Look for Relationships If the remainder in a division problem is zero, what can you say about the dividend?

Notes

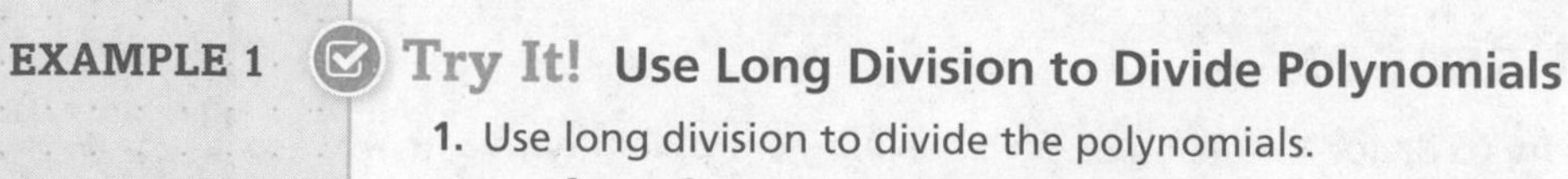

EXAMPLE 1

Try It! Use Long Division to Divide Polynomials

1. Use long division to divide the polynomials.

   a. $x^3 - 6x^2 + 11x - 6$ divided by $x^2 - 4x + 3$

   b. $16x^4 - 85$ divided by $4x^2 + 9$

EXAMPLE 2

Try It! Use Synthetic Division to Divide by $x - a$

2. Use synthetic division to divide $3x^3 - 5x + 10$ by $x - 1$.

HABITS OF MIND

Communicate Precisely Which method would you use to divide a polynomial by $x^2 + 5$? Why?

EXAMPLE 3

Try It! Relate $P(a)$ to the Remainder of $P(x) \div (x - a)$

3. Use synthetic division to show that the remainder of $f(x) = x^3 + 8x^2 + 12x + 5$ divided by $x + 2$ is equal to $f(-2)$.

Notes

Assess

EXAMPLE 4 **Try It! Use the Remainder Theorem to Evaluate Polynomials**

4. A technology company uses the function $R(x) = -x^3 + 12x^2 + 6x + 80$ to model expected annual revenue, in thousands of dollars, for a new product, where x is the number of years after the product is released. Use the Remainder Theorem to estimate the revenue in year 5.

EXAMPLE 5 **Try It! Use the Factor Theorem**

5. Use the Remainder and Factor Theorems to determine whether the given binomial is a factor of $P(x)$.

   a. $P(x) = x^3 - 10x^2 + 28x - 16$; binomial: $x - 4$

   b. $P(x) = 2x^4 + 9x^3 - 2x^2 + 6x - 40$; binomial: $x + 5$

HABITS OF MIND

Make Sense and Persevere Is $x - 2$ a factor of $x^5 + x^4 - 6x^3 + 2x^2 - 11x + 15$? If not, what is the remainder?

Assess

Do You UNDERSTAND?

1. **ESSENTIAL QUESTION** How can you divide polynomials?

2. **Error Analysis** Ella said the remainder of $x^3 + 2x^2 - 4x + 6$ divided by $x + 5$ is 149. Is Ella correct? Explain.

3. **Look for Relationships** You divide a polynomial $P(x)$ by a linear expression $D(x)$. You find a quotient $Q(x)$ and a remainder $R(x)$. How can you check your work?

Do You KNOW HOW?

4. Use long division to divide $x^4 - 4x^3 + 12x^2 - 3x + 6$ by $x^2 + 8$.

5. Use synthetic division to divide $x^3 - 8x^2 + 9x - 5$ by $x - 3$.

6. Use the Remainder Theorem to find the remainder of $2x^4 + x^2 - 10x - 1$ divided by $x + 2$.

7. Is $x + 9$ a factor of the polynomial $P(x) = x^3 + 11x^2 + 15x - 27$? If so, write the polynomial as a product of two factors. If not, explain how you know.

MODEL & DISCUSS

Charlie and Aisha built a small rocket and launched it from their backyard. The rocket fell to the ground 10 s after it launched. The height *h*, in feet, of the rocket relative to the ground at time *t* seconds can be modeled by the function shown.

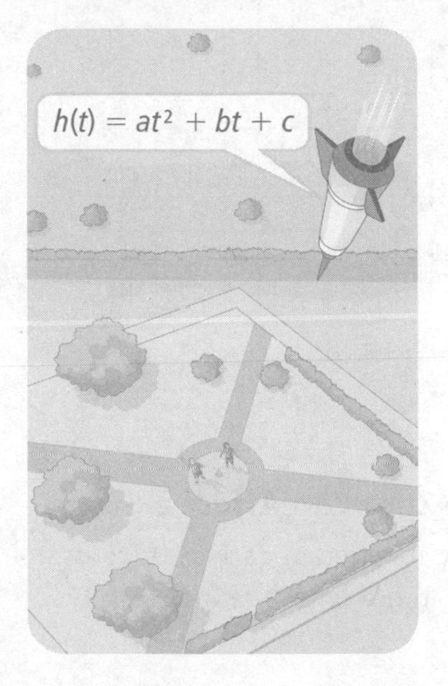

A. How are the launch and landing times related to the modeling function?

B. What additional information about the rocket launch could you use to construct an accurate model for the rocket's height relative to the ground?

C. Construct Arguments Charlie believes that the function $h(t) = -16t^2 + 160t$ models the height of the rocket with respect to time. Do you agree? Explain your reasoning and indicate the domain of this function.

HABITS OF MIND

Reason In Charlie's function, what is the value of c? Why is this the correct value?

Notes

Assess

EXAMPLE 1 Try It! Use Zeros to Graph a Polynomial Function

1. Factor each function. Then use the zeros to sketch its graph.

a. $f(x) = 4x^3 + 4x^2 - 24x$

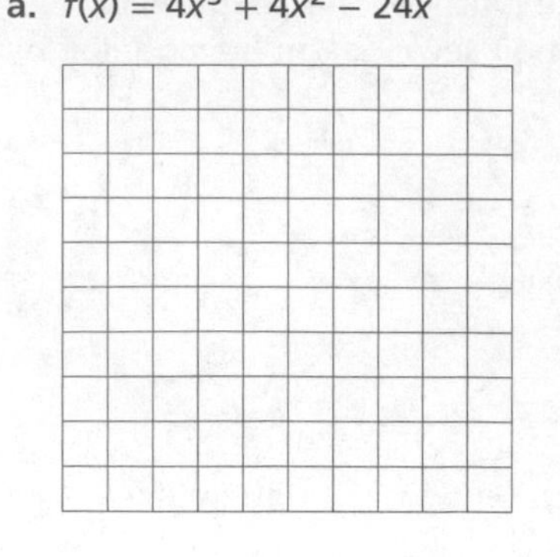

b. $g(x) = x^4 - 81$

EXAMPLE 2 Try It! Understand How a Multiple Zero Can Affect a Graph

2. Describe the behavior of the graph of the function at each of its zeros.

a. $f(x) = x(x + 4)\ (x - 1)^4$

b. $f(x) = (x^2 + 9)(x - 1)^5(x + 2)^2$

HABITS OF MIND

Reason Do the values of a function always change from positive to negative or negative to positive on either side of a zero? Explain.

EXAMPLE 3 Try It! Find Real and Complex Zeros

3. What are all the real and complex zeros of the polynomial function shown in the graph?

a.

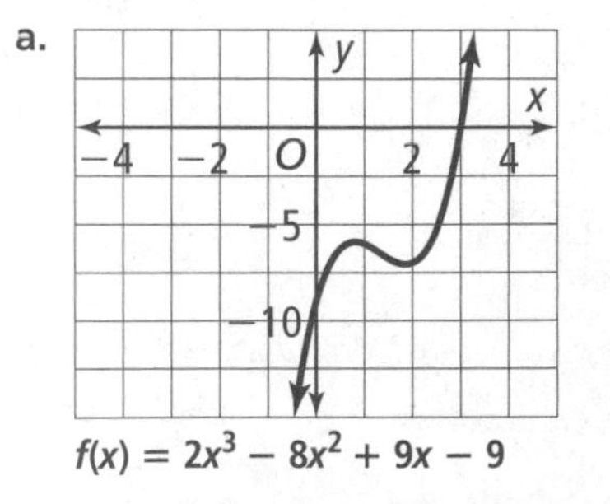

$f(x) = 2x^3 - 8x^2 + 9x - 9$

b.

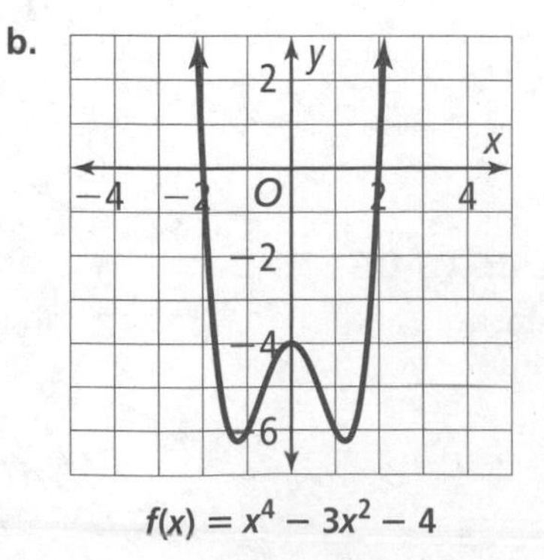

$f(x) = x^4 - 3x^2 - 4$

Notes

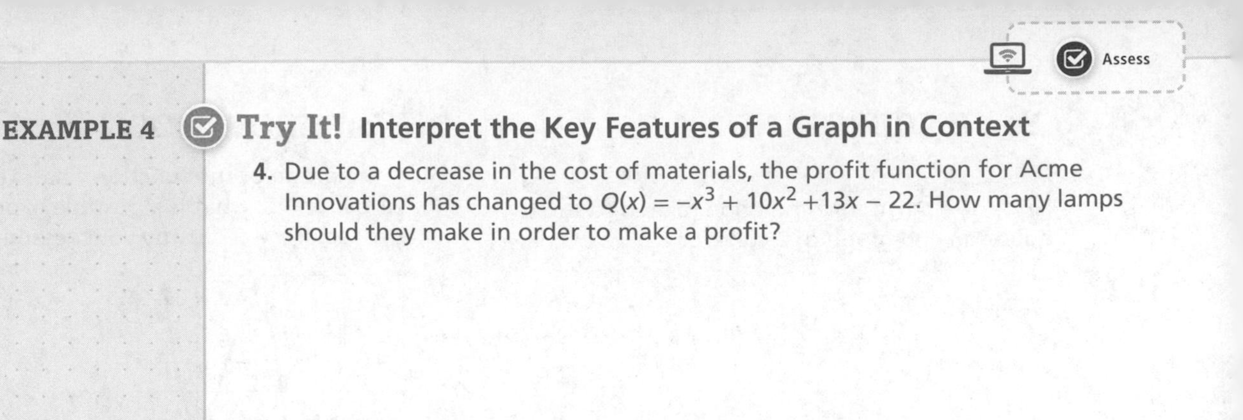

EXAMPLE 4

Try It! Interpret the Key Features of a Graph in Context

4. Due to a decrease in the cost of materials, the profit function for Acme Innovations has changed to $Q(x) = -x^3 + 10x^2 + 13x - 22$. How many lamps should they make in order to make a profit?

HABITS OF MIND

Make Sense and Persevere On a graph, how do complex roots differ from real roots?

EXAMPLE 5

Try It! Solve Polynomial Equations

5. What is the solution of the equation?

a. $x^3 - 7x + 6 = x^3 + 5x^2 - 2x - 24$ b. $x^4 + 2x^2 = -x^3 - 2x$

EXAMPLE 6

Try It! Solve a Polynomial Inequality by Graphing

6. What are the solutions of the inequality?

a. $2x^3 + 12x^2 + 12x < 0$ b. $(x^2 - 1)(x^2 - x - 6) > 0$

HABITS OF MIND

Use Structure How does solving $2x^3 + 12x^2 + 12x = 0$ help you to solve the inequality $2x^3 + 12x^2 + 12x < 0$?

Do You UNDERSTAND?

1. ESSENTIAL QUESTION How are the zeros of a polynomial function related to the equation and graph of a function?

2. **Error Analysis** In order to identify the zeros of the function, a student factored the cubic function $f(x) = x^3 - 3x^2 - 10x$ as follows:

$$\begin{aligned} f(x) &= x^3 - 3x^2 - 10x \\ &= x(x^2 - 3x - 10) \\ &= x(x - 5)(x + 2) \\ x = 0&, x = -5, x = 2 \end{aligned}$$

Describe and correct the error the student made.

3. **Make Sense and Persevere** Explain how you can determine that the function $f(x) = x^3 + 3x^2 + 4x + 2$ has both real and complex zeros.

Do You KNOW HOW?

4. If the graph of the function f has a multiple zero at $x = 2$, what is a possible exponent of the factor $x - 2$? Justify your reasoning.

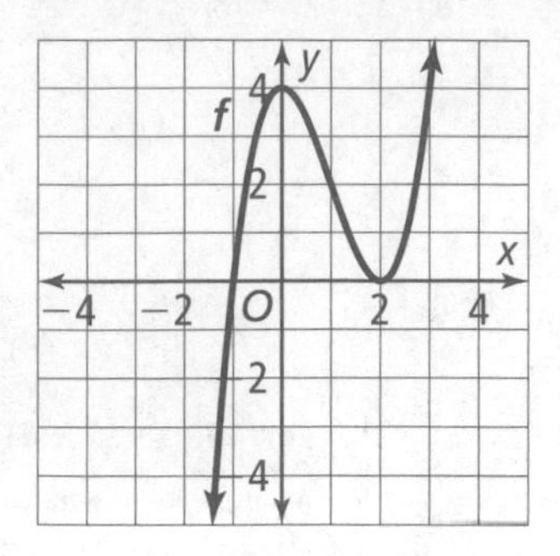

5. Energy Solutions manufactures LED light bulbs. The profit p, in thousands of dollars earned, is a function of the number of bulbs sold, x, in ten thousands. Profit is modeled by the function $-x^3 + 9x^2 - 11x - 21$. For what number of bulbs manufactured is the company profitable?

What Are the Rules?

All games have rules about how to play the game. The rules outline such things as when a ball is in or out, how a player scores points, and how many points a player gets for each winning shot.

If you didn't already know how to play tennis, or some other game, could you figure out what the rules were just by watching? What clues would help you understand the game? Think about this during the Mathematical Modeling in 3 Acts lesson.

ACT 1 Identify the Problem

1. What is the first question that comes to mind after watching the video?

2. Write down the Main Question you will answer.

3. Make an initial conjecture that answers this Main Question.

4. Explain how you arrived at your conjecture.

5. What information will be useful to know to answer the Main Question? How can you get it? How will you use that information?

Video

ACT 2 Develop a Model

6. Use the math that you have learned in the topic to refine your conjecture.

ACT 3 Interpret the Results

7. Did your refined conjecture match the actual answer exactly? If not, what might explain the difference?

Activity

3-6 Theorems about Roots of Polynomial Equations

PearsonRealize.com

CRITIQUE & EXPLAIN

Look at the polynomial functions shown.

$g(x) = x^2 - 7x - 18$
$h(x) = 5x^2 + 24x + 16$

A. Avery has a conjecture that the zeros of a polynomial function have to be positive or negative factors of its constant term. Factor g completely. Are the zeros of g factors of -18?

B. Look for Relationships Now test Avery's conjecture by factoring $h(x)$. Does Avery's conjecture hold? If so, explain why. If not, make a new conjecture.

HABITS OF MIND

Use Structure For the factored function $k(x) = (ax + b)(cx + d)$, what are the coefficients in the expanded expression?

Notes

Assess

EXAMPLE 1

Try It! Identify Possible Rational Solutions

1. List all the possible rational solutions for each equation.

   a. $4x^4 + 13x^3 - 124x^2 + 212x - 8 = 0$

   b. $7x^4 + 13x^3 - 124x^2 + 212x - 45 = 0$

EXAMPLE 2

Try It! Use the Rational Root Theorem

2. A jewelry box measures $2x + 1$ in. long, $2x - 6$ in. wide, and x in. tall. The volume of the box is given by the function $v(x) = 4x^3 - 10x^2 - 6x$. What is the height of the box, in inches, if its volume is 28 in.^{3}?

HABITS OF MIND

Critique Arguments For the jewelry box, a student thought that the rational roots could be $\pm 6, \pm 3, \pm 2, \pm 1, \pm\frac{3}{2}, \pm\frac{1}{2}, \pm\frac{1}{4}$, using factors of -6 for the numerator and factors of 4 for the denominator of the possible rational roots. Is the student correct? Explain.

EXAMPLE 3

Try It! Find All Complex Roots

3. What are all the complex roots of the equation $x^3 - 2x^2 + 5x - 10 = 0$?

Assess

EXAMPLE 4

Try It! Irrational Roots and the Coefficients of a Polynomial

4. Suppose a quadratic polynomial function f has two complex zeros that are a conjugate pair, $a - bi$ and $a + bi$ (where a and b are real numbers). Are all the coefficients of f real? Explain.

HABITS OF MIND

Construct Arguments Could a polynomial equation with rational coefficients have two complex roots that are not conjugates as its only roots? Explain.

EXAMPLE 5

Try It! Write Polynomial Functions Using Conjugates

5. a. What is a quadratic equation in standard form with rational coefficients that has a root of $5 + 4i$?

   b. What is a polynomial function Q of degree 4 with rational coefficients such that $Q(x) = 0$ has roots $2 - \sqrt{3}$ and $5i$?

HABITS OF MIND

Reason Is it possible to write a polynomial function of degree 3 that has rational coefficients and zeros $2 - \sqrt{3}$ and $5i$? Explain.

Do You UNDERSTAND?

1. ESSENTIAL QUESTION How are the roots of a polynomial equation related to the coefficients and degree of the polynomial?

2. **Error Analysis** Renaldo said that a polynomial equation with real coefficients that has zeros $-1 + 2i$ and $3 + \sqrt{5}$ and has a degree of 4. Is Renaldo correct? Explain.

3. **Use Structure** A fifth degree polynomial $P(x)$ with rational coefficients has zeros $2i$ and $\sqrt{7}$. What other zeros does $P(x)$ have? Explain.

4. **Construct Arguments** If one root of a polynomial equation with real coefficients is $4 + 2i$, is it certain that $4 - 2i$ is also a root of the equation? Explain.

Do You KNOW HOW?

List all the possible rational solutions for each equation according to the Rational Roots Theorem. Then find all of the rational roots.

5. $0 = x^3 + 4x^2 - 9x - 36$

6. $0 = x^4 - 2x^3 - 7x^2 + 8x + 12$

7. $0 = 4x^3 + 8x^2 - x - 2$

8. $0 = 9x^4 - 40x^2 + 16$

A polynomial equation with rational coefficients has the given roots. List two more roots of each equation.

9. $1 + \sqrt{11}$ and $-3 + \sqrt{17}$

10. $5 + 12i$ and $-9 - 7i$

11. $12 + 5i$ and $6 - \sqrt{13}$

12. $5 - 15i$ and $17 + \sqrt{23}$

Activity

EXPLORE & REASON

Look at the polynomial graphs below.

$f(x) = x^2$

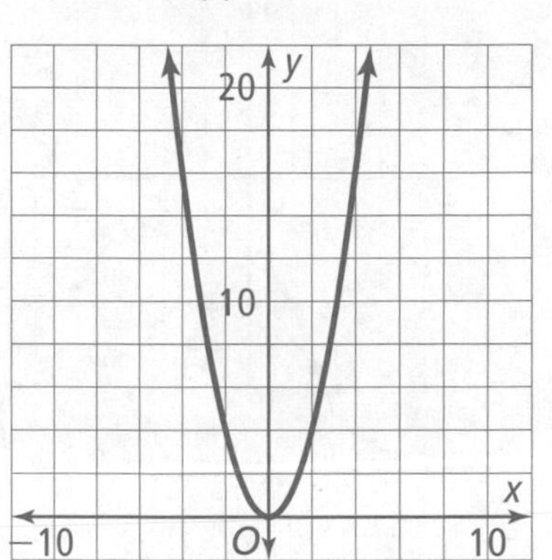

$g(x) = x^3$

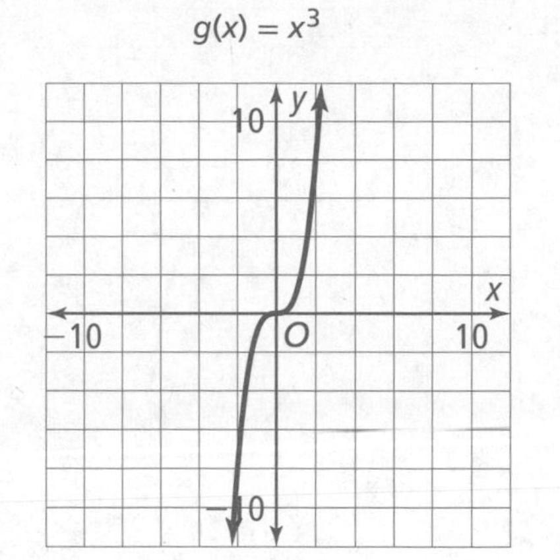

A. Is the graph of f or g symmetric about the y-axis? Is the graph of f or g symmetric about the origin? Explain.

B. **Look for Relationships** Graph more functions of the form $y = x^n$ where n is a natural number. Which of these functions are symmetric about the origin? Which are symmetric about the y-axis? What conjectures can you make?

HABITS OF MIND

Look for Relationships Do you notice any other patterns among the functions with even degree or the functions with odd degree?

Assess

EXAMPLE 1

Try It! Identify Even and Odd Functions From Their Graphs

1. Classify the polynomial functions as even or odd based on the graphs.

a.

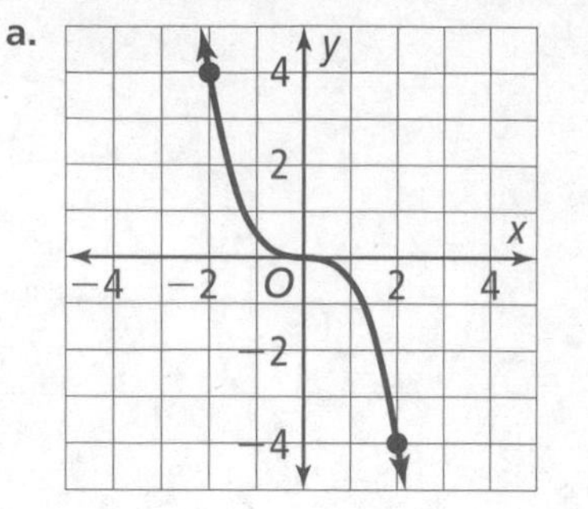

b.

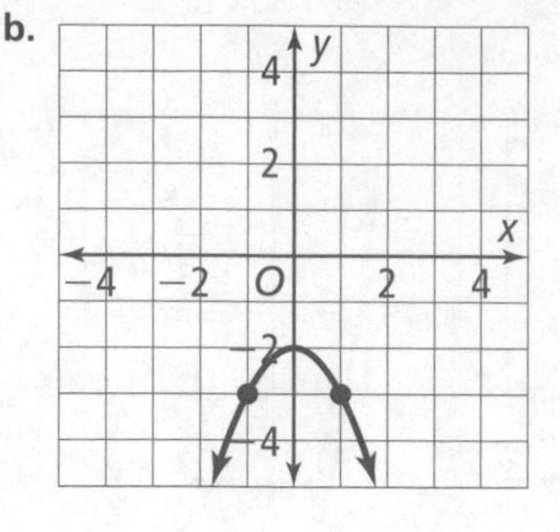

EXAMPLE 2

Try It! Identify Even and Odd Functions From Their Equations

2. Is the function odd, even, or neither?

a. $f(x) = 7x^5 - 2x^2 + 4$

b. $f(x) = x^6 - 2$

HABITS OF MIND

Make Sense and Persevere Why do you replace x with $-x$ when determining if a function is odd, even, or neither?

EXAMPLE 3

Try It! Graph Transformations of Cubic and Quartic Parent Functions

3. How does the graph of the function $g(x) = 2x^3 - 5$ differ from the graph of its parent function?

EXAMPLE 4

Try It! Identify a Transformation

4. Determine the equation of each graph as it relates to its parent cubic function or quartic function.

a.

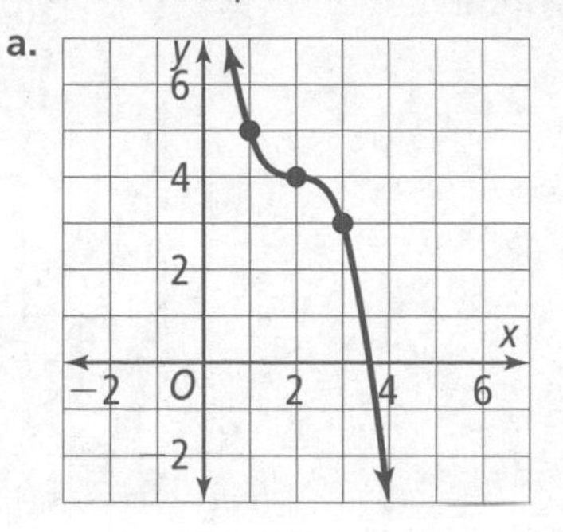

b.

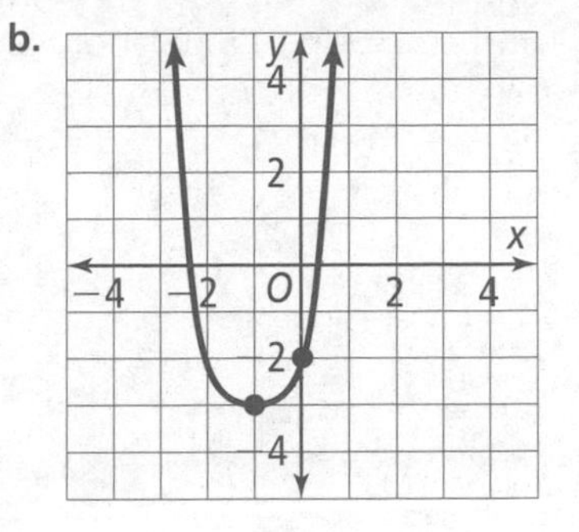

HABITS OF MIND

Look for Relationships What type of transformation would change a function's end behavior?

EXAMPLE 5

Try It! Apply a Transformation of a Cubic Function

5. a. The volume of a cube, in cubic feet, is given by the function $V(x) = x^3$. Write a function for the volume of the cube in cubic inches if x is the edge length in feet.

b. A storage unit is in the shape of a rectangular prism. The volume of the storage unit is given by $V(x) = (x)(x)(x - 1) = x^3 - x^2$, where x is measured in feet. A potential customer wants to compare the volume of this storage unit with that of another storage unit that is 1 foot longer in every dimension. Write a function for the volume of this larger unit.

HABITS OF MIND

Critique Arguments A student thought that, for 5a, the new function should be $V(x) = 144x^3$. What are the two errors the student made?

Do You UNDERSTAND?

1. ESSENTIAL QUESTION How are symmetry and transformations represented in the graph and equation of a polynomial function?

2. **Vocabulary** What is the difference between the graph of an even function and the graph of an odd function?

3. **Error Analysis** A student identified the transformations of the polynomial function $f(x) = 3(x - 1)^3 - 6$ as follows:

   The function is shifted to the left 1 unit, stretched vertically, and is shifted downward 6 units.

   Describe and correct the error the student made.

Do You KNOW HOW?

4. Classify the function on the graph as odd, even, or neither.

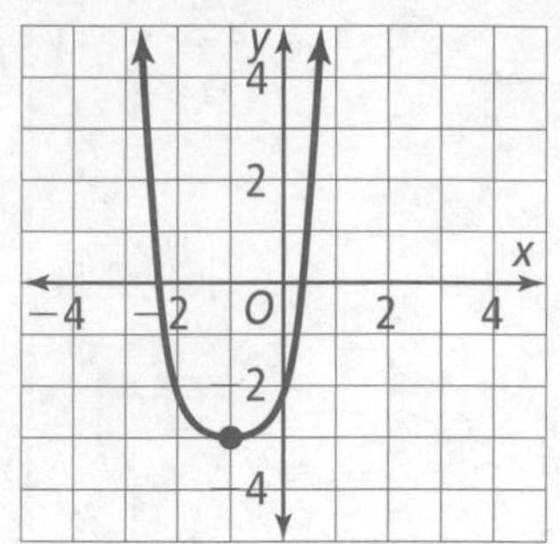

5. Use the equation to classify the function as odd, even, or neither.
   $g(x) = 4x^3 - x$

6. The volume of cardboard box is given by the function $V(x) = x(x - 2)(x) = x^3 - 2x^2$. Write a new function for the volume of a cardboard box that is 2 units longer in every dimension.

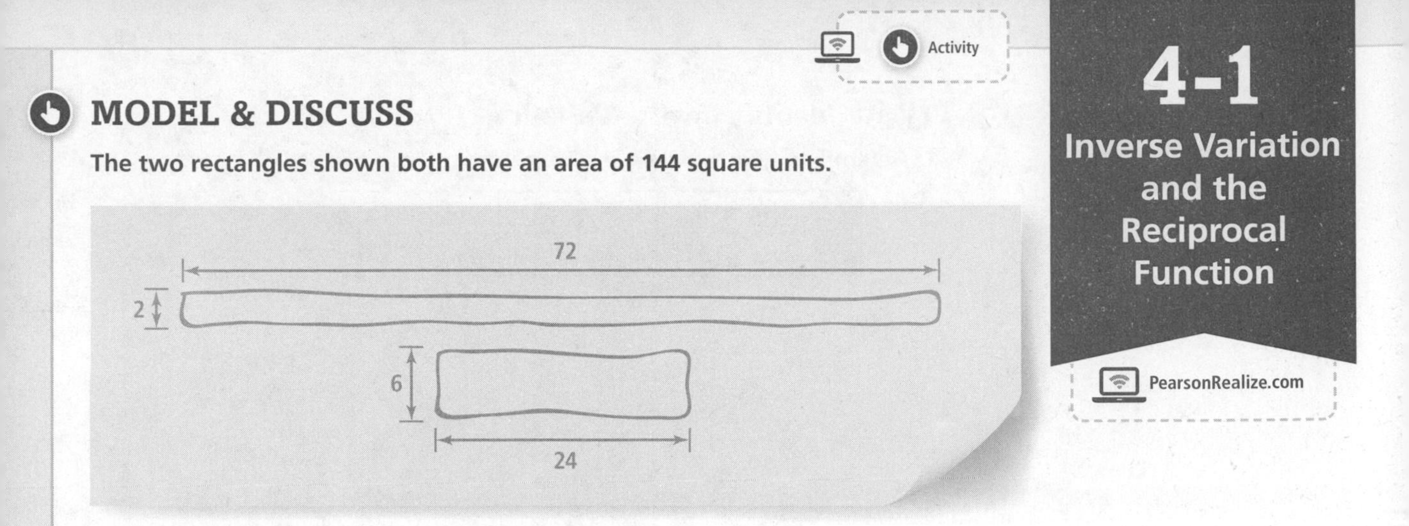

MODEL & DISCUSS

The two rectangles shown both have an area of 144 square units.

A. Sketch as many other rectangles as you can that have the same area. Organize and record your data for the lengths and widths of the rectangles.

B. Use Structure Considering rectangles with an area of 144 square units, what happens to the width of the rectangle as the length increases?

C. Examine at least five other pairs of rectangles, each pair sharing the same area. How would you describe the relationship between the lengths and widths?

HABITS OF MIND

Use Structure How does the formula for the area of a rectangle make sense with the relationships you found?

Notes

Assess

EXAMPLE 1 **Try It!** **Identify Inverse Variation**

1. Determine if each table of values represents an inverse variation.

a.

x	1	2	3	5	6	15
y	25.5	12.75	8.50	5.10	4.25	1.70

b.

x	6.6	5.5	4.4	3.3	2.2	1.1
y	3	5	7	9	11	13

EXAMPLE 2 **Try It!** **Use Inverse Variation**

2. In an inverse variation, $x = 6$ and $y = \frac{1}{2}$

a. What is the equation that represents the inverse variation?

b. What is the value of y when $x = 15$?

HABITS OF MIND

Construct Arguments For rectangles that have a constant perimeter, the length increases as the width decreases. Is the relationship between the length and width an inverse variation? Explain.

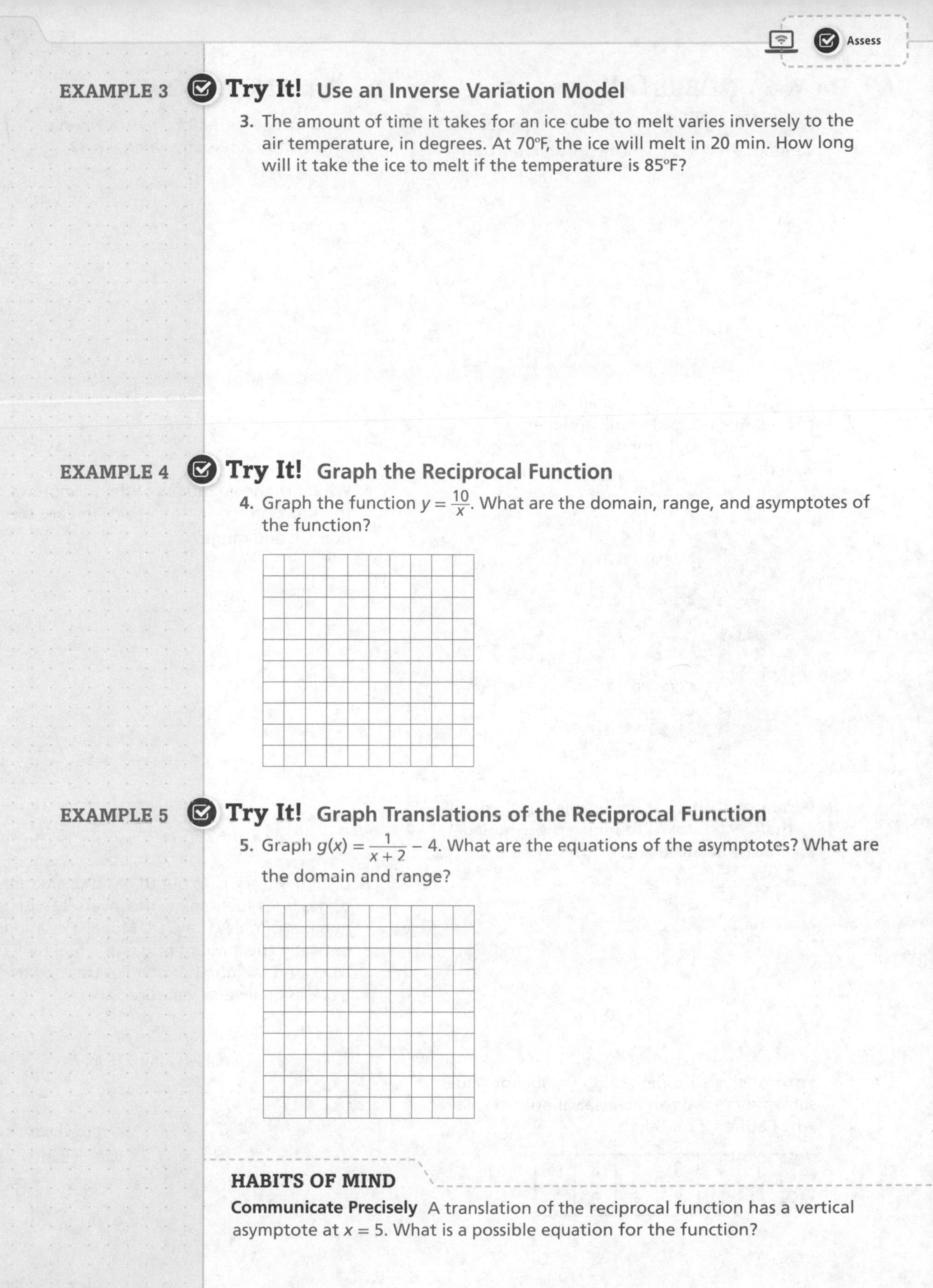

EXAMPLE 3

Try It! Use an Inverse Variation Model

3. The amount of time it takes for an ice cube to melt varies inversely to the air temperature, in degrees. At 70°F, the ice will melt in 20 min. How long will it take the ice to melt if the temperature is 85°F?

EXAMPLE 4

Try It! Graph the Reciprocal Function

4. Graph the function $y = \frac{10}{x}$. What are the domain, range, and asymptotes of the function?

EXAMPLE 5

Try It! Graph Translations of the Reciprocal Function

5. Graph $g(x) = \frac{1}{x + 2} - 4$. What are the equations of the asymptotes? What are the domain and range?

HABITS OF MIND

Communicate Precisely A translation of the reciprocal function has a vertical asymptote at $x = 5$. What is a possible equation for the function?

Do You UNDERSTAND?

1. ESSENTIAL QUESTION How are inverse variations related to the reciprocal function?

2. **Construct Arguments** Explain why the amount of propane in a grill's tank and the time spent grilling could represent an inverse variation.

3. **Vocabulary** Why is it impossible for the graph of the function $y = \frac{1}{x}$ to intersect the horizontal asymptote at the x-axis?

4. **Error Analysis** Carmen said the table of values shown represents an inverse variation. Explain why Carmen is mistaken.

x	1	2	3	4	8	16
y	24	12	8	6	3	2

Do You KNOW HOW?

5. In an inverse variation, $x = -8$ when $y = -\frac{1}{4}$. What is the value of y when $x = 4$?

6. What are the equations of the asymptotes of the function $f(x) = \frac{1}{x-5} + 3$? What are the domain and range?

7. Until the truck runs out of gas, the amount of gas in its fuel tank varies inversely with the number of miles traveled. Model a relationship between the amount of gas in a fuel tank of a truck and the number of miles traveled by the truck as an inverse variation.

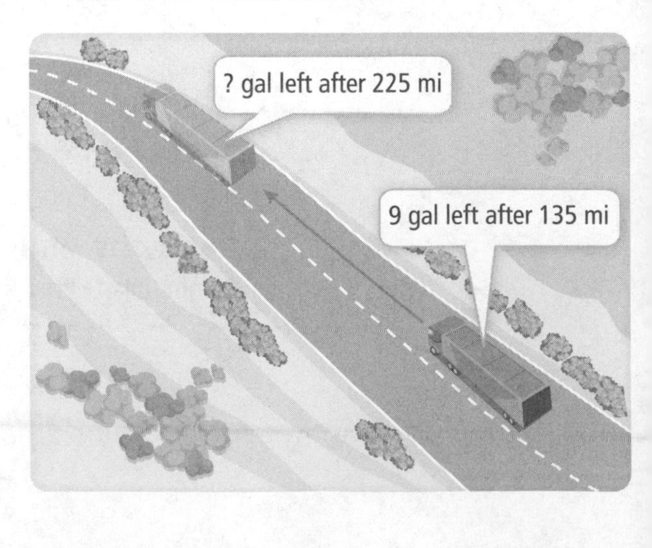

Activity

EXPLORE & REASON

4-2 Graphing Rational Functions

PearsonRealize.com

Look at the three functions shown.

$f(x) = x - 1$

$g(x) = \frac{x-1}{2}$

$h(x) = \frac{x-1}{x-2}$

A. **Look for Relationships** Graph each function. Determine which of the functions are linear. Find the y-intercept of each function and the slope, if appropriate.

B. What is the effect on the graph of f when dividing $x - 1$ by 2?

C. What happens to the graph of h as x approaches 2?

D. **Communicate Precisely** What is the effect on the graph of $f(x)$ when dividing $x - 1$ by $x - 2$? (Hint: Compare it to what you found in part (b).)

HABITS OF MIND

Look for Relationships What similarities do you notice between the graph of $h(x) = \frac{x-1}{x-2}$ and the graph of a reciprocal function?

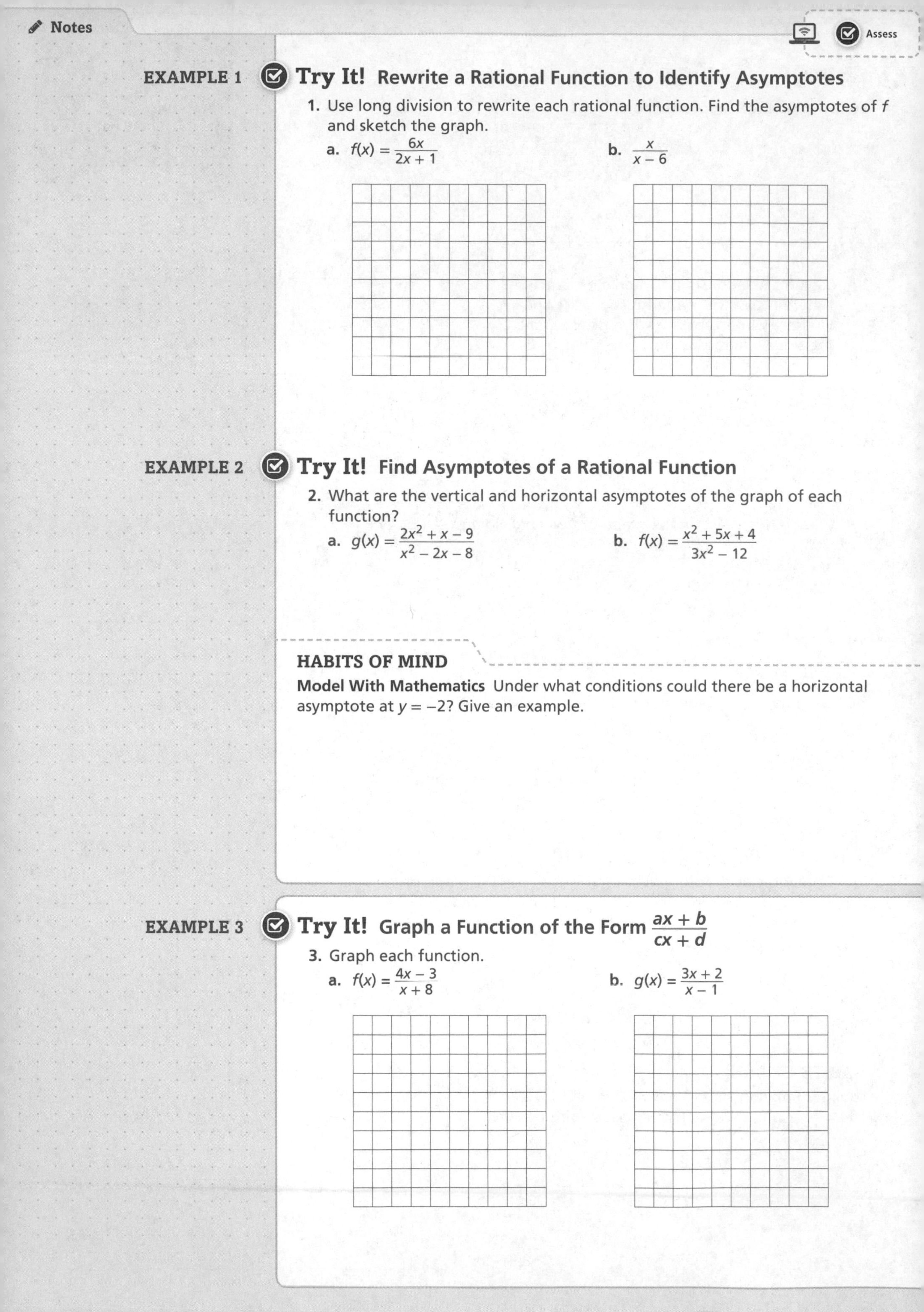

Notes

Assess

EXAMPLE 1

Try It! Rewrite a Rational Function to Identify Asymptotes

1. Use long division to rewrite each rational function. Find the asymptotes of f and sketch the graph.

a. $f(x) = \frac{6x}{2x + 1}$

b. $\frac{x}{x - 6}$

EXAMPLE 2

Try It! Find Asymptotes of a Rational Function

2. What are the vertical and horizontal asymptotes of the graph of each function?

a. $g(x) = \frac{2x^2 + x - 9}{x^2 - 2x - 8}$

b. $f(x) = \frac{x^2 + 5x + 4}{3x^2 - 12}$

HABITS OF MIND

Model With Mathematics Under what conditions could there be a horizontal asymptote at $y = -2$? Give an example.

EXAMPLE 3

Try It! Graph a Function of the Form $\frac{ax + b}{cx + d}$

3. Graph each function.

a. $f(x) = \frac{4x - 3}{x + 8}$

b. $g(x) = \frac{3x + 2}{x - 1}$

Notes

EXAMPLE 4

Try It! Use a Rational Function Model

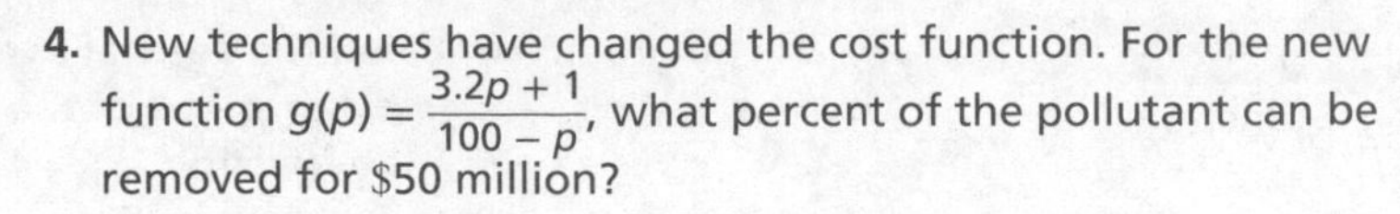

4. New techniques have changed the cost function. For the new function $g(p) = \frac{3.2p + 1}{100 - p}$, what percent of the pollutant can be removed for $50 million?

HABITS OF MIND

Make Sense and Persevere What are the asymptotes for the function $g(p) = \frac{3.2p + 1}{100 - p}$?

EXAMPLE 5

Try It! Graph a Rational Function

5. Identify the asymptotes and sketch the graph of $g(x) = \frac{x^2 - 5x + 6}{2x^2 - 10}$.

HABITS OF MIND

Reason When will the graph of a rational function have two vertical asymptotes?

Do You UNDERSTAND?

1. ESSENTIAL QUESTION How can you graph a rational function?

2. **Vocabulary** Why does it make sense to call the expressions in this lesson *rational* functions?

3. **Error Analysis** Ashton said the graph of $f(x) = \dfrac{x+2}{2x^2+4x-6}$ has a horizontal asymptote at $y = \frac{1}{2}$. Describe and correct Ashton's error.

4. **Reason** When will the graph of a rational function have no vertical asymptotes? Give an example of such a function.

Do You KNOW HOW?

Find the vertical asymptote(s) and horizontal asymptote(s) of the rational function. Then graph the function.

5. $f(x) = \dfrac{x+2}{x-3}$

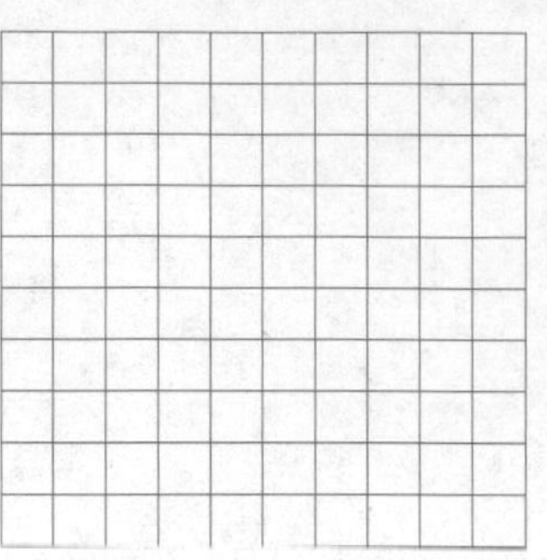

6. $f(x) = \dfrac{x-1}{2x+1}$

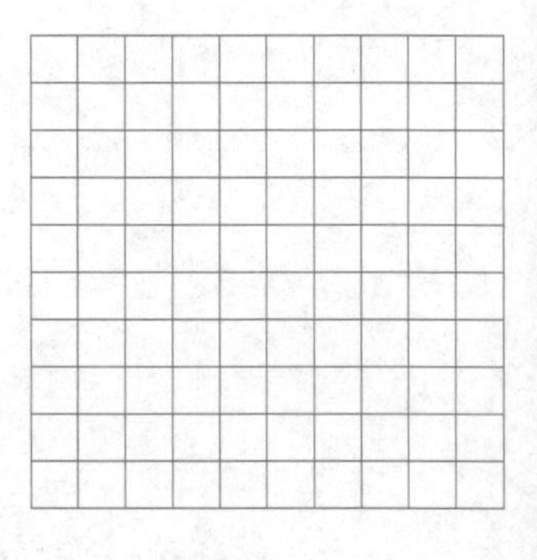

7. A trainer mixed water with an electrolyte solution. The relationship can be modeled by $f(x) = \dfrac{4}{x+12}$. Graph the function.

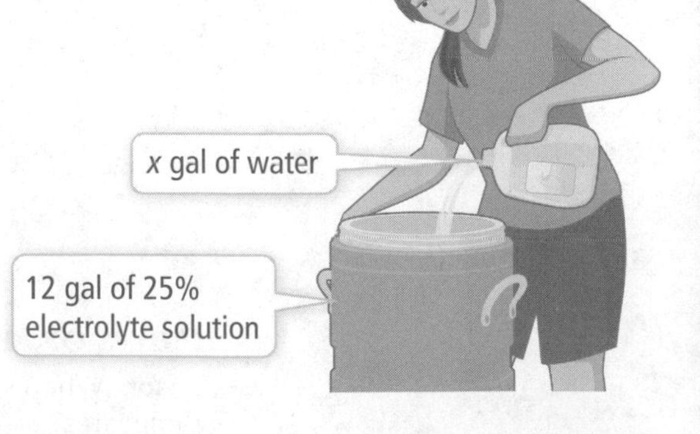

Activity

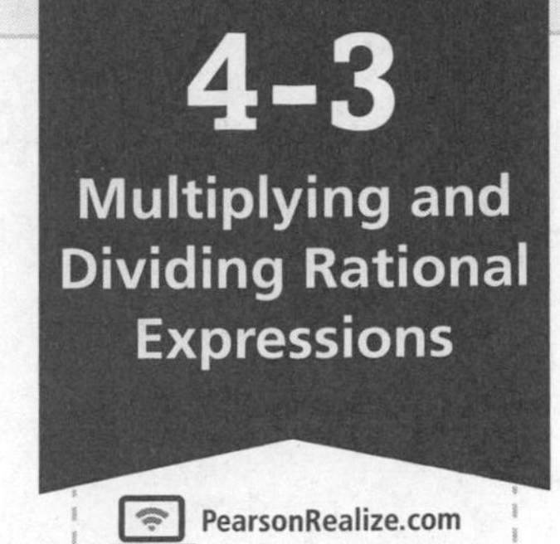

EXPLORE & REASON

Consider the following graph of the function $y = x + 2$.

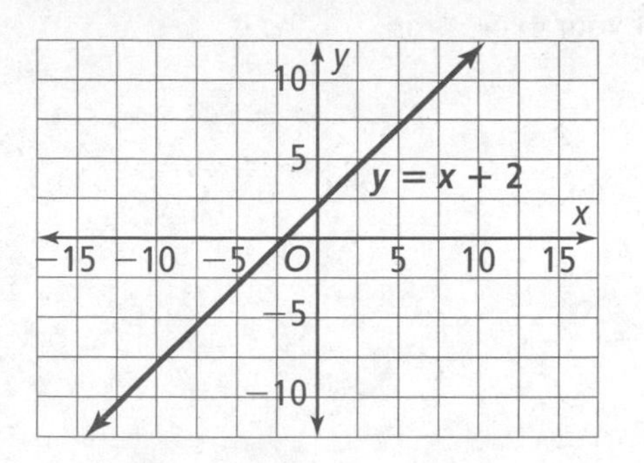

A. What is the domain of this function?

B. Sketch a function that resembles the graph, but restrict its domain to exclude 2.

C. Use Structure Consider the function you have sketched. What kind of function might have a graph like this? Explain.

HABITS OF MIND

Reason Does the graph of $y = \frac{2x + 6}{x + 3}$ have a vertical asymptote at $x = -3$? Explain.

Assess

EXAMPLE 1

Try It! Write Equivalent Rational Expressions

1. Write an expression equivalent to $\frac{3x^5 - 18x^4 - 21x^3}{2x^6 - 98x^4}$. Remember to give the domain for your expression.

EXAMPLE 2

Try It! Simplify a Rational Expression

2. Simplify each expression and show the domain for which the identity with the two expressions is valid.

   a. $\frac{x^2 + 2x + 1}{x^3 - 2x^2 - 3x}$

   b. $\frac{x^3 + 4x^2 - x - 4}{x^2 + 3x - 4}$

HABITS OF MIND

Critique Reasoning Bailey simplified the rational expression $\frac{x^2 + 2x + 4}{x^2 + x + 2}$ by dividing out the x^2-terms, and then dividing out a factor of $x + 2$ to get 2 as the simplified form of the rational expression. Is Bailey correct? Why or why not?

EXAMPLE 3

Try It! Multiply Rational Expressions

3. Find the simplified form of each product, and give the domain.

   a. $\frac{x^2 - 16}{9 - x} \cdot \frac{x^2 + x - 90}{x^2 + 14x + 40}$

   b. $\frac{x + 3}{4x} \cdot \frac{3x - 18}{6x + 18} \cdot \frac{x^2}{4x + 12}$

Notes

Assess

EXAMPLE 4

Try It! Multiply a Rational Expression by a Polynomial

4. Find the simplified form of each product and the domain.

a. $\frac{x^3 - 4x}{6x^2 - 13x - 5} \cdot (2x^3 - 3x^2 - 5x)$

b. $\frac{3x^2 + 6x}{x^2 - 49} \cdot (x^2 + 9x + 14)$

HABITS OF MIND

Generalize Why is it important to identify the domain of a rational expression before you simplify it rather than after?

EXAMPLE 5

Try It! Divide Rational Expressions

5. Find the simplified quotient and the domain of each expression.

a. $\frac{1}{x^2 + 9x} \div \left(\frac{6 - x}{3x^2 - 18x}\right)$

b. $\frac{2x^2 - 12x}{x + 5} \div \left(\frac{x - 6}{x + 5}\right)$

EXAMPLE 6

Try It! Use Division of Rational Expressions

6. The company compares the ratios of surface area to volume for two more containers. One is a rectangular prism with a square base. The other is a rectangular prism with a rectangular base. One side of the base is equal to the side-length of the first container, and the other side is twice as long. The surface area of this second container is $4x^2 + 6xh$. The heights of the two containers are equal. Which has the smaller surface area-to-volume ratio?

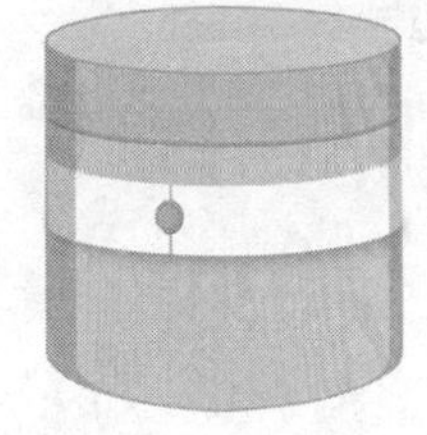

HABITS OF MIND

Use Structure Is the domain of the quotient $\frac{2x^2 - 12x}{x + 5} \div \left(\frac{x - 6}{x + 5}\right)$ different from the domain of the product $\left(\frac{2x^2 - 12x}{x + 5}\right)\left(\frac{x - 6}{x + 5}\right)$? Explain.

Do You UNDERSTAND?

1. **ESSENTIAL QUESTION** How does understanding operations with fractions help you multiply and divide rational expressions?

2. **Vocabulary** In your own words, define rational expression and provide an example of a rational expression.

3. **Error Analysis** A student divided the rational expressions as follows:

$$\frac{4x}{5y} \div \frac{20x^2}{25y^2} = \frac{4x}{\cancel{5}y} \div \frac{^{4}\cancel{20}x^2}{25y^2} = \frac{16x^3}{25y^3}.$$

Describe and correct the errors the student made.

4. **Communicate Precisely** Why do you have to state the domain when simplifying rational expressions?

Do You KNOW HOW?

5. What is the simplified form of the rational expression $\frac{x^2 - 36}{x^2 + 3x - 18}$? What is the domain?

6. Find the product and give the domain of $\frac{y + 3}{y + 2} \cdot \frac{y^2 + 4y + 4}{y^2 - 9}$.

7. Find and simplify the ratio of the volume of Figure A to the volume of Figure B.

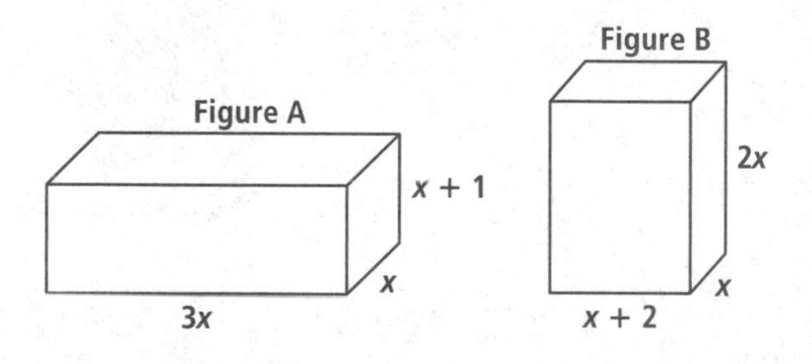

Activity

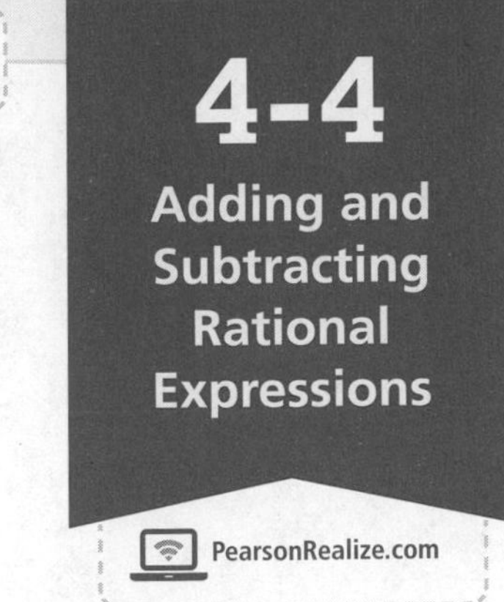

CRITIQUE & EXPLAIN

Teo and Shannon find the following exercise in their homework:

$$\frac{1}{2} + \frac{1}{3} + \frac{1}{9}$$

A. Teo claims that a common denominator of the sum is $2 + 3 + 9 = 14$. Shannon claims that it is $2 \cdot 3 \cdot 9 = 54$. Is either student correct? Explain why or why not.

B. Find the sum, explaining the method you use.

C. Construct Arguments Timothy states that the quickest way to find the sum of any two fractions with unlike denominators is to multiply their denominators to find a common denominator, and then rewrite each fraction with that denominator. Do you agree?

HABITS OF MIND

Look for Relationships For two fractions with denominators 10 and x, when is $10x$ the least common multiple? When is $10x$ NOT the least common multiple?

Notes

Assess

EXAMPLE 1

Try It! Add Rational Expressions With Like Denominators

1. Find the sum.

a. $\frac{10x-5}{2x+3}+\frac{8-4x}{2x+3}$

b. $\frac{x-5}{x+5}+\frac{3x-21}{x+5}$

HABITS OF MIND

Make Sense and Persevere Explain why it does not make sense to add the denominators when adding rational numbers. Use numerical fractions to support your thinking.

EXAMPLE 2

Try It! Identify the Least Common Multiple of Polynomials

2. Find the LCM for each set of expressions.

a. $x^3+9x^2+27x+27,\ x^2-4x-21$

b. $10x^2-10y^2,\ 15x^2-30xy+15y^2,\ x^2+3xy+2y^2$

EXAMPLE 3

Try It! Add Rational Expressions With Unlike Denominators

3. Find the sum.

a. $\frac{x+6}{x^2-4}+\frac{2}{x^2-5x+6}$

b. $\frac{2x}{3x+4}+\frac{4x^2-11x-12}{6x^2+5x-4}$

Assess

EXAMPLE 4

Try It! Subtract Rational Expressions

4. Simplify.

a. $\frac{1}{3x} + \frac{1}{6x} - \frac{1}{x^2}$

b. $\frac{3x - 5}{x^2 - 25} - \frac{2}{x + 5}$

HABITS OF MIND

Communicate Precisely How does finding the LCM of two or more polynomials help you to add and subtract rational expressions?

EXAMPLE 5

Try It! Find a Rate

5. On the way to work Juan carpools with a fellow co-worker, and then takes the city bus back home in the evening. The average speed of the 20-mi trip is 5 mph faster in the carpool. Write an expression that represents Juan's total travel time.

HABITS OF MIND

Construct Arguments Does Juan spend more time in the carpool or riding the bus? How do you know?

EXAMPLE 6

Try It! Simplify a Compound Fraction

6. Simplify.

a. $\dfrac{\frac{1}{x - 1}}{\frac{x + 1}{3} + \frac{4}{x - 1}}$.

b. $\dfrac{2 - \frac{1}{x}}{\frac{x + 2}{x}}$

HABITS OF MIND

Reason Edwin multiplied the top and bottom of the fraction in problem 6 part (a) by $\frac{3}{x + 1} + \frac{x - 1}{4}$. Will this technique work to simplify the compound fraction? Explain.

Do You UNDERSTAND?

1. **ESSENTIAL QUESTION** How do you rewrite rational expressions to find sums and differences?

2. **Vocabulary** In your own words, define **compound fraction** and provide an example of one.

3. **Error Analysis** A student added the rational expressions as follows:
$\frac{5x}{x+7} + \frac{7}{x} = \frac{5x}{x+7} + \frac{7(7)}{x+7} = \frac{5x+49}{x+7}$.
Describe and correct the error the student made.

4. **Construct Arguments** Explain why, when stating the domain of a sum or difference of rational expressions, not only should the simplified sum or difference be considered but the original expression should also be considered.

5. **Make Sense and Persevere** In adding or subtracting rational expressions, why is the L in LCD significant?

Do You KNOW HOW?

6. Find the sum of $\frac{3}{x+1} + \frac{11}{x+1}$.

Find the LCM of the polynomials.

7. $x^2 - y^2$ and $x^2 - 2xy + y^2$

8. $5x^3y$ and $15x^2y^2$

Find the sum or difference.

9. $\frac{3x}{4y^2} - \frac{y}{10x}$

10. $\frac{9y+2}{3y^2-2y-8} + \frac{7}{3y^2+y-4}$

11. Find the perimeter of the quadrilateral in simplest form.

Sides: x, $\frac{2}{3x}$, $2x$, $\frac{1}{x}$

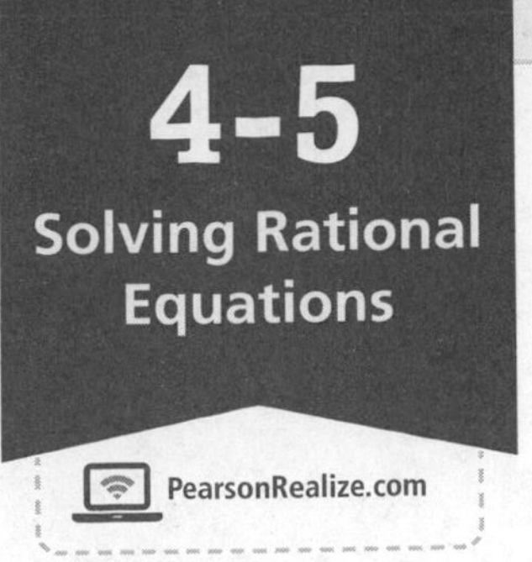

CRITIQUE & EXPLAIN

Nicky and Tavon used different methods to solve the equation $\frac{1}{2}x + \frac{2}{5} = \frac{9}{10}$.

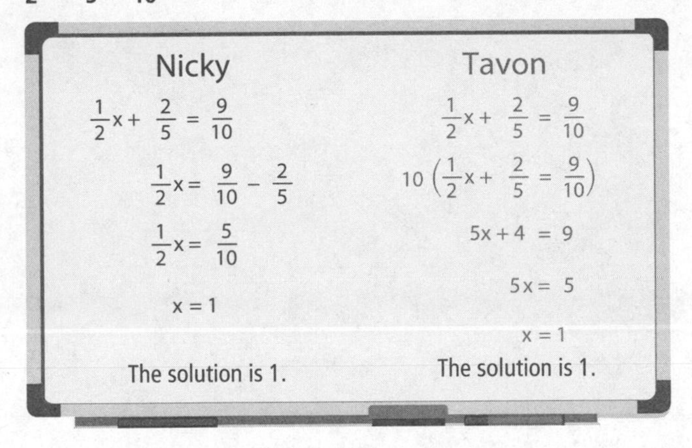

Nicky
$\frac{1}{2}x + \frac{2}{5} = \frac{9}{10}$
$\frac{1}{2}x = \frac{9}{10} - \frac{2}{5}$
$\frac{1}{2}x = \frac{5}{10}$
$x = 1$
The solution is 1.
Tavon
$\frac{1}{2}x + \frac{2}{5} = \frac{9}{10}$
$10\left(\frac{1}{2}x + \frac{2}{5} = \frac{9}{10}\right)$
$5x + 4 = 9$
$5x = 5$
$x = 1$
The solution is 1.

A. Explain the different strategies that Nicky and Tavon used and the advantages or disadvantages of each.

B. Did Nicky use a correct method to solve the equation? Did Tavon?

C. Use Structure Why might Tavon have chosen to multiply both sides of the equation by 10? Could he have used another number? Explain.

HABITS OF MIND

Reason If Tavon had multiplied both sides of the equation by 100, would his answer have been 10 times as much? Explain.

Notes

Assess

EXAMPLE 1

Try It! Solve a Rational Equation

1. What is the solution to each equation?

a. $\frac{2}{x+5} = 4$

b. $\frac{1}{x-7} = 2$

HABITS OF MIND

Critique Reasoning For part (b), Kaitlyn wrote $1 = 2x - 7$, then $8 = 2x$, and $4 = x$. Is she correct? Explain.

EXAMPLE 2

Try It! Solve a Work-Rate Problem

2. It takes 12 hours to fill a pool with two pipes, where the water in one pipe flows three times as fast as the other pipe. How long will it take the slower pipe to fill the pool by itself?

HABITS OF MIND

Reason In a Work-Rate problem, explain why you can't average the individual rates to determine how long it will take to complete a job together.

Notes

Assess

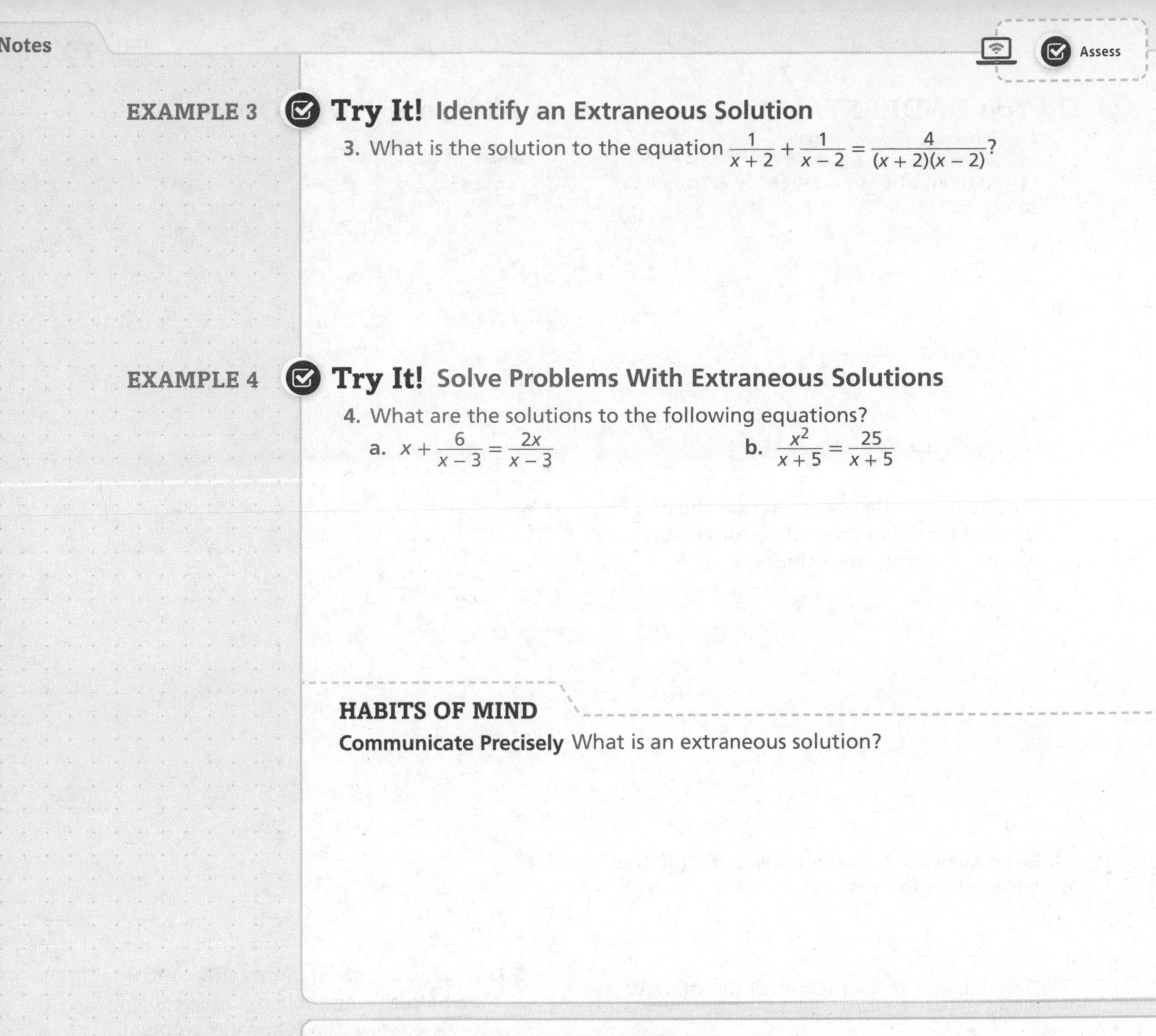

EXAMPLE 3

Try It! Identify an Extraneous Solution

3. What is the solution to the equation $\frac{1}{x+2} + \frac{1}{x-2} = \frac{4}{(x+2)(x-2)}$?

EXAMPLE 4

Try It! Solve Problems With Extraneous Solutions

4. What are the solutions to the following equations?

a. $x + \frac{6}{x-3} = \frac{2x}{x-3}$

b. $\frac{x^2}{x+5} = \frac{25}{x+5}$

HABITS OF MIND

Communicate Precisely What is an extraneous solution?

EXAMPLE 5

Try It! Solve a Rate Problem

5. Three people are planting tomatoes in a community garden. Marta takes 50 minutes to plant the garden alone, Benito takes x minutes and Tyler takes $x + 15$ minutes. If the three of them take 20 minutes to finish the garden, how long would it have taken Tyler alone?

HABITS OF MIND

Make Sense and Persevere What does the fraction $\frac{1}{50}$ mean with regards to Marta?

Do You UNDERSTAND?

1. **ESSENTIAL QUESTION** How can you solve rational equations and identify extraneous solutions?

2. **Vocabulary** Write your own example of a rational equation that, when solved, has at least one **extraneous solution**.

3. **Error Analysis** A student solved the rational equation as follows:

   $\frac{1}{2x} - \frac{2}{5x} = \frac{1}{10x} - 3;\ x = 0$

   Describe and correct the error the student made.

4. **Construct Arguments** Yuki says, *"You can check the solution(s) of rational equations in any of the steps of the solution process."* Explain why her reasoning is incorrect.

Do You KNOW HOW?

Solve.

5. $\frac{4}{x+6} = 2$

6. $\frac{x^2}{x+3} = \frac{9}{x+3}$

7. Organizing given information into a table can be helpful when solving rate problems. Use this table to solve the following problem.

	Distance	Rate	Time
Upstream			
Downstream			

The speed of a stream is 4 km/h. A boat can travel 6 km upstream in the same time it takes to travel 12 km downstream. Find the speed of the boat in still water.

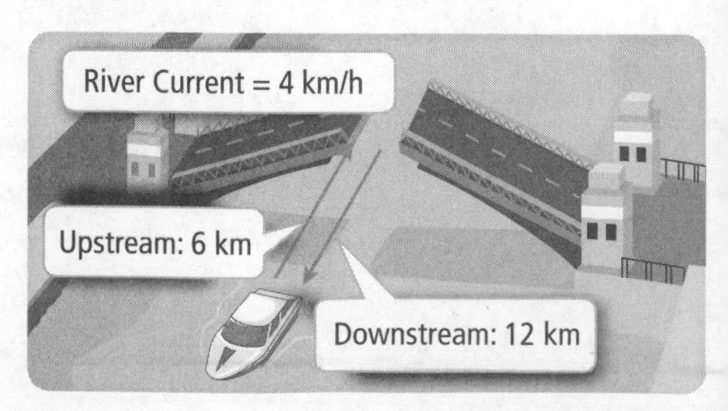

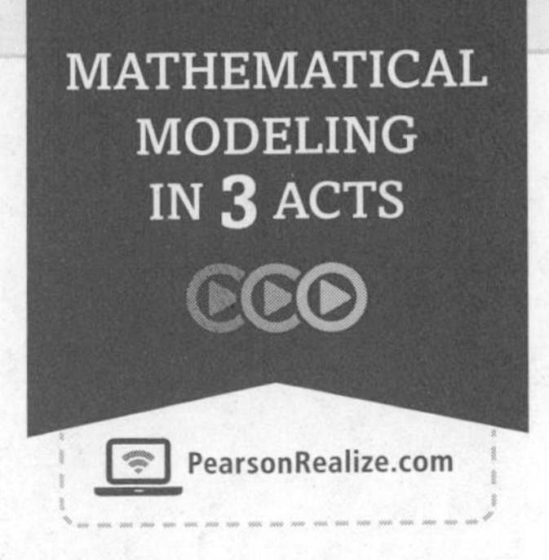

Real Cool Waters

Nothing feels better on a hot day than jumping into a pool! Many cities have swimming pools that people can go to for a small fee. Some people have swimming pools in their backyards that they can enjoy any time.

If neither of these options are available, you can always create your own beach paradise! Get a kiddie pool, a lawn chair, and a beach umbrella. Think about your beach paradise as during the Mathematical Modeling in 3 Acts lesson.

ACT 1 Identify the Problem

1. What is the first question that comes to mind after watching the video?

2. Write down the main question you will answer about what you saw in the video.

3. Make an initial conjecture that answers this main question.

4. Explain how you arrived at your conjecture.

5. Write a number that you know is too small.

6. Write a number that you know is too large.

7. What information will be useful to know to answer the main question? How can you get it? How will you use that information?

Video

ACT 2 Develop a Model

8. Use the math that you have learned in this Topic to refine your conjecture.

ACT 3 Interpret the Results

9. Is your refined conjecture between the highs and lows you set up earlier?

10. Did your refined conjecture match the actual answer exactly? If not, what might explain the difference?

5-1

nth Roots, Radicals, and Rational Exponents

PearsonRealize.com

EXPLORE & REASON

The graph shows $y = x^2$.

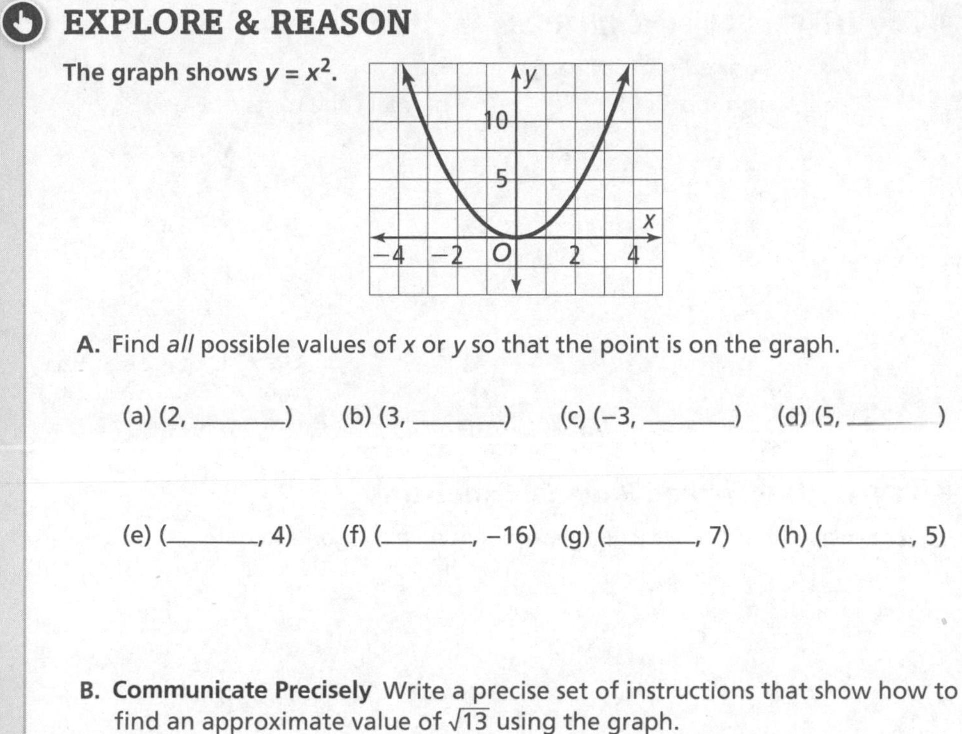

A. Find *all* possible values of x or y so that the point is on the graph.

(a) (2, ______) (b) (3, ______) (c) (−3, ______) (d) (5, ______)

(e) (______, 4) (f) (______, −16) (g) (______, 7) (h) (______, 5)

B. Communicate Precisely Write a precise set of instructions that show how to find an approximate value of $\sqrt{13}$ using the graph.

C. Draw a graph of $y = x^3$. Use the graph to approximate each value.

(a) $\sqrt[3]{5}$ (b) $\sqrt[3]{-5}$ (c) $\sqrt[3]{8}$

(d) A solution to $x^3 = 5$ (e) A solution to $x^3 = -5$ (f) A solution to $x^3 = 8$

HABITS OF MIND

Look for Relationships How is $\sqrt[6]{5}$ related to $\sqrt[3]{5}$?

Notes

Assess

EXAMPLE 1

Try It! Find All Real *n*th Roots

1. Find the specified roots of each number.

a. real fourth roots of 81

b. real cube roots of 64

EXAMPLE 2

Try It! Understand Rational Exponents

2. Explain what each fractional exponent means, then evaluate.

a. $25^{\frac{1}{2}}$

b. $32^{\frac{2}{5}}$

HABITS OF MIND

Generalize What is true about the denominators of fractional exponents in which absolute value must be considered?

EXAMPLE 3

Try It! Evaluate Expressions With Rational Exponents

3. What is the value of each expression? Round to the nearest hundredth if necessary.

a. $-\left(16^{\frac{3}{4}}\right)$

b. $\sqrt[5]{3.5^4}$

Notes

Assess

EXAMPLE 4

Try It! Simplify *n*th Roots

4. Simplify each expression.

   a. $\sqrt[3]{-8a^3b^9}$

   b. $\sqrt[4]{256x^{12}y^{24}}$

HABITS OF MIND

Make Sense and Persevere What is an example of a variable expression that has both a cube root and a fourth root which can be simplified to an expression without a radical?

EXAMPLE 5

Try It! Use *n*th Roots to Solve Equations

5. a. Solve the equation $5x^3 = 320$.

   b. Solve the equation $2p^4 = 162$.

EXAMPLE 6

Try It! Use *n*th Roots to Solve Problems

6. One cube has an edge length 3 cm shorter than the edge length of a second cube. The volume of the smaller cube is 200 cm^3. What is the volume of the larger cube?

HABITS OF MIND

Communicate Precisely What are the steps necessary to solve the equation $ax^n = b$?

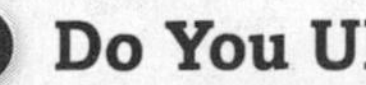

Do You UNDERSTAND?

1. ESSENTIAL QUESTION How are exponents and radicals used to represent roots of real numbers?

2. **Error Analysis** Kaitlyn said $\sqrt[3]{10} = 10^3$. Explain Kaitlyn's error.

3. **Vocabulary** In the radical expression $\sqrt[5]{125}$, what is the index? What is the radicand?

4. **Use Structure** Why is $75^{\frac{3}{5}}$ equal to $\left(75^{\frac{1}{5}}\right)^3$?

5. **Construct Arguments** Anastasia said that $(x^8)^{\frac{1}{4}} = \frac{x^8}{x^4} = x^4$. Is Anastasia correct? Explain.

6. **Make Sense and Persevere** Is it possible for a rational exponent to be an improper fraction? Explain how $27^{\frac{4}{3}}$ is evaluated or why it cannot be evaluated.

Do You KNOW HOW?

Write each expression in radical form.

7. $a^{\frac{1}{5}}$

8. $7^{\frac{2}{3}}$

Write each expression in exponential form.

9. $\sqrt[3]{b}$

10. $\sqrt[4]{p^7}$

11. How many real third roots does 1,728 have?

12. How many real sixth roots does 15,625 have?

13. Solve the equation $4x^3 = 324$.

14. Solve the equation $2x^4 = 2{,}500$.

Simplify each expression.

15. $\sqrt[3]{27x^{12}y^6}$

16. $\sqrt[5]{-32x^5y^{30}}$

17. A snow globe is packaged in a cubic container that has volume 64 in.^{3} A large shipping container is also a cube, and its edge length is 8 inches longer than the edge length of the snow globe container. How many snow globes can fit into the larger shipping container?

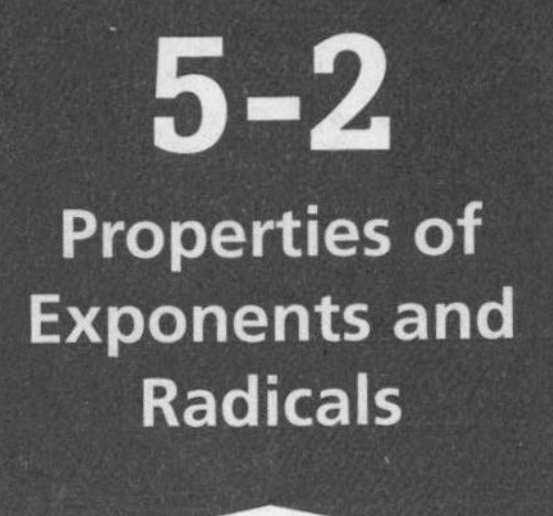

CRITIQUE & EXPLAIN

Olivia was practicing evaluating and simplifying expressions. Her work for three expressions is shown.

1. $24^2 = 400 + 16 = 416$
2. $3^6 = 9(27) = 270 - 27 = 243$
3. $\sqrt{625} = \sqrt{400} + \sqrt{225} = 20 + 15 = 35$

A. Is Olivia's work in the first example correct? Explain your thinking.

B. Is Olivia's work in the second example correct? Explain your thinking.

C. Is Olivia's work in the third example correct? Explain your thinking.

D. Make Sense and Persevere What advice would you give Olivia on simplifying expressions?

HABITS OF MIND

Construct Arguments You know that $3^2 + 4^2 = 5^2$. Does $\sqrt{3^2} + \sqrt{4^2} = \sqrt{5^2}$? If not, how could you rewrite the equation using radicals so that it is true?

Notes

Assess

EXAMPLE 1

Try It! Use Properties of Exponents

1. How can you rewrite each expression using the properties of exponents?

a. $\left(\frac{3}{32^{\frac{2}{5}}}\right)^{\frac{1}{2}}$

b. $2a^{\frac{1}{3}}\left(ab^{\frac{1}{2}}\right)^{\frac{2}{3}}$

EXAMPLE 2

Try It! Use Properties of Exponents to Rewrite Radicals

2. How can you rewrite each expression?

a. $\sqrt[4]{81a^8b^5}$

b. $\sqrt[3]{\frac{x^4y^2}{125x}}$

HABITS OF MIND

Make Sense and Persevere What do you have to check to be sure that an expression is in simplest radical form?

EXAMPLE 3

Try It! Rewrite the Product or Quotient of a Radical

3. What is the reduced radical form of each expression?

a. $\sqrt[5]{\frac{7}{16x^3}}$

b. $\sqrt[4]{27x^2} \cdot \sqrt{3x}$

Notes

Assess

EXAMPLE 4 **Try It! Add and Subtract Radical Expressions**

4. How can you rewrite each expression in a simpler form?

a. $\sqrt[3]{2{,}000} + \sqrt{2} - \sqrt[3]{128}$

b. $\sqrt{20} - \sqrt{600} - \sqrt{125}$

HABITS OF MIND

Critique Reasoning Divit says that you can simplify the product of any two radical expressions, but not necessarily the sum. Is he correct? Give an example.

EXAMPLE 5 **Try It! Multiply Binomial Radical Expressions**

5. Multiply.

a. $(x - \sqrt{10})(x + \sqrt{10})$

b. $\sqrt{6}(5 + \sqrt{3})$

EXAMPLE 6 **Try It! Rationalize a Binomial Denominator**

6. What is the reduced radical form of each expression?

a. $\dfrac{5 - \sqrt{2}}{2 - \sqrt{3}}$

b. $\dfrac{-4x}{1 - \sqrt{x}}$

HABITS OF MIND

Reason Is the product of two irrational binomials always irrational? Explain.

Do You UNDERSTAND?

1. **ESSENTIAL QUESTION** How can properties of exponents and radicals be used to rewrite radical expressions?

2. **Vocabulary** How can you determine if a radical expression is in reduced form?

3. **Use Structure** Explain why $(-64)^{\frac{1}{3}}$ equals $-64^{\frac{1}{3}}$ but $(-64)^{\frac{1}{2}}$ does not equal $-64^{\frac{1}{2}}$.

4. **Error Analysis** Explain the error in Julie's work in rewriting the radical expression.

$$\sqrt{-3} \cdot \sqrt{-12} = \sqrt{-3(-12)} = \sqrt{36} = 6$$

Do You KNOW HOW?

What is the reduced radical form of each expression?

5. $49^{\frac{3}{4}} \cdot 49^{\frac{-1}{4}}$

6. $\left(\dfrac{a^2b^8}{a^{\frac{1}{3}}}\right)^{\frac{3}{4}}$

7. $\sqrt[4]{1{,}024x^9y^{12}}$

8. $\sqrt[3]{\dfrac{4}{9m^2}}$

9. $\sqrt{63} - \sqrt{700} - \sqrt{112}$

10. $\sqrt{5}(6 + \sqrt{2})$

11. $\dfrac{3}{\sqrt{6}}$

12. $\dfrac{\sqrt{7}}{\sqrt{5} + 3}$

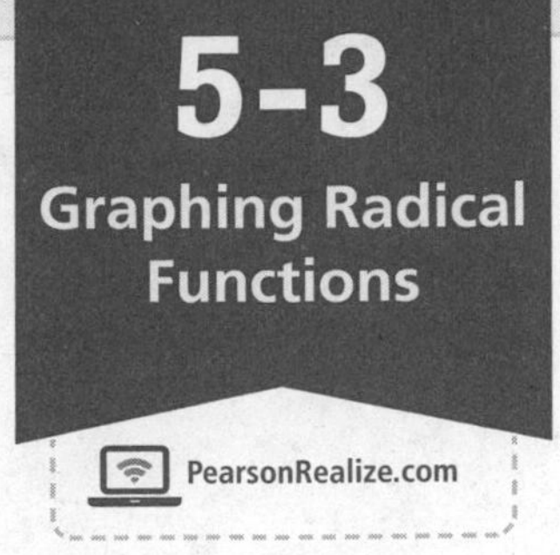

Activity

EXPLORE & REASON

Consider the formula for the area of a square: $A = s^2$.

A. Graph the function that represents area as a function of side length.

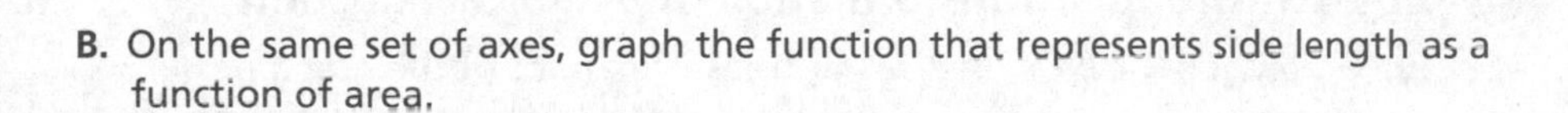

B. On the same set of axes, graph the function that represents side length as a function of area.

C. Look for Relationships How are the two graphs related?

HABITS OF MIND

Communicate Precisely What is the domain and range of each function?

EXAMPLE 1

Try It! Graph Square Root and Cube Root Functions

1. Graph the following functions. What are the domain and range of each function? Is the function increasing or decreasing?

   a. $f(x) = \sqrt{x - 5}$

   b. $g(x) = \sqrt[3]{x + 1}$

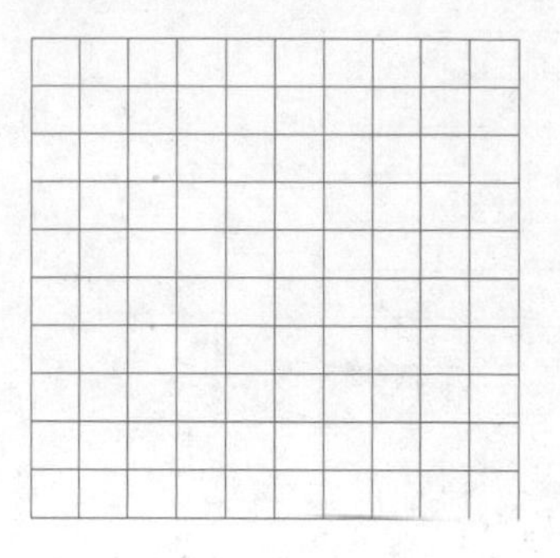

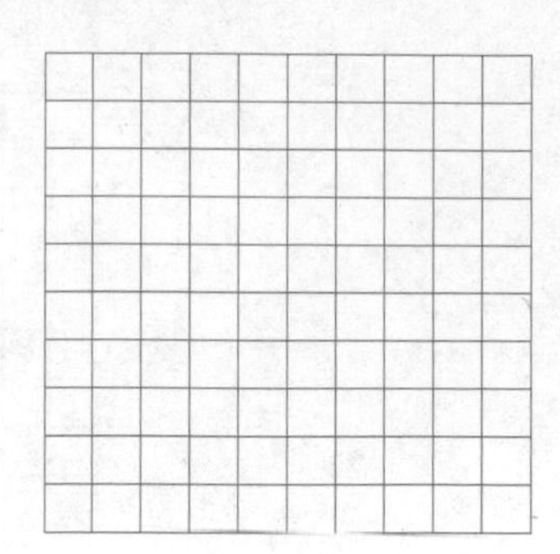

EXAMPLE 2

Try It! Graph a Transformation of a Radical Function

2. Graph $g(x) = \frac{1}{2}\sqrt{x - 1} - 3$. What transformations of the graph of $f(x) = \sqrt{x}$ produce the graph of g? What is the effect of the transformations on the domain and range of g?

HABITS OF MIND

Use Structure How does the graph of $y = \sqrt{x - a} + b$ compare to the graph of $y = \sqrt{x}$?

Notes

Assess

EXAMPLE 3

Try It! Rewrite Radical Functions to Identify Transformations

3. What transformations of the parent graph of $f(x) = \sqrt{x}$ produce the graphs of the following functions?

a. $m(x) = \sqrt{7x - 3.5} - 10$

b. $j(x) = -2\sqrt{12x} + 4$

EXAMPLE 4

Try It! Write an Equation of a Transformation

4. What radical function is represented in each graph below?

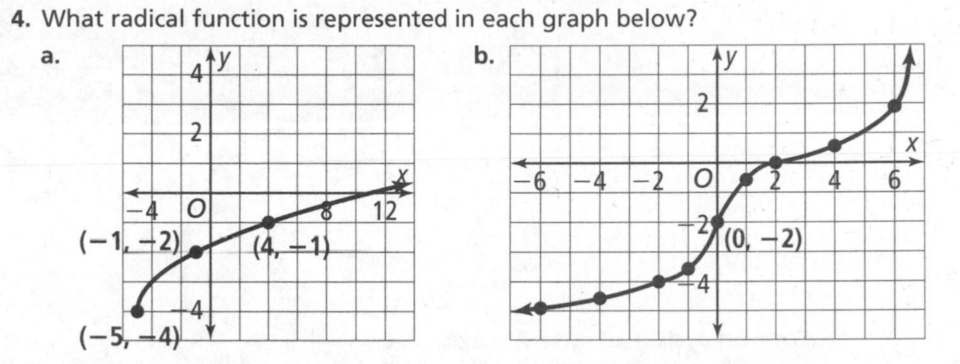

HABITS OF MIND

Model With Mathematics What is an example of a radical function whose domain is $x \geq -3$ and range is $y \geq 2$?

EXAMPLE 5

Try It! Interpret a Radical Function Model

5. Use the same function as in Example 5. Suppose Sasha's brother walks through elevations ranging from 8 ft to 48 ft. What are the minimum and maximum distances that he can see?

HABITS OF MIND

Generalize What transformations result in a cube root function being an odd function?

Assess

Do You UNDERSTAND?

1. ESSENTIAL QUESTION How can you use what you know about transformations of functions to graph radical functions?

2. **Error Analysis** Parker said the graph of the radical function $g(x) = -\sqrt{x+2} - 1$ is a translation 2 units left and 1 unit down from the parent function $f(x) = \sqrt{x}$. Describe and correct the error.

3. **Reason** What effect does a have on the graph of $f(x) = a\sqrt{x}$?

Do You KNOW HOW?

Graph each function. Then identify its domain and range.

4. $f(x) = \sqrt{x-2}$

5. $f(x) = \sqrt[3]{x+2}$

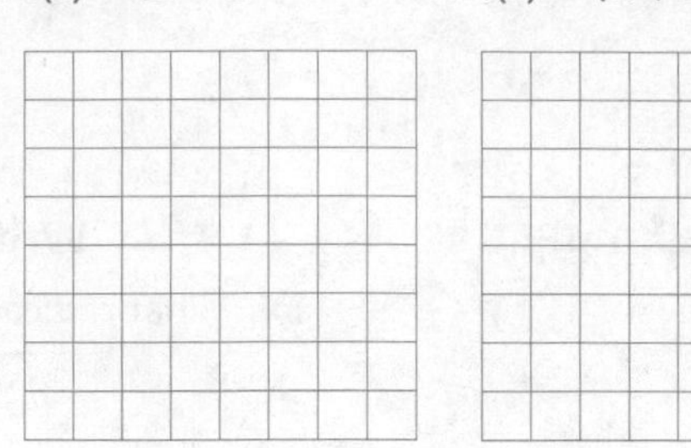

6. $f(x) = \sqrt{x+1} - 2$

7. $f(x) = \sqrt[3]{x-3} + 2$

8. $f(x) = 3\sqrt{x-5}$

9. $f(x) = \frac{1}{2}\sqrt[3]{x} + 1$

10. The volume of a cube is a function of the cube's side length. The function can be written as $V(s) = s^3$, where s is the side length and V is the volume.

    a. Express a cube's side length as a function of its volume, $s(V)$.

    b. Graph $V(s)$ and $s(V)$. What are the domain and range of the functions? Explain.

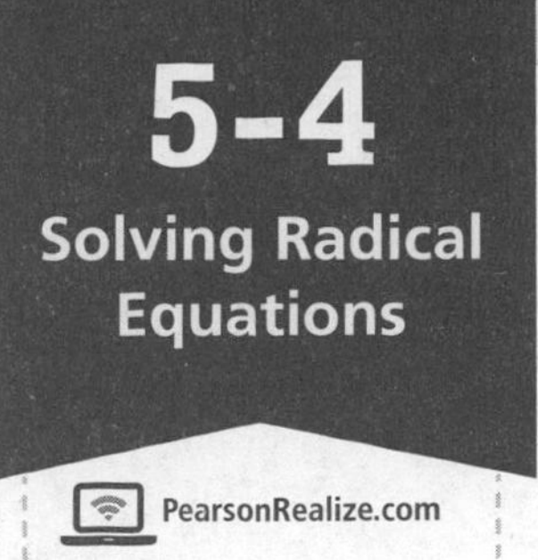

EXPLORE & REASON

A. Solve $3(a + 1)^2 + 2 = 11$. Use at least two different methods.

B. Try each of the methods you used in part (a) to solve $\sqrt[3]{(a + 1)} + 2 = 11$.

C. **Generalize** Which of the methods is better suited for solving an equation with a radical? What problems arise when using the other method?

HABITS OF MIND

Construct Arguments The squares of two numbers are equal. Does that mean that the two numbers themselves must also be equal? Explain.

Notes

Assess

EXAMPLE 1

Try It! Solve an Equation With One Radical

1. Solve each radical equation.

   a. $\sqrt{x-2}+3=5$

   b. $\sqrt[3]{x-1}=2$

EXAMPLE 2

Try It! Rewrite a Formula

2. The speed, v, of a vehicle in relation to its stopping distance, d, is represented by the equation $v=3.57\sqrt{d}$. What is the equation for the stopping distance in terms of the vehicle's speed?

HABITS OF MIND

Reason Reese solved the equation in **1(a)** by first squaring both sides. Is this an appropriate first step? Why or why not?

EXAMPLE 3

Try It! Identify an Extraneous Solution

3. Solve each radical equation. Identify any extraneous solutions.

   a. $x=\sqrt{7x+8}$

   b. $x+2=\sqrt{x+2}$

Notes

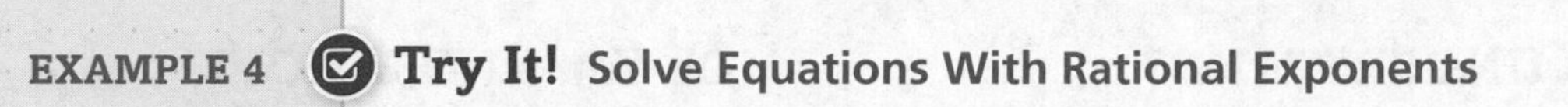

EXAMPLE 4

Try It! Solve Equations With Rational Exponents

4. Solve each equation.

a. $(x^2 - 3x - 6)^{\frac{3}{2}} - 14 = -6$

b. $(x + 8)^2 = (x - 10)^{\frac{5}{2}}$

EXAMPLE 5

Try It! Solve an Equation With Two Radicals

5. Solve each radical equation. Check for extraneous solutions.

a. $\sqrt{x + 4} - \sqrt{3x} = -2$

b. $\sqrt{15 - x} - \sqrt{6x} = -3$

HABITS OF MIND

Reason Why are extraneous solutions a possibility for radical equations?

EXAMPLE 6

Try It! Solve a Radical Inequality

6. A doctor calculates that a particular dose of medicine is appropriate for an individual whose BSA is less than 1.8. If the mass of the individual is 75 kg, how many centimeters tall can he or she be for the dose to be appropriate?

HABITS OF MIND

Make Sense and Persevere How are the steps for solving a radical inequality different from the steps for solving a radical equation?

Do You UNDERSTAND?

1. ESSENTIAL QUESTION How can you solve equations that include radicals or rational exponents?

2. **Construct Arguments** How can you use a graph to show that the solution to $\sqrt[3]{84x+8} = 8$ is 6?

3. **Vocabulary** Why does solving a radical equation sometimes result in an extraneous solution?

4. **Error Analysis** Neil said that −3 and 6 are the solutions to $\sqrt{3x+18} = x$. What error did Neil make?

5. **Communicate Precisely** Describe how you would solve the equation $x^{\frac{2}{3}} = n$. How is this solution method to be interpreted if the equation had been written in radical form instead?

Do You KNOW HOW?

Solve for *x*.

6. $3\sqrt{x+22} = 21$

7. $\sqrt[3]{5x} = 25$

In exercises 8 and 9, find the extraneous solution.

8. $\sqrt{8x+9} = x$

9. $x = \sqrt{24-2x}$

10. Rewrite the equation $y = \sqrt{\frac{x-48}{6}}$ to isolate *x*.

11. Use a graph to find the solution to the equation $9 = \sqrt{3x+11}$.

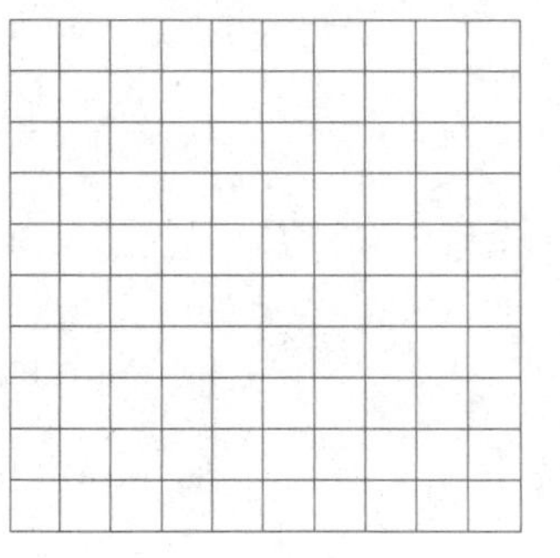

Solve each equation.

12. $(3x+2)^{\frac{2}{5}} = 4$

13. $\sqrt{2x-5} - \sqrt{x-3} = 1$

14. $\sqrt{x+2} + \sqrt{3x+4} = 2$

The Snack Shack

Americans seem to love the beach! When the weather is warm, people flock to the beach. Some people bring coolers packed with food and drinks. Others prefer to take advantage of snack bars and shops set up along the beach.

Some beachside communities have built long wooden walkways, or boardwalks, to make it easier for beachgoers to walk to the snack bars and stores. How easy do you find walking in the sand? Think about this during the Mathematical Modeling in 3 Acts lesson.

ACT 1 Identify the Problem

1. What is the first question that comes to mind after watching the video?

2. Write down the main question you will answer about what you saw in the video.

3. Make an initial conjecture that answers this main question.

4. Explain how you arrived at your conjecture.

5. What information will be useful to know to answer the main question? How can you get it? How will you use that information?

Video

ACT 2 Develop a Model

6. Use the math that you have learned in this Topic to refine your conjecture.

ACT 3 Interpret the Results

7. Did your refined conjecture match the actual answer exactly? If not, what might explain the difference?

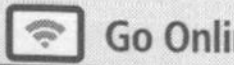

5-5 Function Operations

PearsonRealize.com

MODEL & DISCUSS

In business, the term *profit* is used to describe the difference between the money the business earns (revenue) and the money the business spends (cost).

A. Grooming USA charges $25 for every pet that is groomed. Let x represent the number of pets groomed in a month. Define a revenue function for the business.

B. Materials and labor for each pet groomed costs $15. The business also has fixed costs of $1,000 each month. Define a cost function for this business.

C. Last month, Grooming USA groomed 95 pets. Did they earn a profit? What would the profit be if the business groomed 110 pets in a month?

D. Generalize Explain your procedure for calculating the profit for Grooming USA. Suppose you wanted to calculate the profit for several different scenarios. How could you simplify your process?

HABITS OF MIND

Make Sense and Persevere A business "breaks even" when its revenue equals its costs. How many pets would Grooming USA have to groom in order to break even?

Notes

Assess

EXAMPLE 1

Try It! Add and Subtract Functions

1. Let $f(x) = 2x^2 + 7x - 1$ and $g(x) = 3 - 2x$. Identify rules for the following functions.

   a. $f + g$

   b. $f - g$

EXAMPLE 2

Try It! Multiply Functions

2. Suppose demand, d, for a company's product at cost, x, is predicted by the function $d(x) = -0.25x^2 + 1{,}000$, and the price, p, that the company can charge for the product is given by $p(x) = x + 16$. Find the company's revenue function.

EXAMPLE 3

Try It! Divide Functions

3. Identify the rule and domain for $\frac{f}{g}$ for each pair of functions.

   a. $f(x) = x^2 - 3x - 18$, $g(x) = x + 3$

   b. $f(x) = x - 3$, $g(x) = x^2 - x - 6$

HABITS OF MIND

Communicate Precisely How are the domains of $f + g$, $f - g$, $f \cdot g$, and $\frac{f}{g}$ related to the domains of f and g?

Notes

Assess

EXAMPLE 4

Try It! Compose Functions

4. Let $f(x) = 2x - 1$ and $g(x) = 3x$. Identify the rules for the following functions.
   a. $f(g(2))$
   b. $f(g(x))$

EXAMPLE 5

Try It! Write a Rule for a Composite Function

5. Identify the rules for $f \circ g$ and $g \circ f$.
   a. $f(x) = x^3$, $g(x) = x + 1$
   b. $f(x) = x^2 + 1$, $g(x) = x - 5$

EXAMPLE 6

Try It! Use a Composite Function Model

6. As a member of the Games Shop rewards program, you get a 20% discount on purchases. All sales are subject to a 6% sales tax. Write functions to model the discount and the sales tax, then identify the rule for the composition function that calculates the final price you would pay at the Games Shop.

HABITS OF MIND

Reason Let $f(x) = \frac{1}{3}(x - 2)$ and $g(x) = 3x + 2$. Find the rules for $f \circ g$ and $g \circ f$. Are they equivalent? If so, does this prove that the composition of two functions is commutative?

Do You UNDERSTAND?

1. ESSENTIAL QUESTION How do you combine, multiply, divide, and compose functions, and how do you find the domain of the resulting function?

2. **Vocabulary** In your own words, define and provide an example of a composite function.

3. **Error Analysis** Reagan said the domain of $\frac{f}{g}$ when $f(x) = 5x^2$ and $g(x) = x + 3$ is the set of real numbers. Explain why Reagan is incorrect.

4. **Use Structure** Explain why changing the order in which two functions occur affects the result when subtracting and dividing the functions.

Do You KNOW HOW?

Let $f(x) = 3x^2 + 5x + 1$ and $g(x) = 2x - 1$.

5. Identify the rule for $f + g$.

6. Identify the rule for $f - g$.

7. Identify the rule for $g - f$.

Let $f(x) = x^2 + 2x + 1$ and $g(x) = x - 4$.

8. Identify the rule for $f \cdot g$.

9. Identify the rule for $\frac{f}{g}$, and state the domain.

10. Identify the rule for $\frac{g}{f}$, and state the domain.

11. If $f(x) = 2x^2 + 5$ and $g(x) = -3x$, what is $f(g(x))$?

Activity

5-6 Inverse Relations and Functions

PearsonRealize.com

EXPLORE & REASON

Each number path will lead you from a number in the domain, the set of all real numbers, to a number in the range.

Number Path f: $x \rightarrow f(x)$

- Start with x.
- Subtract 3.
- Multiply by -2.
- Add 5.

Number Path g: $x \rightarrow g(x)$

- Start with x.
- Add 1.
- Square the value.
- Subtract 2.

A. Follow the number paths to find $f(1)$ and $g(1)$.

B. Identify all possible values of x that lead to $f(x) = 7$ and all values that lead to $g(x) = 7$.

C. Communicate Precisely Based on the two number paths, under what conditions can you follow a path back to a unique value in the domain?

HABITS OF MIND

Model With Mathematics Write a rule for Number Path f. Write a rule for the process of following the number path backward. How do the two rules compare?

Notes

Assess

EXAMPLE 1

Try It! Represent the Inverse of a Relation

1. Identify the inverse relation. Is it a function?

x	−1	0	1	2	3	4
y	9	7	5	3	1	−1

EXAMPLE 2

Try It! Find an Equation of an Inverse Relation

2. Let $f(x) = 2x + 1$.

   a. Write an equation to represent the inverse of f.

   b. How can you use the graph of f to determine if the inverse of f is a function? Explain your answer.

HABITS OF MIND

Communicate Precisely Think of $f(x) = 2x + 1$ as a number path: start with x, multiply by 2, and add 1. How could you describe the path from the result back to x?

EXAMPLE 3

Try It! Restrict a Domain to Produce an Inverse Function

3. Find the inverse of each function by identifying an appropriate restriction of its domain.

   a. $f(x) = x^2 + 8x + 16$

   b. $f(x) = x^2 - 9$

Assess

EXAMPLE 4

Try It! Find an Equation of an Inverse Function

4. Let $f(x) = 2 - \sqrt[3]{x + 1}$.

a. Sketch the graph of f.

b. Verify that the inverse will be a function and write an equation for $f^{-1}(x)$.

EXAMPLE 5

Try It! Use Composition to Verify Inverse Functions

5. Use composition to determine whether f and g are inverse functions.

a. $f(x) = \frac{1}{4}x + 7$, $g(x) = 4x - 7$

b. $f(x) = \sqrt[3]{x - 1}$, $g(x) = x^3 + 1$

HABITS OF MIND

Construct Arguments Dana says that the functions $f(x) = (x - 2)^2 + 5$ and $g(x) = \sqrt{x - 5} + 2$ are inverses. Keegan says that the functions are inverses only if the domain is restricted. Is either person correct? Explain.

EXAMPLE 6

Try It! Rewrite a Formula

6. The manufacturer of a gift box designs a box with length and width each twice as long as its height. Find a formula that gives the height h of the box in terms of its volume V. Then give the length of the box if the volume is 640 cm^3.

HABITS OF MIND

Make Sense and Persevere In the formula $V = \frac{4}{3}\pi r^3$, which variable is the dependent variable? In the formula $r = \sqrt[3]{\frac{3}{4\pi}V}$, which variable is the dependent variable?

Do You UNDERSTAND?

1. **ESSENTIAL QUESTION** How can you find the inverse of a function and verify the two functions are inverses?

2. **Error Analysis** Abi said the inverse of $f(x) = 3x + 1$ is $f^{-1}(x) = \frac{1}{3}x - 1$. Is she correct? Explain.

3. **Construct Arguments** Is the inverse of a function always a function? Explain.

Do You KNOW HOW?

Consider the function $f(x) = -\frac{1}{2}x + 5$.

4. Write an equation for the inverse of $f(x)$.

5. Use composition to show that $f(x)$ and the equation you wrote are inverses.

6. Sketch a graph of f and its inverse.

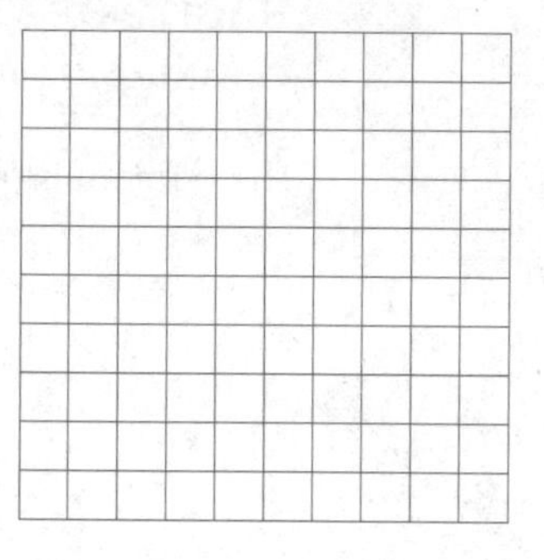

7. How can you verify by the graph of f and its inverse that they are indeed inverses?

8. Is the inverse of $f(x)$ a function? Explain.

6-1 Key Features of Exponential Functions

PearsonRealize.com

EXPLORE & REASON

Margaret investigates three functions: $y = 3x$, $y = x^3$, and $y = 3^x$. She is interested in the differences and ratios between consecutive y-values. Here is the table she started for $y = 3x$.

Investigating $y = 3x$			
x	y	Difference between y-values	Ratio between y-values
1	3		
2	6	$6 - 3 = 3$	$\frac{6}{3} = 2$
3	9	$9 - 6 = 3$	$\frac{9}{6} = 1.5$
4	12	$12 - 9 = 3$	$\frac{12}{9} \approx 1.33$

A. Create tables like Margaret's for all three functions and fill in more rows.

B. Which functions have a constant difference between consecutive y-values? Constant ratio?

C. Use Structure Which of these three functions will have y-values that increase the fastest as x increases? Why?

HABITS OF MIND

Generalize Let b represent a whole number. For $b > 1$, which function do you think will increase at a faster rate as x increases, $f(x) = b^x$ or $g(x) = x^b$? Explain.

Notes

Assess

EXAMPLE 1

Try It! Identify Key Features of Exponential Functions

1. Graph $f(x) = 4(0.5)^x$. What are the domain, range, intercepts, asymptote, and the end behavior for this function?

EXAMPLE 2

Try It! Graph Transformations of Exponential Functions

2. How do the asymptote and intercept of the given function compare to the asymptote and intercept of the function $f(x) = 5^x$?

   a. $g(x) = 5^{x+3}$

   b. $h(x) = 5^{-x}$

HABITS OF MIND

Reason What kinds of transformations will affect the asymptote or the intercept(s) of an exponential function? Explain.

Notes

Assess

EXAMPLE 3

Try It! Model with Exponential Functions

3. A factory purchased a 3D Printer on January 2, 2010. The value of the printer is modeled by the function $f(x) = 30(0.93)^x$, where x is the number of years since 2010.
   a. What is the value of the printer after 10 years?
   b. Does the printer lose more of its value in the first 10 years or in the second?

EXAMPLE 4

Try It! Interpret an Exponential Function

4. Two-hundred twenty hawks were released into a region in 2016. The function $f(x) = 220(1.05)^x$ can be used to model the number of red-tailed hawks in the region x years after 2016.
   a. Is the population increasing or decreasing? Explain.
   b. In what year will the number of hawks reach 280?

HABITS OF MIND

Use Structure How can you determine the growth or decay factor by looking at an exponential function? The growth or decay rate?

EXAMPLE 5

Try It! Compare Two Exponential Functions

5. In Example 5, will the value of the painting ever surpass the value of the sculpture according to the models? Explain.

HABITS OF MIND

Reason For two functions $f(x) = b^x$ and $g(x) = b^{x+n}$, where $n > 0$, is it possible that the two graphs will intersect? Explain.

Do You UNDERSTAND?

1. ESSENTIAL QUESTION How do graphs and equations reveal key features of exponential growth and decay functions?

2. **Vocabulary** How do *exponential functions* differ from polynomial and rational functions?

3. **Error Analysis** Charles claimed the function $f(x) = \left(\frac{3}{2}\right)^x$ represents exponential decay. Explain the error Charles made.

4. **Communicate Precisely** How are exponential growth functions similar to exponential decay functions? How are they different?

Do You KNOW HOW?

5. Graph the function $f(x) = 4 \times 3^x$. Identify the domain, range, intercept, asymptote, and describe the end behavior.

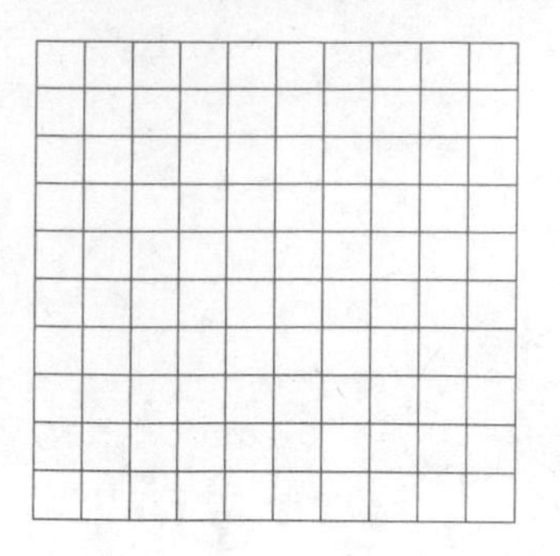

6. The exponential function $f(x) = 2500(0.4)^x$ models the amount of money in Zachary's savings account over the last 10 years. Is Zachary's account balance increasing or decreasing? Write the base in terms of the rate of growth or decay.

7. Describe how the graph of $g(x) = 4(0.5)^{x-3}$ compares to the graph of $f(x) = 4(0.5)^x$.

8. Two trucks were purchased by a landscaping company in 2016. Their values are modeled by the functions $f(x) = 35(0.85)^x$ and $g(x) = 46(0.75)^x$ where x is the number of years since 2016. Which function models the truck that is worth the most after 5 years? Explain.

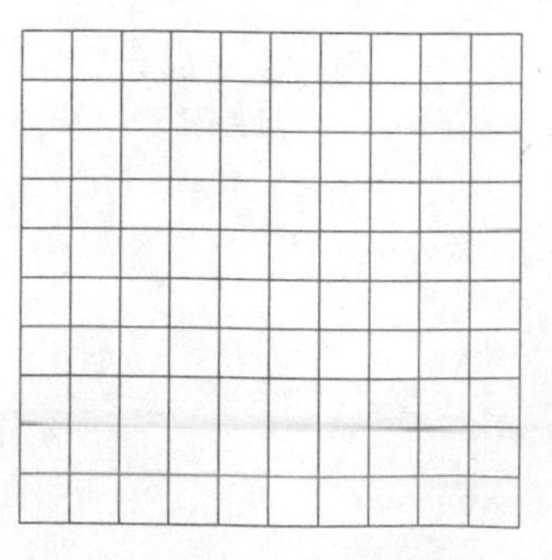

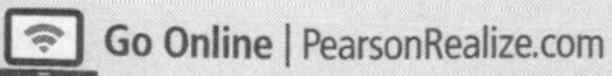

Activity

6-2 Exponential Models

PearsonRealize.com

EXPLORE & REASON

Juan is studying exponential growth of bacteria cultures. Each is carefully controlled to maintain a specific growth rate. Copy and complete the table to find the number of bacteria cells in each culture.

Culture	Initial Number of Bacteria	Growth Rate per Day	Time (days)	Final Number of Bacteria
A	10,000	8%	1	
B	10,000	4%	2	
C	10,000	2%	4	
D	10,000	1%	8	

A. What is the relationship between the daily growth rate and the time in days for each culture?

B. Look for Relationships Would you expect a culture with a growth rate of $\frac{1}{2}$% and a time of 16 days to have more or fewer cells than the others in the table? Explain.

HABITS OF MIND

Model With Mathematics Describe another situation that you could represent using an exponential function.

Assess

EXAMPLE 1

Try It! Rewrite an Exponential Function to Identify a Rate

1. The population in a small town is increasing annually at 1.8%. What is the quarterly rate of population increase?

HABITS OF MIND

Generalize Why can't you just divide an annual interest rate by 4 to obtain a quarterly interest rate?

EXAMPLE 2

Try It! Understand Continuously Compounded Interest

2. \$3,000 is invested in an account that earns 3% annual interest, compounded monthly.

   a. What is the value of the account after 10 years?

   b. What is the value of the account after 100 years?

EXAMPLE 3

Try It! Understanding Continuously Compounded Interest

3. If you continued the table for $n = 1{,}000{,}000$, would the value in the account increase or decrease? How do you know?

HABITS OF MIND

Generalize Which yields the greatest return on investment: compounding quarterly, hourly, or continuously? Explain.

Notes

Assess

EXAMPLE 4

Try It! Find Continuously Compounded Interest

4. You invest \$125,000 in an account that earns 4.75% annual interest, compounded continuously.

   a. What is the value of the account after 15 years?

   b. What is the value of the account after 30 years?

EXAMPLE 5

Try It! Use Two Points to Find an Exponential Model

5. A surveyor determined the value of an area of land over a period of several years since 1950. The land was worth \$31,000 in 1954 and \$35,000 in 1955. Use the data to determine an exponential model that describes the value of the land.

EXAMPLE 6

Try It! Use Regression to Find an Exponential Model

6. According to the model in Example 6, what was the approximate temperature 35 minutes after cooling started?

HABITS OF MIND

Generalize How can a graph help you determine whether an exponential model is appropriate for a data set? Explain.

Do You UNDERSTAND?

1. ESSENTIAL QUESTION Why do you develop exponential models to represent and interpret situations?

2. **Error Analysis** The exponential model $y = 5{,}000(1.05)^t$ represents the amount Yori earns in an account after t years when \$5,000 is invested. Yori said the monthly interest rate of the exponential model is 5%. Explain Yori's error.

3. **Vocabulary** Explain the similarities and differences between compound interest and continuously compounded interest.

4. **Communicate Precisely** Kylee is using a calculator to find an exponential regression model. How would you explain to Kylee what the variables in the model $y = ab^x$ represent?

Do You KNOW HOW?

The exponential function models the annual rate of increase. Find the monthly and quarterly rates.

5. $f(t) = 2{,}000(1.03)^t$

6. $f(t) = 500(1.055)^t$

Find the total amount of money invested in an account at the end of the given time period.

7. compounded monthly, $P = \$2{,}000$, $r = 3\%$, $t = 5$ years

8. continuously compounded, $P = \$1{,}500$, $r = 1.5\%$, $t = 6$ years

Write an exponential model given two points.

9. (3, 55) and (4, 70)

10. (7, 12) and (8, 25)

11. Paul invests \$6,450 in an account that earns continuously compounded interest at an annual rate of 2.8%. What is the value of the account after 8 years?

The Crazy Conditioning

Like all sports, soccer requires its players to be well trained. That is why players often have to run sprints in practice.

To make sprint drills more interesting, many coaches set up competitions. Coaches might split the players into teams and have them run relay races against each other. Or they might have the players sprint around cones and over barriers. What other ways would make doing sprints more fun? Think about this during this Mathematical Modeling in 3 Acts lesson.

ACT 1 Identify the Problem

1. What is the first question that comes to mind after watching the video?

2. Write down the main question you will answer about the video.

3. Make an initial conjecture that answers this main question.

4. Explain how you arrived at your conjecture.

5. Write a number that you know is too small.

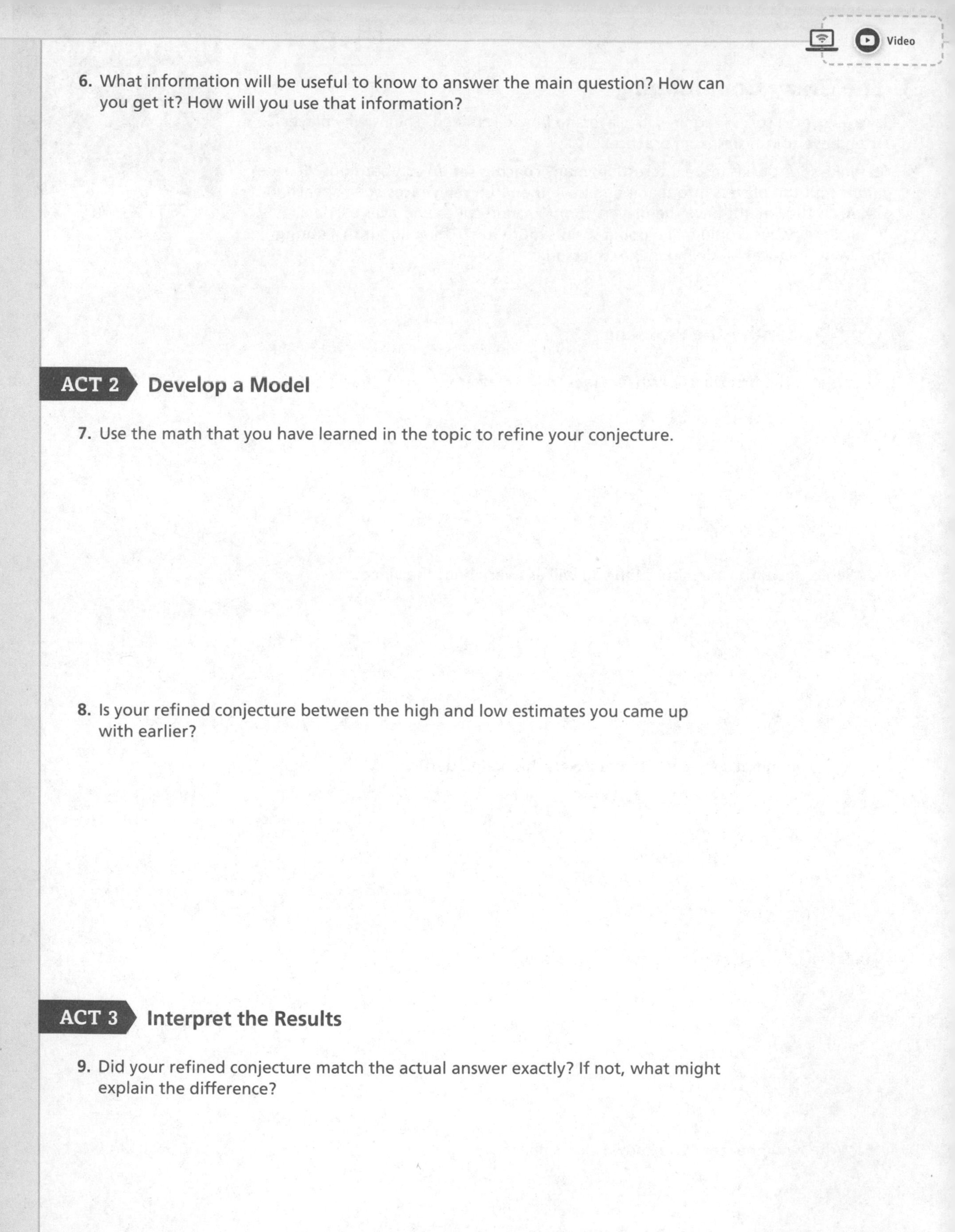

6. What information will be useful to know to answer the main question? How can you get it? How will you use that information?

ACT 2 Develop a Model

7. Use the math that you have learned in the topic to refine your conjecture.

8. Is your refined conjecture between the high and low estimates you came up with earlier?

ACT 3 Interpret the Results

9. Did your refined conjecture match the actual answer exactly? If not, what might explain the difference?

Activity

CRITIQUE & EXPLAIN

Earthquakes make seismic waves through the ground. The equation $y = 10^x$ relates the height, or amplitude, in microns, of a seismic wave, y, and the power, or magnitude, x, of the ground-shaking it can cause.

Taylor and Chen used different methods to find the magnitude of the earthquake with amplitude 5,500.

Magnitude, x	Amplitude, y
2	100
3	1,000
?	4,500
4	10,000

Taylor

5,500 is halfway between 1,000 and 10,000.

3.5 is halfway between 3 and 4.

The magnitude is about 3.5.

Chen

$y = 10^x$

$10^3 = 1{,}000$
$10^4 = 10{,}000$
$10^{3.5} \approx 3{,}162$
$10^{3.7} \approx 5{,}012$
$10^{3.8} \approx 6{,}310$
$10^{3.74} \approx 5{,}500$

The magnitude is about 3.74.

A. What is the magnitude of an earthquake with amplitude 100,000? How do you know?

B. Construct Arguments Critique Taylor's and Chen's work. Is each method valid? Could either method be improved?

C. Describe how to express the exact value of the desired magnitude.

HABITS OF MIND

Reason Taylor reasoned that since 5,500 was halfway between 1,000 and 10,000, that the magnitude had to be halfway between 3 and 4. What is incorrect about Taylor's reasoning?

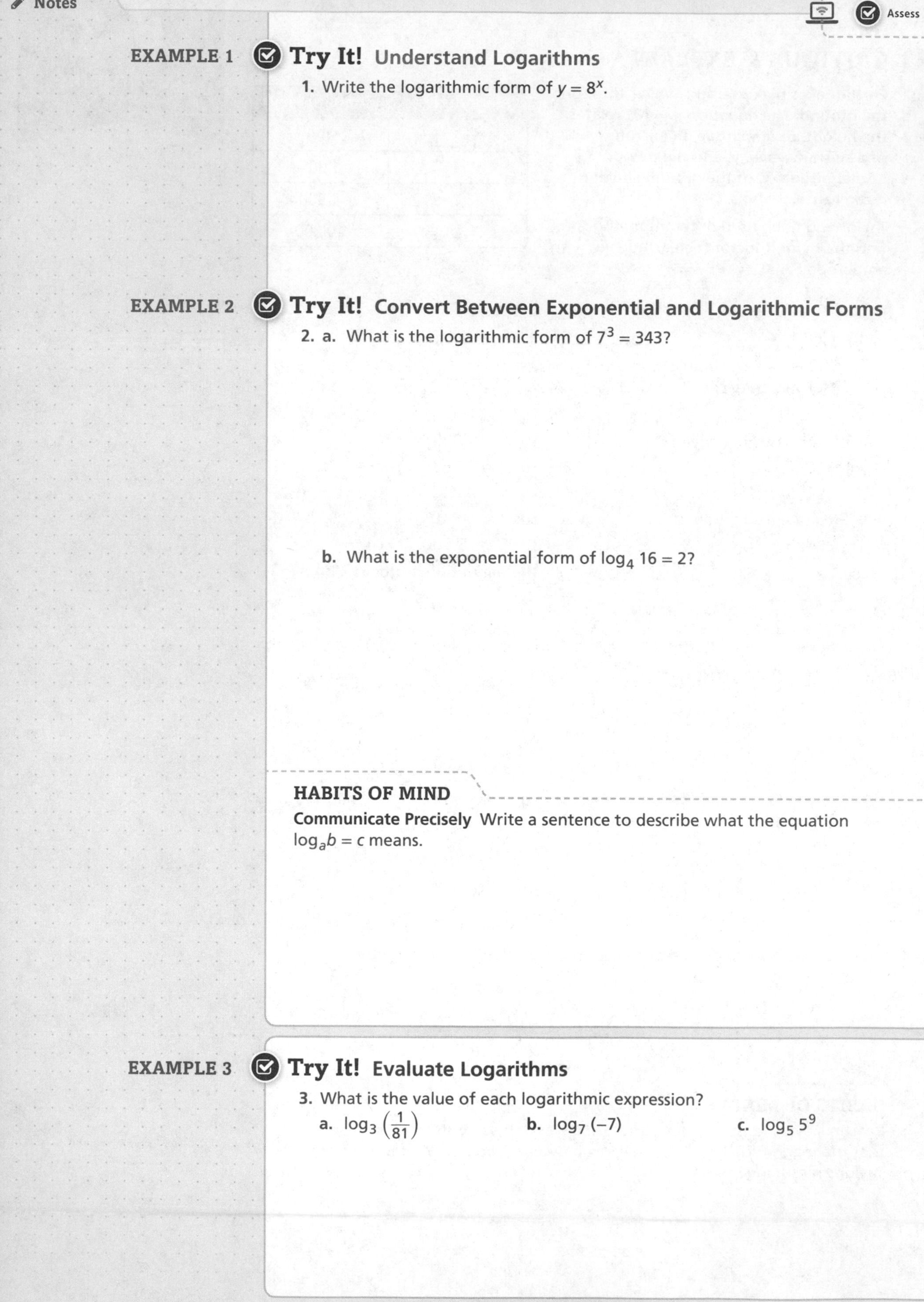

Notes

Assess

EXAMPLE 1

Try It! Understand Logarithms

1. Write the logarithmic form of $y = 8^x$.

EXAMPLE 2

Try It! Convert Between Exponential and Logarithmic Forms

2. a. What is the logarithmic form of $7^3 = 343$?

b. What is the exponential form of $\log_4 16 = 2$?

HABITS OF MIND

Communicate Precisely Write a sentence to describe what the equation $\log_a b = c$ means.

EXAMPLE 3

Try It! Evaluate Logarithms

3. What is the value of each logarithmic expression?

a. $\log_3 \left(\frac{1}{81}\right)$

b. $\log_7 (-7)$

c. $\log_5 5^9$

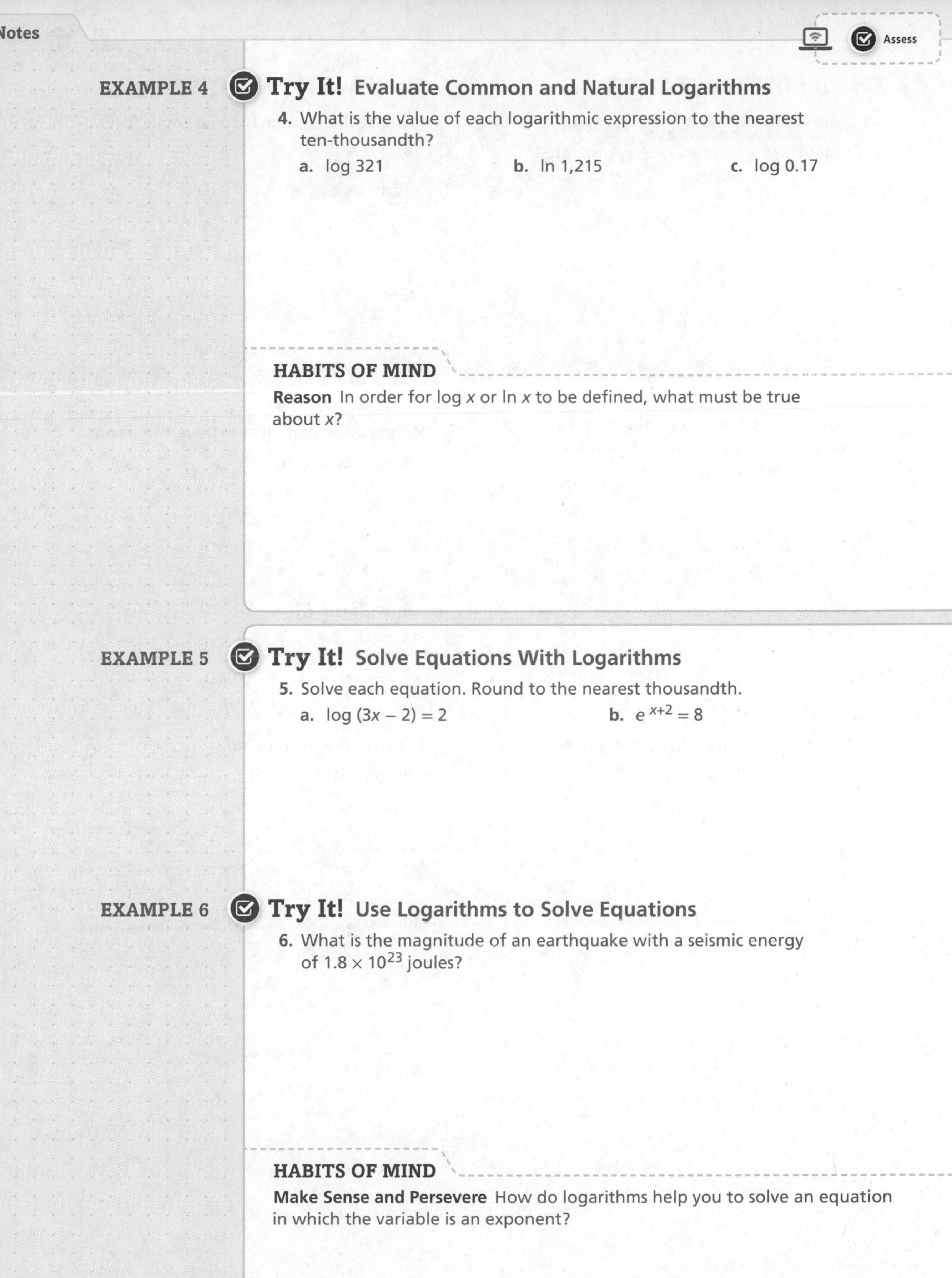

Notes

Assess

EXAMPLE 4

Try It! Evaluate Common and Natural Logarithms

4. What is the value of each logarithmic expression to the nearest ten-thousandth?

a. log 321

b. ln 1,215

c. log 0.17

HABITS OF MIND

Reason In order for log x or ln x to be defined, what must be true about x?

EXAMPLE 5

Try It! Solve Equations With Logarithms

5. Solve each equation. Round to the nearest thousandth.

a. $\log(3x - 2) = 2$

b. $e^{x+2} = 8$

EXAMPLE 6

Try It! Use Logarithms to Solve Equations

6. What is the magnitude of an earthquake with a seismic energy of 1.8×10^{23} joules?

HABITS OF MIND

Make Sense and Persevere How do logarithms help you to solve an equation in which the variable is an exponent?

Do You UNDERSTAND?

1. ESSENTIAL QUESTION What are logarithms and how are they evaluated?

2. **Error Analysis** Amir said the expression $\log_5(-25)$ simplifies to -2. Explain Amir's possible error.

3. **Vocabulary** Explain the difference between the common logarithm and the natural logarithm.

4. **Make Sense and Persevere** How can logarithms help to solve an equation such as $10^t = 656$?

Do You KNOW HOW?

Write each equation in logarithmic form.

5. $2^{-6} = \frac{1}{64}$

6. $e^4 \approx 54.6$

Write each equation in exponential form.

7. $\log 200 \approx 2.301$

8. $\ln 25 \approx 3.22$

Evaluate the expression.

9. $\log_4 64$

10. $\log \frac{1}{100}$

11. $\ln e^5$

12. Solve for x. $4e^x = 7$.

Activity

EXPLORE & REASON

Compare the graphs.

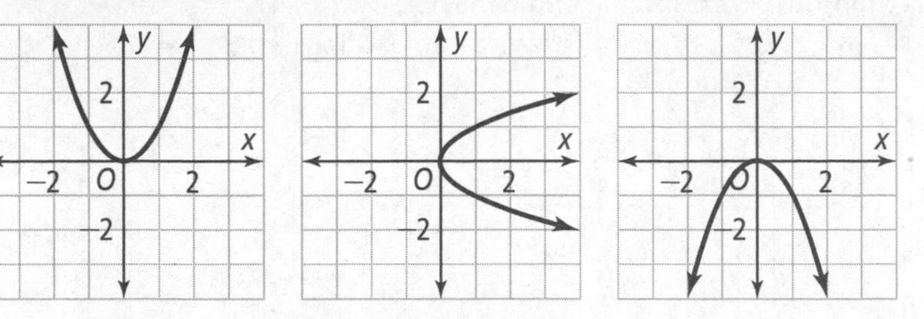

A. Which two graphs represent the inverse of each other? Explain.

B. Look for Relationships What is the relationship between the domain and the range of the two inverse relations?

HABITS OF MIND

Communicate Precisely How are the points on graphs of functions that are inverses of each other related?

EXAMPLE 1 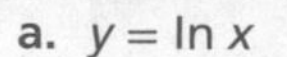

Try It! Identify Key Features of Logarithmic Functions

1. Graph each function and identify the domain and range. List any intercepts or asymptotes. Describe the end behavior.

a. $y = \ln x$

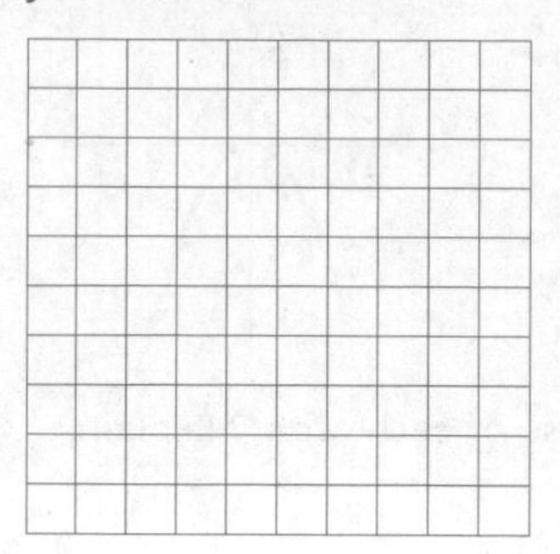

b. $y = \log_{\frac{1}{2}} x$

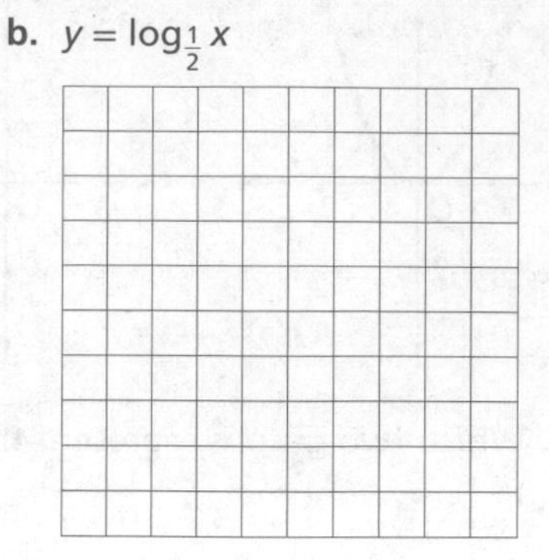

EXAMPLE 2

Try It! Graph Transformations of Logarithmic Functions

2. Describe how each graph compares to the graph of $f(x) = \ln x$.

a. $g(x) = \ln x + 4$

b. $h(x) = 5 \ln x$

HABITS OF MIND

Use Structure Does the graph of either $y = \ln x + 4$ or $y = \ln (x + 4)$ have an intercept that is different from the intercept of $y = \ln x$? Explain.

Assess

EXAMPLE 3 Try It! Inverses of Exponential and Logarithmic Functions

3. Find the inverse of each function.

   a. $f(x) = 3^{x+2}$

   b. $g(x) = \log_7 x - 2$

EXAMPLE 4 Try It! Interpret the Inverse of a Formula Involving Logarithms

4. Describe what happens to the amount of monthly revenue as the amount of advertising increases. How might you determine the optimal advertising budget? Explain.

HABITS OF MIND

Generalize How would you explain, in your own words, how to find the inverse of a logarithmic function?

EXAMPLE 5 Try It! Compare Two Logarithmic Functions

5. For which plane do you think the altitude will change more quickly over the interval $15 \le t \le 20$? Explain your reasoning.

HABITS OF MIND

Look for Relationships How does the average rate of change of the function $f(x) = \log x$ change as x increases?

Do You UNDERSTAND?

1. ESSENTIAL QUESTION How is the relationship between logarithmic and exponential functions revealed in the key features of their graphs?

2. **Error Analysis** Raynard claims the domain of the function $y = \log_3 x$ is all real numbers. Explain the error Raynard made.

3. **Communicate Precisely** How are the graphs of $f(x) = \log_5 x$ and $g(x) = -\log_5 x$ related?

Do You KNOW HOW?

4. Graph the function $y = \log_4 x$ and identify the domain and range. List any intercepts or asymptotes. Describe the end behavior.

5. Write the equation for the function $g(x)$, which can be described as a vertical shift $1\frac{1}{2}$ units up from the function $f(x) = \ln x - 1$.

6. The function $y = 5 \ln (x + 1)$ gives y, the number of downloads, in hundreds, x minutes after the release of a song. Find the equation of the inverse and interpret its meaning.

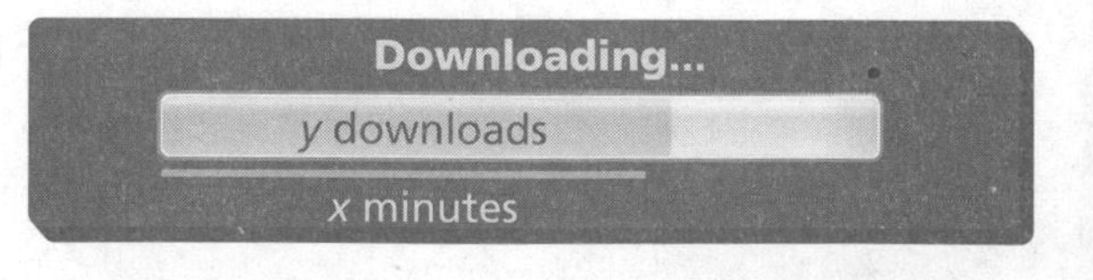

Activity

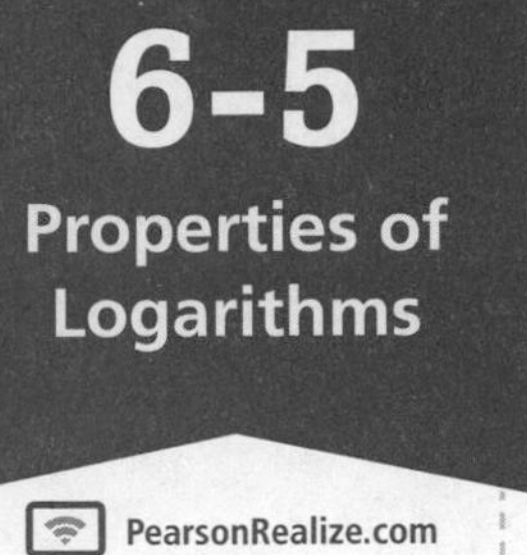

EXPLORE & REASON

Look at the graph of $y = \log x$ and the ordered pairs shown.

$y = \log x$

(3, 0.477)

(5, 0.699)

(15, 1.176)

A. Complete the table shown.

x	3	5	15
$\log x$			

B. Look for Relationships What is the relationship between the numbers 3, 5, and 15? What is the relationship between the logarithms of 3, 5, and 15?

C. What is your prediction for the value of log 45? log 75? Explain.

HABITS OF MIND

Generalize Do you think that the relationships you found in the Explore & Reason activity would also hold for natural logarithms? Give an example.

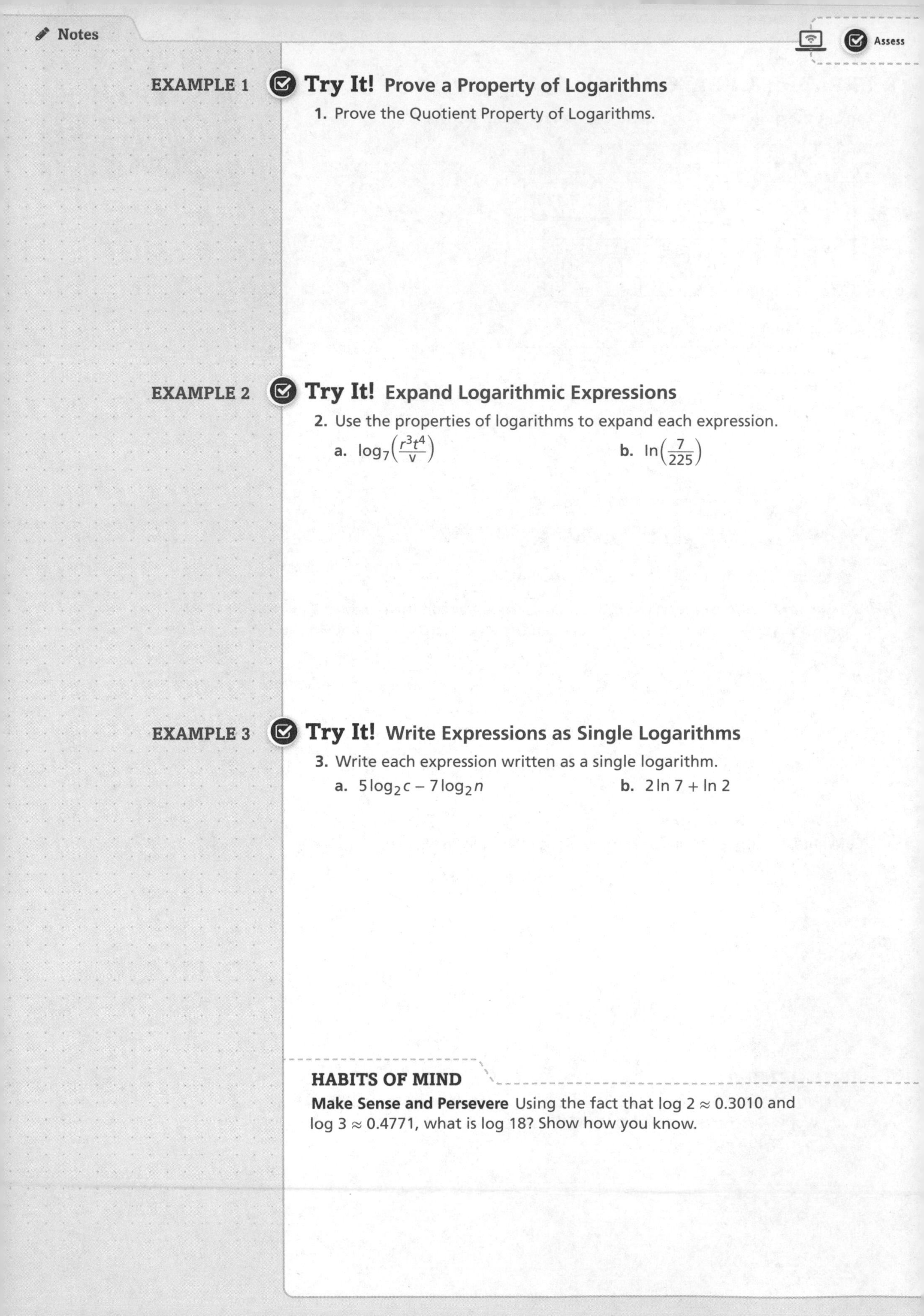

Notes

Assess

EXAMPLE 1

Try It! Prove a Property of Logarithms

1. Prove the Quotient Property of Logarithms.

EXAMPLE 2

Try It! Expand Logarithmic Expressions

2. Use the properties of logarithms to expand each expression.

a. $\log_7\left(\frac{r^3t^4}{v}\right)$

b. $\ln\left(\frac{7}{225}\right)$

EXAMPLE 3

Try It! Write Expressions as Single Logarithms

3. Write each expression written as a single logarithm.

a. $5\log_2 c - 7\log_2 n$

b. $2\ln 7 + \ln 2$

HABITS OF MIND

Make Sense and Persevere Using the fact that $\log 2 \approx 0.3010$ and $\log 3 \approx 0.4771$, what is log 18? Show how you know.

Assess

EXAMPLE 4

Try It! Apply Properties of Logarithms

4. What is the concentration of hydrogen ions in a liter of orange juice?

HABITS OF MIND

Generalize What types of numbers have logarithms that are negative? Explain.

EXAMPLE 5

Try It! Evaluate Logarithmic Expressions by Changing the Base

5. Estimate the value of each loqarithm. Then use a calculator to find the value of each logarithm to the nearest thousandth.

   a. $\log_2 7$

   b. $\log_5 3$

EXAMPLE 6

Try It! Use the Change of Base Formula

6. What is the solution to the equation $3^x = 15$? Express the solution as a logarithm and then evaluate. Round to the nearest thousandth.

HABITS OF MIND

Use Appropriate Tools Why is the Change of Base Formula useful when evaluating a logarithm with a calculator?

Do You UNDERSTAND?

1. ESSENTIAL QUESTION How are the properties of logarithms used to simplify expressions and solve logarithmic equations?

2. **Vocabulary** While it is not necessary to change to base 10 when applying the Change of Base Formula, why is it common to do so?

3. **Error Analysis** Amanda claimed the expanded form of the expression $\log_4(c^2d^5)$ is $5\log_4 c + 5\log_4 d$. Explain the error Amanda made.

Do You KNOW HOW?

4. Use the properties of logarithms to expand the expression $\log_6\left(\frac{49}{5}\right)$.

5. Use the properties of logarithms to write the expression $5 \ln s + 6 \ln t$ as a single logarithm.

6. Use the formula $\text{pH} = \log\frac{1}{[H^+]}$ to write an expression for the concentration of hydrogen ions, $[H^+]$, in a container of baking soda with a pH of 8.9.

Activity

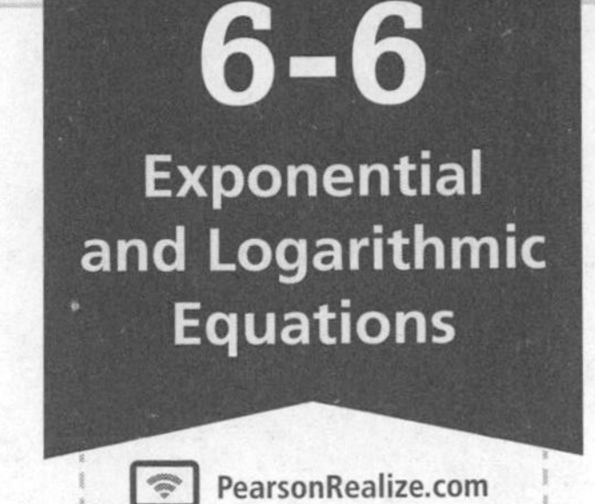

MODEL & DISCUSS

A store introduces two new models of fitness trackers to its product line. A glance at the data is enough to see that sales of both types of fitness trackers are increasing. Unfortunately, the store has limited space for the merchandise. The manager decides that the store will sell both models until sales of TrackSmart exceed those of FitTracker.

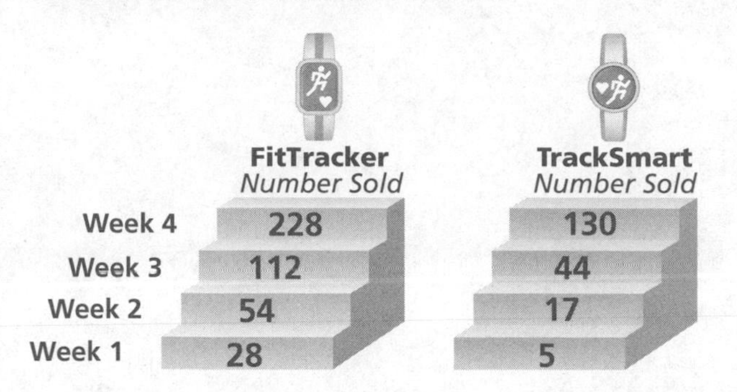

A. **Model With Mathematics** Find an equation of an exponential that models the sales for each fitness tracker. Describe your method.

B. Based on the equations that you wrote, determine when the store will stop selling FitTracker.

HABITS OF MIND

Look for Relationships How do you know that the sales data is modeled by an exponential function?

Notes

Assess

EXAMPLE 1

Try It! Solve Exponential Equations Using a Common Base

1. Solve each equation using a common base.

a. $25^{3x} = 125^{x+2}$

b. $0.001 = 10^{6x}$

EXAMPLE 2

Try It! Rewrite Exponential Equations Using Logarithms

2. Rewrite the equation $5^x = 12$ using logarithms.

HABITS OF MIND

Communicate Precisely In order to set the exponents of two exponential expressions equal to each other, what must be true about the exponential expressions?

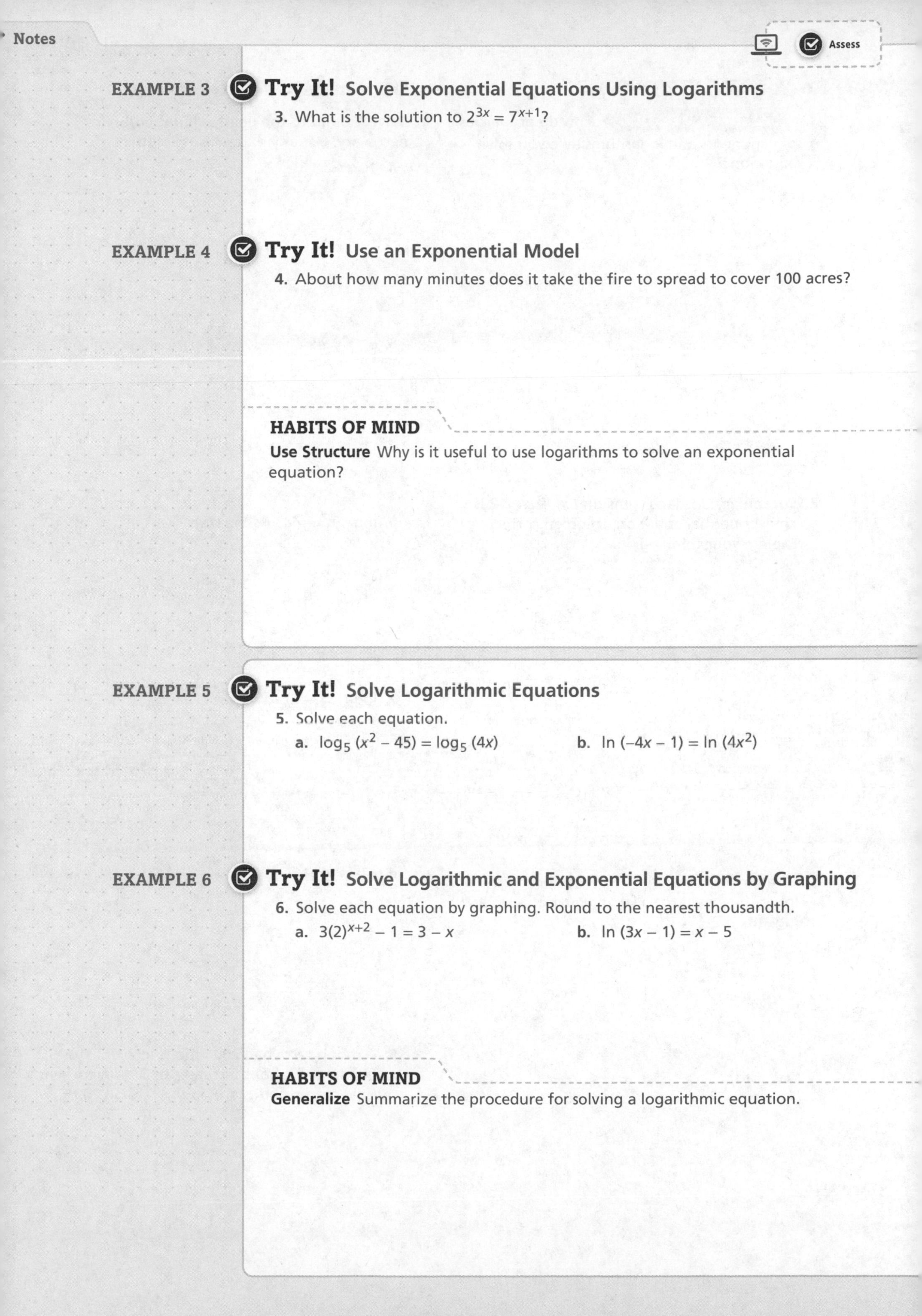

Notes

Assess

EXAMPLE 3

Try It! Solve Exponential Equations Using Logarithms

3. What is the solution to $2^{3x} = 7^{x+1}$?

EXAMPLE 4

Try It! Use an Exponential Model

4. About how many minutes does it take the fire to spread to cover 100 acres?

HABITS OF MIND

Use Structure Why is it useful to use logarithms to solve an exponential equation?

EXAMPLE 5

Try It! Solve Logarithmic Equations

5. Solve each equation.

a. $\log_5 (x^2 - 45) = \log_5 (4x)$

b. $\ln (-4x - 1) = \ln (4x^2)$

EXAMPLE 6

Try It! Solve Logarithmic and Exponential Equations by Graphing

6. Solve each equation by graphing. Round to the nearest thousandth.

a. $3(2)^{x+2} - 1 = 3 - x$

b. $\ln (3x - 1) = x - 5$

HABITS OF MIND

Generalize Summarize the procedure for solving a logarithmic equation.

Do You UNDERSTAND?

1. ESSENTIAL QUESTION How do properties of exponents and logarithms help you solve equations?

2. **Vocabulary** Jordan claims that $x^2 + 3 = 12$ is an exponential equation. Is Jordan correct? Explain your thinking.

3. **Communicate Precisely** How can properties of logarithms help to solve an equation such as $\log_6 (8x - 2)^3 = 12$?

Do You KNOW HOW?

Solve. Round to the nearest hundredth, if necessary. List any extraneous solutions.

4. $16^{3x} = 256^{x+1}$

5. $6^{x+2} = 4^x$

6. $\log_5 (x^2 - 44) = \log_5 (7x)$

7. $\log_2 (3x - 2) = 4$

8. $4^{2x} = 9^{x-1}$

9. A rabbit farm had 200 rabbits in 2015. The number of rabbits increases by 30% every year. How many rabbits are on the farm in 2031?

6-7 Geometric Sequences and Series

PearsonRealize.com

EXPLORE & REASON

A store offered customers two plans for getting bonus points:

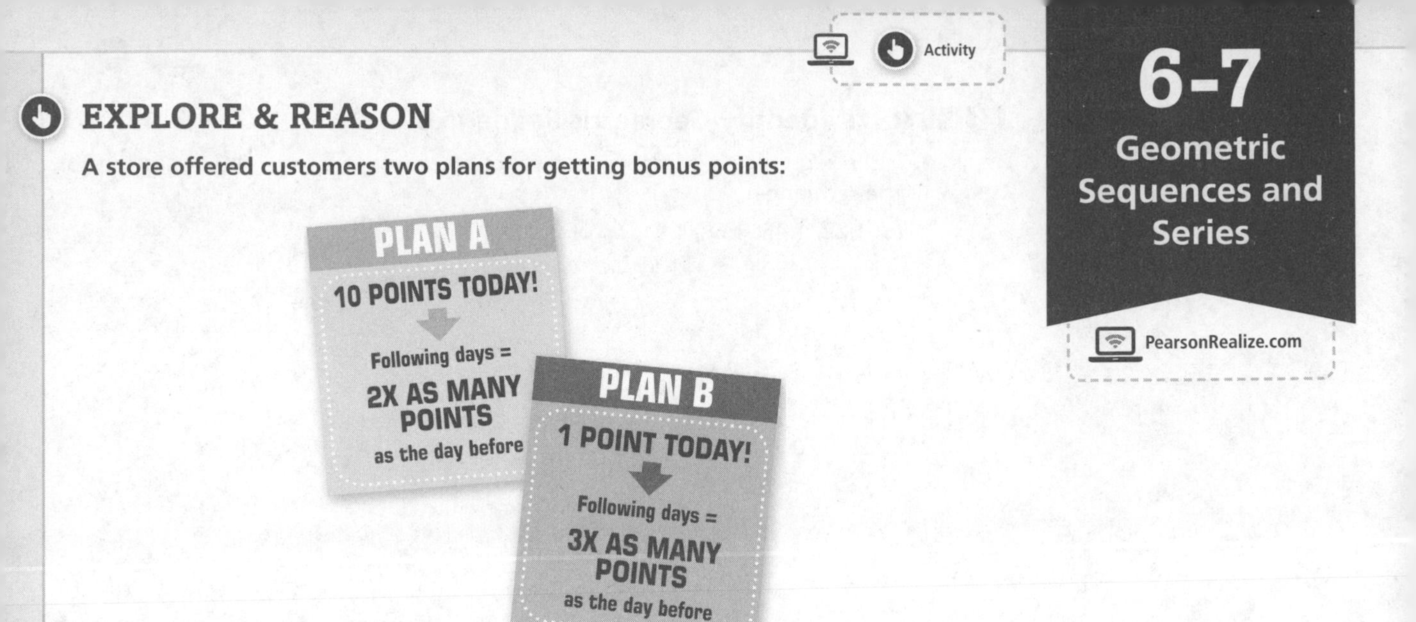

A. What expression represents the number of points received each day for Plan A?

B. What expression represents the number of points received each day for Plan B?

C. **Reason** On the 7th day, which plan would offer the most bonus points? Explain.

HABITS OF MIND

Reason Does Plan B always offer more points than Plan A? Explain.

 Notes

Assess

EXAMPLE 1

Try It! Identify Geometric Sequences

1. Is the sequence a geometric sequence? If so, write a recursive definition for the sequence.

   a. 1.22, 1.45, 1.68, 1.91, ...

   b. −1.5, 0.75, −0.375, 0.1875, ...

EXAMPLE 2

Try It! Translate Between Recursive and Explicit Definitions

2. a. Given the recursive definition $a_n = \begin{cases} 12, & n = 1 \\ \frac{1}{3}a_{n-1}, & n > 1 \end{cases}$; what is the explicit definition for the sequence?

   b. Given the explicit definition $a_n = 6(1.2)^{n-1}$; what is the recursive definition?

EXAMPLE 3

Try It! Solve Problems with Geometric Sequences

3. A geometric sequence can be used to describe the growth of bacteria in an experiment. On the first day of the experiment there were 9 bacteria in a Petri dish. On the 10th day, there are 3^{20} bacteria in the dish. How many bacteria were in the dish on the 7th day of the experiment?

HABITS OF MIND

Use Appropriate Tools How can you use the recursive definition for a geometric sequence to find the 19th term?

Notes

EXAMPLE 4

Try It! Formula for the Sum of a Finite Geometric Series

4. a. Write the expanded form of the series $\sum_{n=1}^{5} \frac{1}{2}(3)^{n-1}$. What is the sum?

b. Write the series $-2 + \left(\frac{-2}{3}\right) + \ldots + \left(\frac{-2}{243}\right)$ using sigma notation. What is the sum?

EXAMPLE 5

Try It! Find the Number of Terms in a Finite Geometric Series

5. a. How many terms are in the geometric series $3 + 6 + 12 + \ldots + 768$?

b. The sum of a geometric series is 155. The first term of the series is 5, and its common ratio is 2. How many terms are in the series?

EXAMPLE 6

Try It! Use a Finite Geometric Series

6. What is the monthly payment for a \$40,000 loan for 4 years with an annual interest rate of 4.8%?

HABITS OF MIND

Make Sense and Persevere Why is using a formula easier than calculating and adding all 10 terms?

Do You UNDERSTAND?

1. ESSENTIAL QUESTION How can you represent and use geometric sequences and series?

2. **Error Analysis** Denzel claims the sequence 0, 7, 49, 343, ... is a geometric sequence and the next number is 2,401. What error did he make?

3. **Vocabulary** Describe the similarities and differences between a common difference and a common ratio.

4. **Use Structure** What happens to the terms of a sequence if a_1 is positive and $r > 1$? What happens if $0 < r < 1$? Explain.

Do You KNOW HOW?

Find the common ratio and the next three terms of each geometric sequence.

5. 2, −4, 8, −16, ...

6. −64, −16, −4, −1, ...

7. 0.8, 2.4, 7.2, 21.6, ...

8. 2, −10, 50, −250, ...

9. 100, 50, 25, 12.5, ...

10. In a video game, players earn 10 points for finishing the first level and twice as many points for each additional level. How many points does a player earn for finishing the fifth level? How many points will the player have earned in the game up to that point?

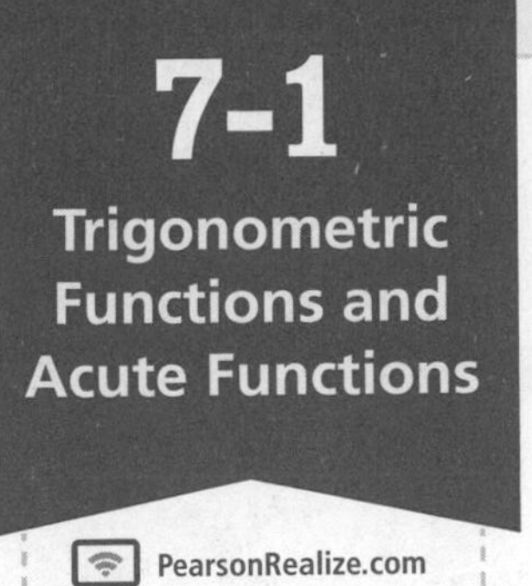

EXPLORE & REASON

In the figure below, △*ABC* ~ △*DEF*.

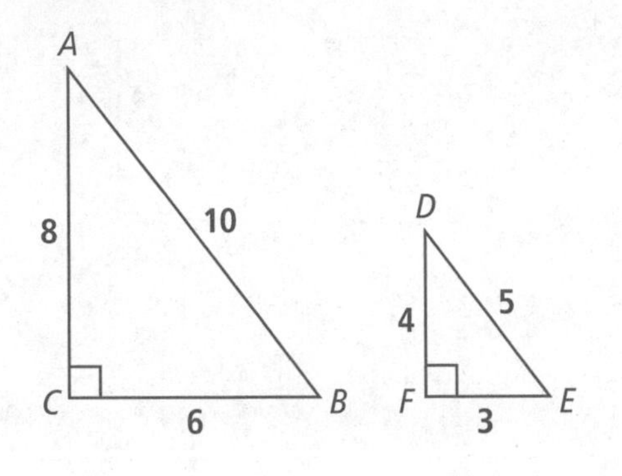

A. Write as many ratios as you can using two side lengths from △*ABC*.

B. Write as many ratios as you can using two side lengths from △*DEF*.

C. Look for Relationships What do the results from parts (a) and (b) suggest about the ratios of side lengths in similar right triangles?

HABITS OF MIND

Look for Relationships Find the side lengths of two right triangles, one that is similar to the triangles above and one that is not. How do the ratios in these triangles compare to the ones above?

Assess

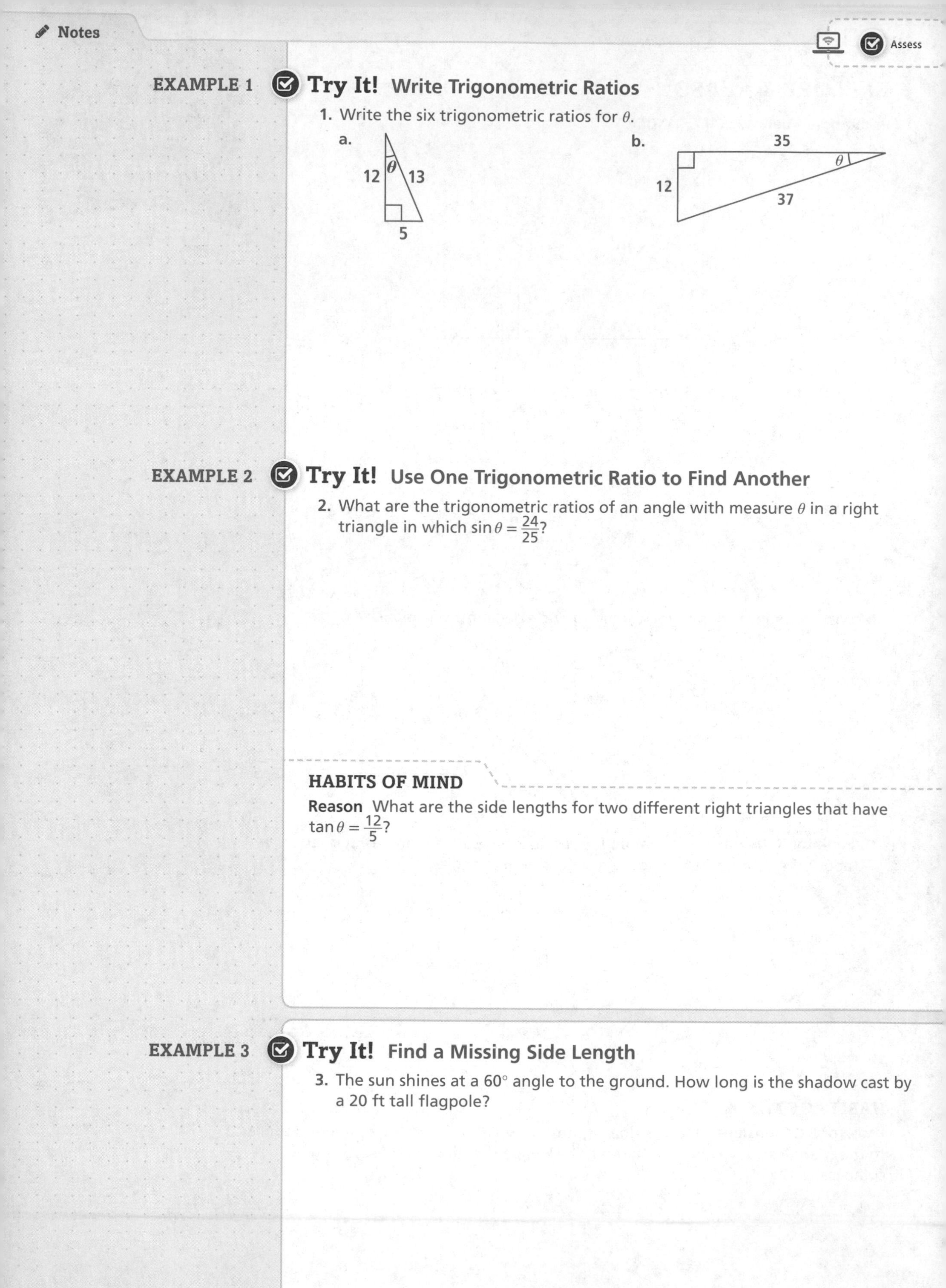

EXAMPLE 1

Try It! Write Trigonometric Ratios

1. Write the six trigonometric ratios for θ.

a.

b.

EXAMPLE 2

Try It! Use One Trigonometric Ratio to Find Another

2. What are the trigonometric ratios of an angle with measure θ in a right triangle in which $\sin\theta = \frac{24}{25}$?

HABITS OF MIND

Reason What are the side lengths for two different right triangles that have $\tan\theta = \frac{12}{5}$?

EXAMPLE 3

Try It! Find a Missing Side Length

3. The sun shines at a 60° angle to the ground. How long is the shadow cast by a 20 ft tall flagpole?

Notes

Assess

EXAMPLE 4

Try It! Evaluate Trigonometric Ratios in Special Triangles

4. The length of the hypotenuse in a 45° –45° –90° triangle is $5\sqrt{2}$. What are the sine and secant ratios for a 45° angle?

HABITS OF MIND

Construct Arguments Is it true that if $\sec\theta = \sqrt{2}$ for θ in a right triangle that the triangle must be isosceles? Explain.

EXAMPLE 5

Try It! Explain Trigonometric Identities

5. What are the cofunction identities for tangent and cotangent?

HABITS OF MIND

Communicate Precisely What is an equation that relates the three functions cosecant, secant, and cotangent?

Do You UNDERSTAND?

1. ESSENTIAL QUESTION How can ratios of lengths of sides within right triangles help determine other lengths and angle measures in the triangles?

2. **Error Analysis** Terrell said that cos θ is the reciprocal of sin θ. Explain and correct Terrell's error.

3. **Vocabulary** Explain what it means to say that $\tan \theta = \frac{1}{\cot \theta}$ is an identity.

4. **Construct Arguments** Why are the cofunction identities true for all right triangles?

5. **Generalize** How does knowing one trigonometric ratio allow you to find the other five trigonometric ratios?

6. **Look for Relationships** Why do secant and cosecant always have to be greater than 1 or less than −1?

Do You KNOW HOW?

Find sin θ using the given trigonometric ratio.

7. $\csc \theta = \frac{7}{3}$

8. $\tan \theta = \frac{5}{12}$

Use the trigonometric ratio given to write the other five trigonometric ratios for θ.

9. $\cos \theta = \frac{5}{13}$

10. $\tan \theta = \frac{3}{4}$

Write the reciprocal identity of the given trigonometric ratio.

11. $\cos \theta$

12. $\sec \theta$

Write the cofunction identity of the given trigonometric ratio.

13. $\csc \theta$

14. $\sec \theta$

15. A right triangle has a side of 16 m adjacent to an angle of 37°. What is the length of the hypotenuse rounded to the nearest whole meter?

16. A flagpole is 24 ft tall. A support wire runs from the top of the flagpole to an anchor in the ground. The wire makes a 73° angle with the ground. To the nearest tenth of a foot, how far from the base of the flagpole is the anchor?

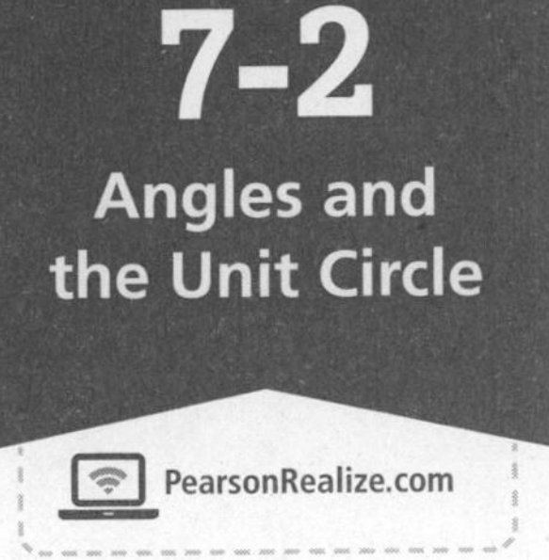

EXPLORE & REASON

A bug is placed at the point (1, 0) of the coordinate plane as shown. It starts walking counterclockwise along a circle with radius 1.

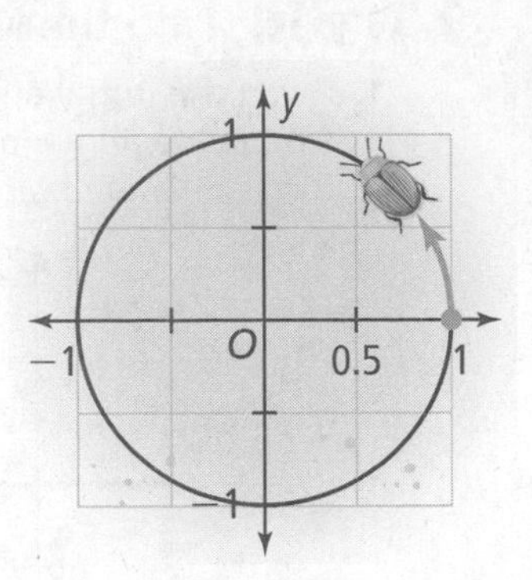

A. **Model With Mathematics** How can you calculate the distance along the circle the bug has traveled? How can you determine the measure of the central angle?

B. When the bug has traveled $\frac{1}{8}$ of the way along the circle, how far has it traveled? What central angle does its path travel through?

C. What are the distances traveled and the central angles when the bug has traveled $\frac{1}{6}$ of the way around the circle and $\frac{4}{5}$ of the way around the circle?

HABITS OF MIND

Look for Relationships A second bug is placed on a circle with radius 2. After it has traveled $\frac{4}{5}$ of the way along this new circle, how far has it traveled compared to the first bug? How do the central angles of the two bugs' paths compare?

Assess

EXAMPLE 1

Try It! Find the Measure of an Angle in Standard Position

1. Given the initial and terminal sides, find a positive angle measure, a negative angle measure, and an angle measure greater than 360° for each angle below.

a. b.

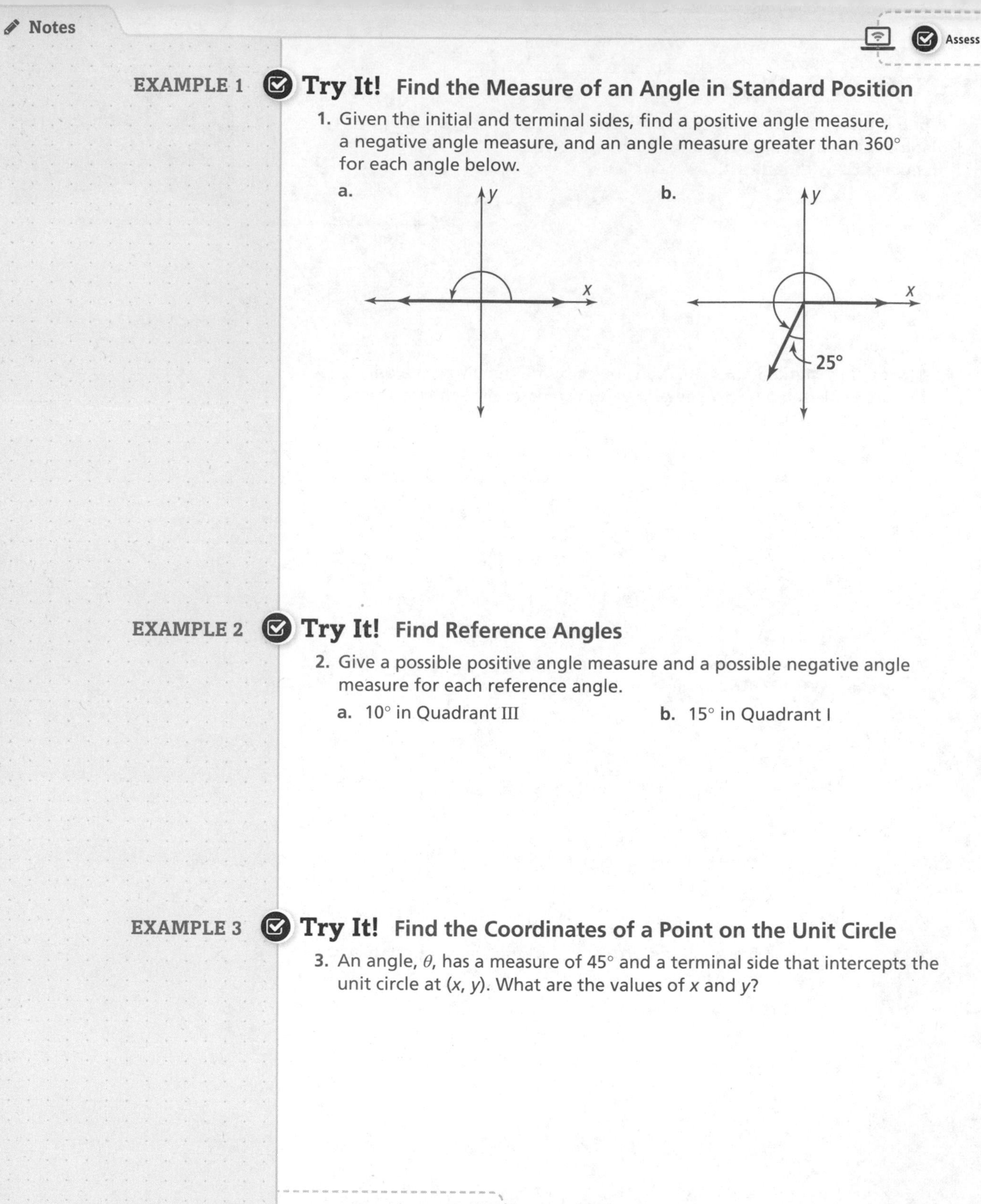

EXAMPLE 2

Try It! Find Reference Angles

2. Give a possible positive angle measure and a possible negative angle measure for each reference angle.

a. 10° in Quadrant III

b. 15° in Quadrant I

EXAMPLE 3

Try It! Find the Coordinates of a Point on the Unit Circle

3. An angle, θ, has a measure of 45° and a terminal side that intercepts the unit circle at (x, y). What are the values of x and y?

HABITS OF MIND

Make Sense and Persevere Why is the reference angle the angle between the terminal side and the x-axis instead of the y-axis?

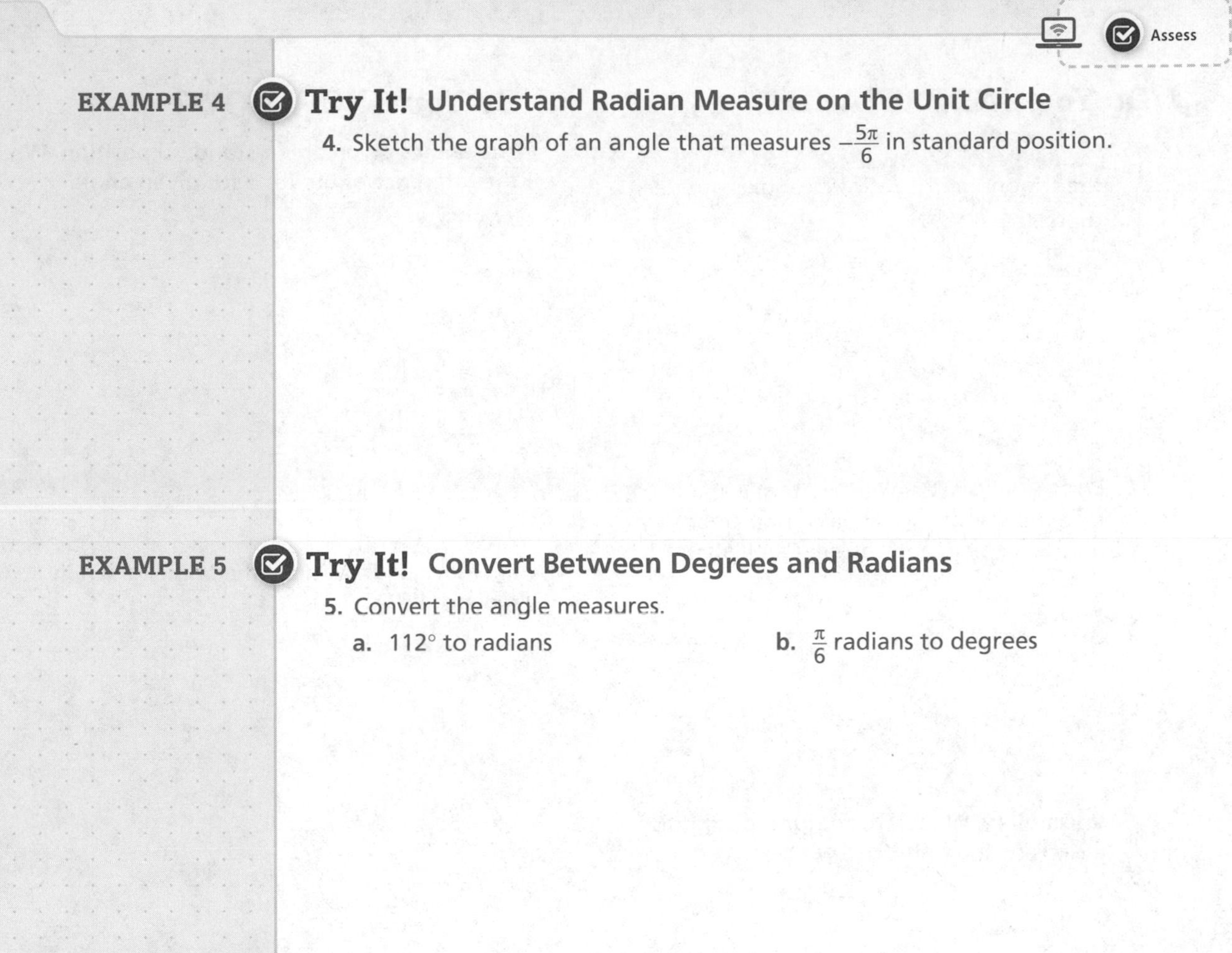

EXAMPLE 4

Try It! Understand Radian Measure on the Unit Circle

4. Sketch the graph of an angle that measures $-\frac{5\pi}{6}$ in standard position.

EXAMPLE 5

Try It! Convert Between Degrees and Radians

5. Convert the angle measures.

   a. 112° to radians

   b. $\frac{\pi}{6}$ radians to degrees

EXAMPLE 6

Try It! Use Radians to Find Arc Length

6. If the satellite could be tracked for 5,000 km, what angle in radians would it pass through?

HABITS OF MIND

Reason Which angle is larger, an angle measuring 180° or an angle measuring 3 radians? Explain.

Do You UNDERSTAND?

1. ESSENTIAL QUESTION How can we extend the trigonometric ratios to angles greater than 90°?

2. **Error Analysis** Camilla said that θ and its reference angle are always supplementary angles. Explain and correct Camilla's error.

3. **Vocabulary** What two features distinguish a circle as the unit circle?

4. **Reason** If given an angle measure in radians, how can you determine in which quadrant its terminal side will be, without converting to degrees?

5. **Make Sense and Persevere** If you are using a calculator to find the measure of an angle in degrees, what type of measure might make you question whether your calculator is actually in radian mode? Explain.

Do You KNOW HOW?

The angles given are in standard position. What is the reference angle for each given angle?

6. 65°

7. 145°

In what quadrant does the angle, given in radians, lie?

8. $\frac{\pi}{6}$

9. $\frac{5\pi}{3}$

What is the negative angle of rotation for the angle with given positive angle of rotation?

10. 270°

11. 110°

Convert each radian measure to a degree measure.

12. $\frac{\pi}{3}$

13. $\frac{7\pi}{4}$

Convert each degree measure to a radian measure.

14. –30°

15. 480°

PearsonRealize.com

EXPLORE & REASON

The graph shows the terminal sides of an angle with measure θ and its supplement, $180 - \theta$, on the unit circle.

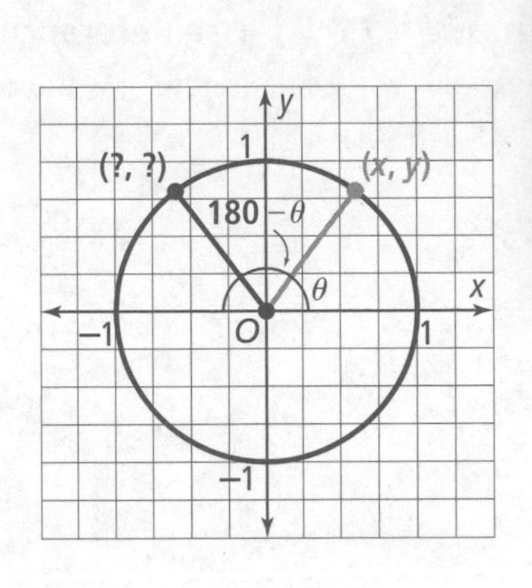

A. How are the coordinates of the intersection of the terminal side of an angle with measure θ and the unit circle related to the sine and cosine of the angle?

B. What do you notice about θ and about the acute angle formed by the terminal side of $180 - \theta$ and the x-axis?

C. Draw the terminal sides of angles in Quadrants III and IV that form the same acute angle with the x-axis as the angles in Quadrants I and II. How are these angles related to θ?

D. **Communicate Precisely** How are all four terminal sides related geometrically on the coordinate plane?

HABITS OF MIND

Reason When you connect the four points on the unit circle above, the figure is a rectangle. For what angle θ is that rectangle a square?

Notes

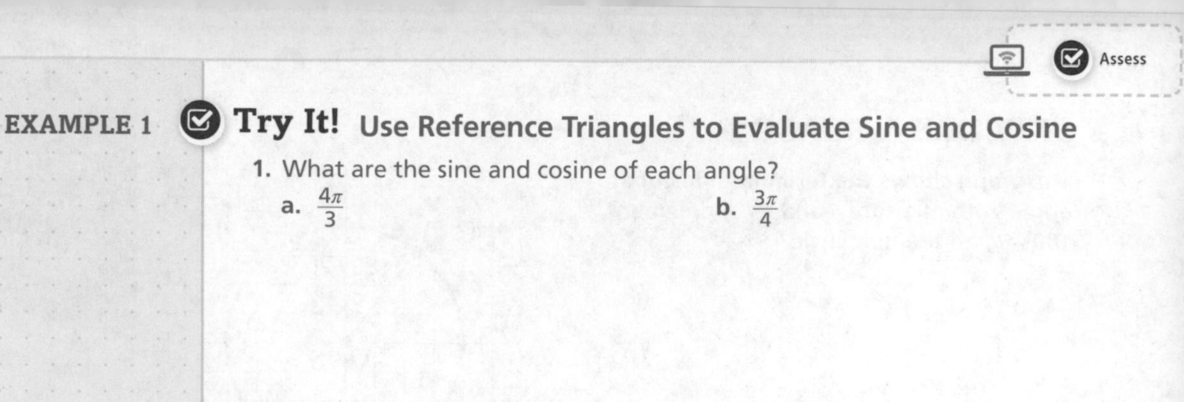

Assess

EXAMPLE 1

Try It! Use Reference Triangles to Evaluate Sine and Cosine

1. What are the sine and cosine of each angle?

a. $\frac{4\pi}{3}$

b. $\frac{3\pi}{4}$

HABITS OF MIND

Use Structure In which quadrants do the coordinates of the terminal point of an angle θ result in a negative value for $\tan \theta$? Explain.

EXAMPLE 2

Try It! Use the Pythagorean Identity $\sin^2 \theta + \cos^2 \theta = 1$

2. a. What is $\sin \theta$ if $\cos \theta = \frac{\sqrt{2}}{2}$ and $0 < \theta < \frac{\pi}{2}$?

b. What is $\cos \theta$ if $\sin \theta = -0.8$ and θ is in Quadrant IV?

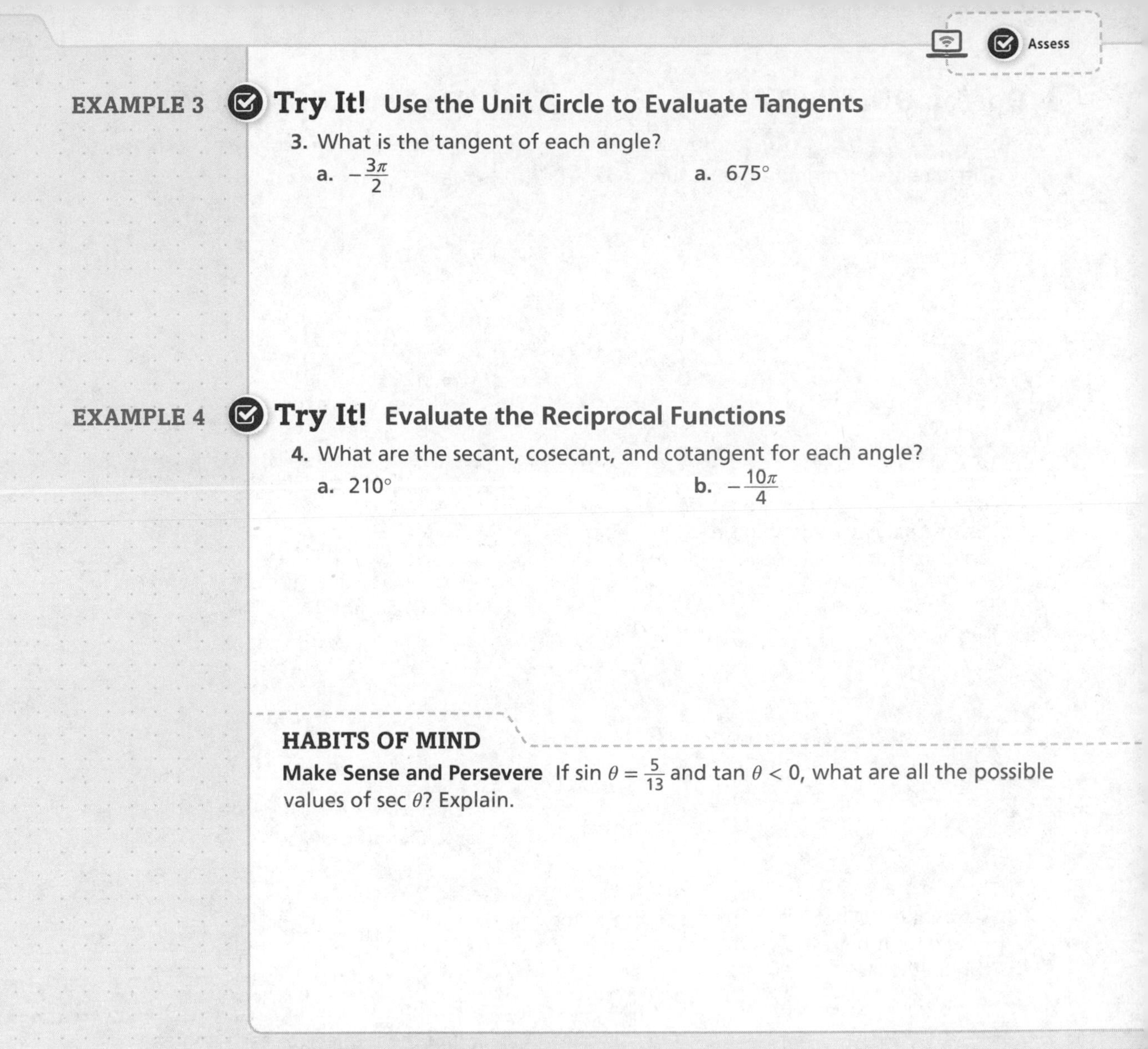

EXAMPLE 3

Try It! Use the Unit Circle to Evaluate Tangents

3. What is the tangent of each angle?

a. $-\frac{3\pi}{2}$

a. 675°

EXAMPLE 4

Try It! Evaluate the Reciprocal Functions

4. What are the secant, cosecant, and cotangent for each angle?

a. 210°

b. $-\frac{10\pi}{4}$

HABITS OF MIND

Make Sense and Persevere If $\sin \theta = \frac{5}{13}$ and $\tan \theta < 0$, what are all the possible values of $\sec \theta$? Explain.

EXAMPLE 5

Try It! Use Any Circle Centered at the Origin

5. What is the final position of a search team relative to the camp if they travel 30° north of due west, or 150°, for 5 mi from their base camp?

HABITS OF MIND

Look for Relationships How does the length of the radius of the circle affect the value of cosine and sine of 150°?

Assess

Do You UNDERSTAND?

1. ESSENTIAL QUESTION How is the unit circle related to trigonometric functions?

2. **Error Analysis** Hugo said $\sin \frac{5\pi}{2} = -1$. Explain an error Hugo could have made.

3. **Vocabulary** What is a reference triangle, and how does it help you work with the angles on the unit circle?

4. **Reason** Why is $\cos 30° = \cos(-30°)$?

Do You KNOW HOW?

Find the sine and cosine of each angle.

5. $\frac{5\pi}{4}$

6. $120°$

7. What is $\sin \theta$ if $\cos \theta = \frac{4}{5}$ and θ is in Quadrant II?

8. What is $\cos \theta$ if $\sin \theta = -\frac{1}{2}$ and θ is in Quadrant III?

Find the tangent of each angle.

9. $\frac{\pi}{6}$

10. $-45°$

11. Evaluate the secant, cosecant, and tangent of a $135°$ angle.

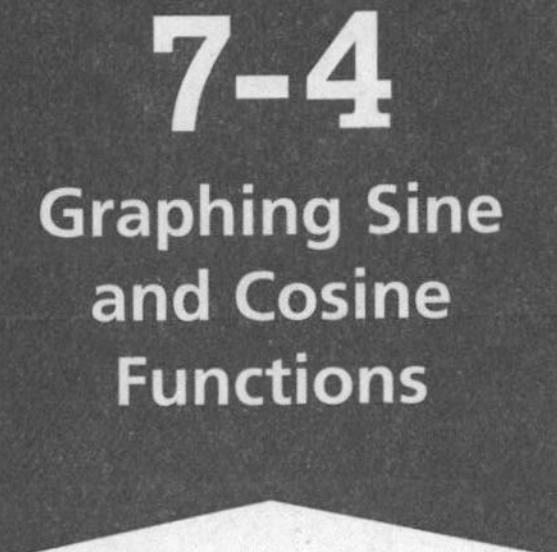

EXPLORE & REASON

The graph shows a rider's height above the platform when riding a Ferris wheel *t* minutes after entering the Ferris wheel car.

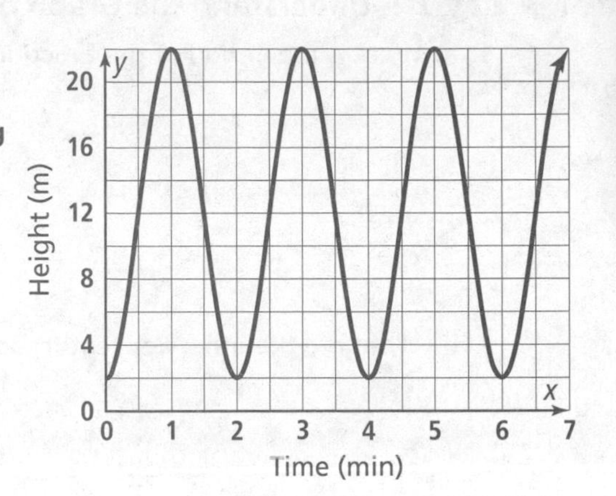

A. Sketch a graph of a rider's height if the Ferris wheel is twice as high. How does the graph represent the change in height?

B. Sketch a graph of a rider's height if the Ferris wheel is the same height as the first but goes twice as fast. How does the graph represent the change in speed?

C. **Communicate Precisely** How are the three graphs similar? How are they different?

HABITS OF MIND

Reason In the section of the graph shown, how many revolutions did the Ferris wheel make? Explain.

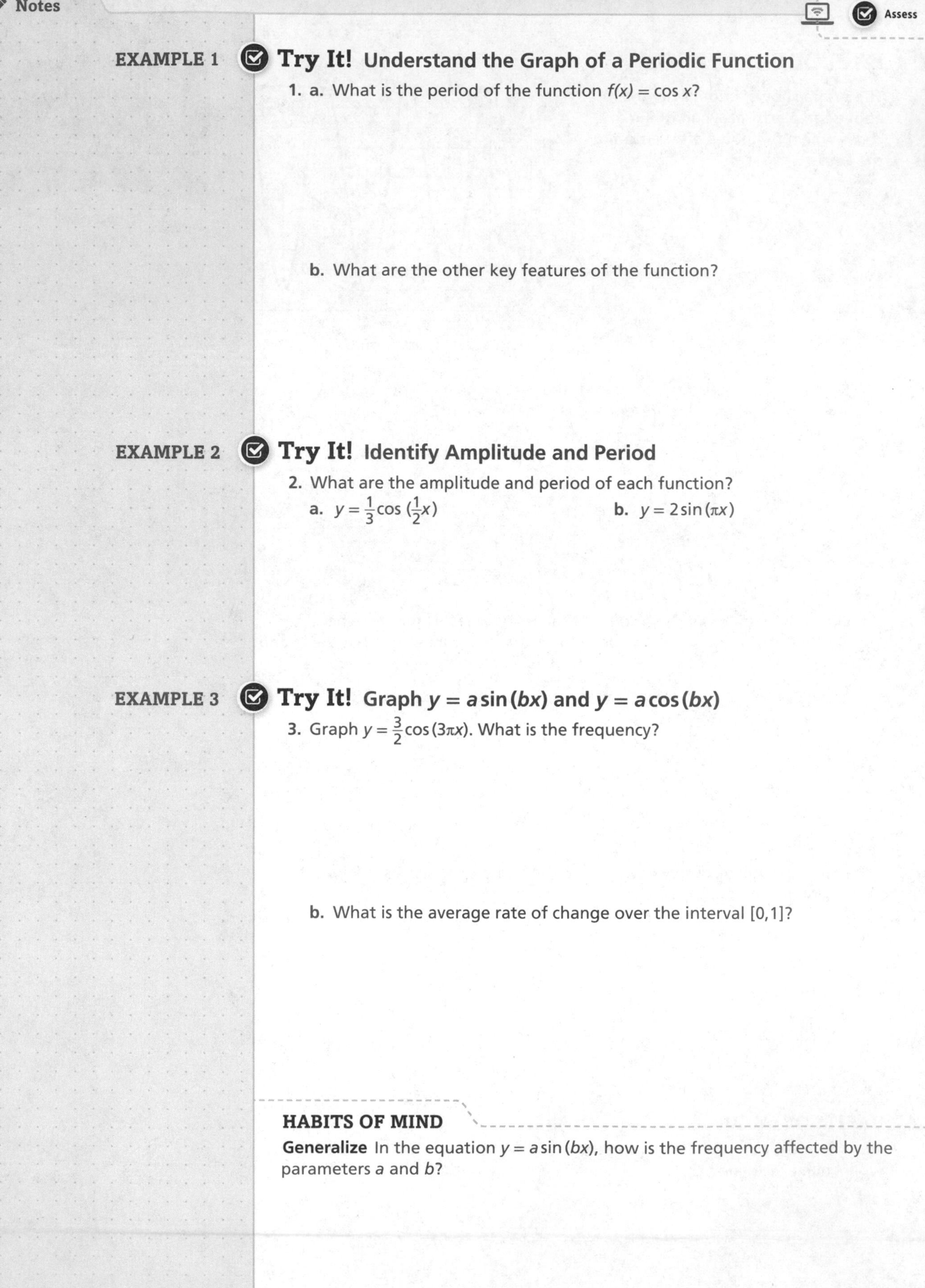

Notes

Assess

EXAMPLE 1

Try It! Understand the Graph of a Periodic Function

1. a. What is the period of the function $f(x) = \cos x$?

b. What are the other key features of the function?

EXAMPLE 2

Try It! Identify Amplitude and Period

2. What are the amplitude and period of each function?

a. $y = \frac{1}{3}\cos\left(\frac{1}{2}x\right)$

b. $y = 2\sin(\pi x)$

EXAMPLE 3

Try It! Graph $y = a\sin(bx)$ and $y = a\cos(bx)$

3. Graph $y = \frac{3}{2}\cos(3\pi x)$. What is the frequency?

b. What is the average rate of change over the interval [0,1]?

HABITS OF MIND

Generalize In the equation $y = a\sin(bx)$, how is the frequency affected by the parameters a and b?

Notes

Assess

EXAMPLE 4

Try It! Develop a Graph and an Equation From a Description

4. Construct a graph over 3 h for the tip of the minute hand *t* minutes after noon if the minute hand is 8 in. long. What is the period?

EXAMPLE 5

Try It! Compare Key Features of Two Periodic Functions

5. a. How do the frequencies of *f* and *g* compare?

b. What else is different about the two functions? Explain.

HABITS OF MIND

Use Structure Suppose you have two graphs, $y = a\sin(bx)$ and $y = c\cos(dx)$. The amplitude of the sine graph is larger than that of the cosine graph. The period of the cosine graph is larger than that of the sine graph. How are the parameters *a*, *b*, *c*, and *d* related?

Do You UNDERSTAND?

1. **ESSENTIAL QUESTION** How can you identify, use, and interpret key features of sine and cosine functions?

2. **Error Analysis** Christy said that the function $y = 3\cos(4x)$ has an amplitude of 3 and a period of $\frac{\pi}{4}$. Explain and correct Christy's error.

3. **Vocabulary** Explain the difference between the period and the amplitude of a periodic function.

4. **Reason** What is the range of the cosine function? How does the range compare to the amplitude of the function?

Do You KNOW HOW?

Find the period and amplitude of each function.

5.

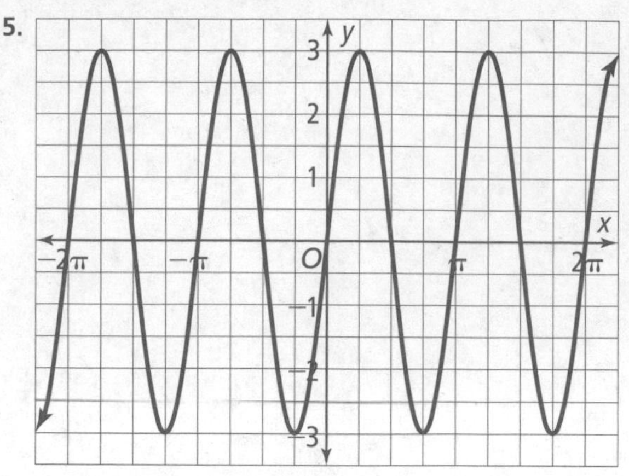

6.

7. Use the graph from Exercise 6. How many cycles does the function have in the interval from 0 to 2π?

MATHEMATICAL MODELING IN 3 ACTS

PearsonRealize.com

What Note Was That?

Sounds are created by vibrations. As the vibrations travel through the air, they create sound waves. The frequency of a sound is the measurement of the number of cycles of that wave per second, in a unit called hertz (Hz). Music notes can be identified by their frequency.

What information do you need to determine the frequency of a note? How accurate does your data need to be? Think about this during the Mathematical Modeling in 3 Acts lesson.

ACT 1 Identify the Problem

1. What is the first question that comes to mind after watching the video?

2. Write down the Main Question you will answer.

3. Make an initial conjecture that answers this Main Question.

4. Explain how you arrived at your conjecture.

5. What information will be useful to know to answer the main question? How can you get it? How will you use that information?

Video

ACT 2 Develop a Model

6. Use the math that you have learned in the topic to refine your conjecture.

ACT 3 Interpret the Results

7. Did your refined conjecture match the actual answer exactly? If not, what might explain the difference?

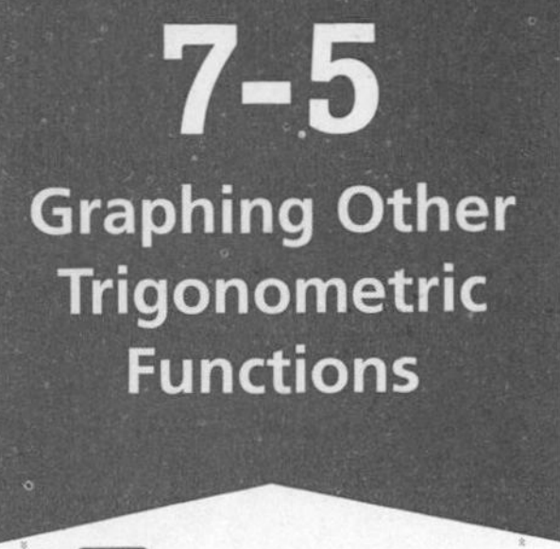

EXPLORE & REASON

Use the graphs of $f(x) = x + 3$ and $g(x) = \frac{1}{x+3}$ to compare these reciprocal functions.

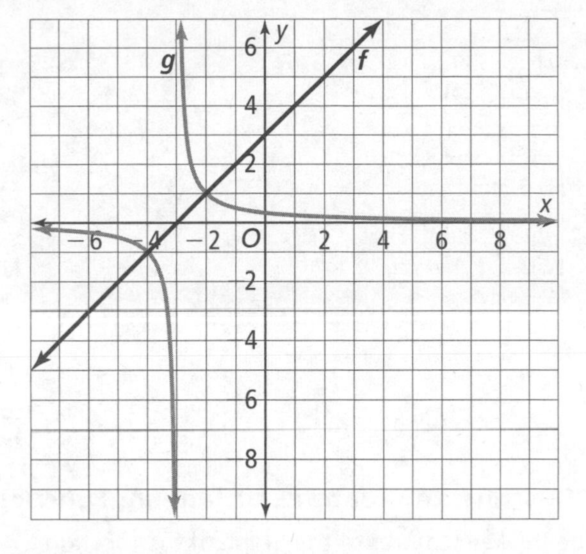

A. Identify the zeros of each function.

B. Identify the asymptotes of $y = g(x)$. Describe how the rule for g can be used to predict the horizontal and vertical asymptotes of its graph.

C. **Look for Relationships** How can you use the graph of f to predict a vertical asymptote in the graph of g, the reciprocal of f?

HABITS OF MIND

Reason What is causing the vertical asymptote at $x = -3$ in g? Explain.

Notes

Assess

EXAMPLE 1

Try It! Graph $y = \tan x$

1. Create a table of values, and use the unit circle to help you sketch the graph of $y = \cot x$. Plot the function's zeros and asymptotes in your sketch.

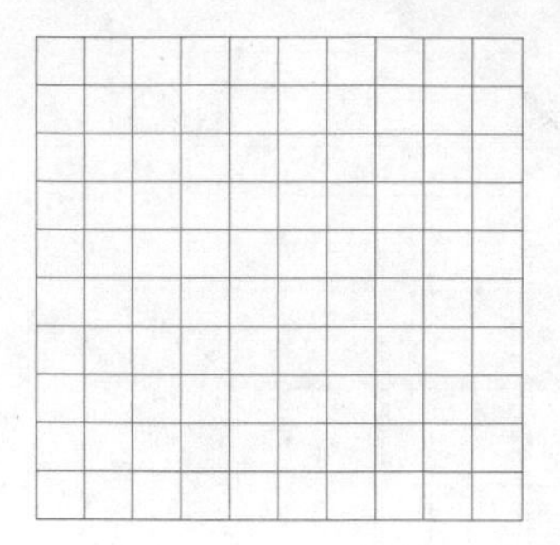

EXAMPLE 2

Try It! Describe Key Features of Tangent Functions

2. Describe the key features of the graph of the function $y = \cot x$. Refer to your graph from Example 1, Try It!

HABITS OF MIND

Make Sense and Persevere Why is there no discussion of amplitude as a key feature of the graphs of tangent and cotangent?

EXAMPLE 3

Try It! Graph $y = a \tan bx$

3. Sketch the graph of the function $y = \frac{1}{2}\cot 3x$.

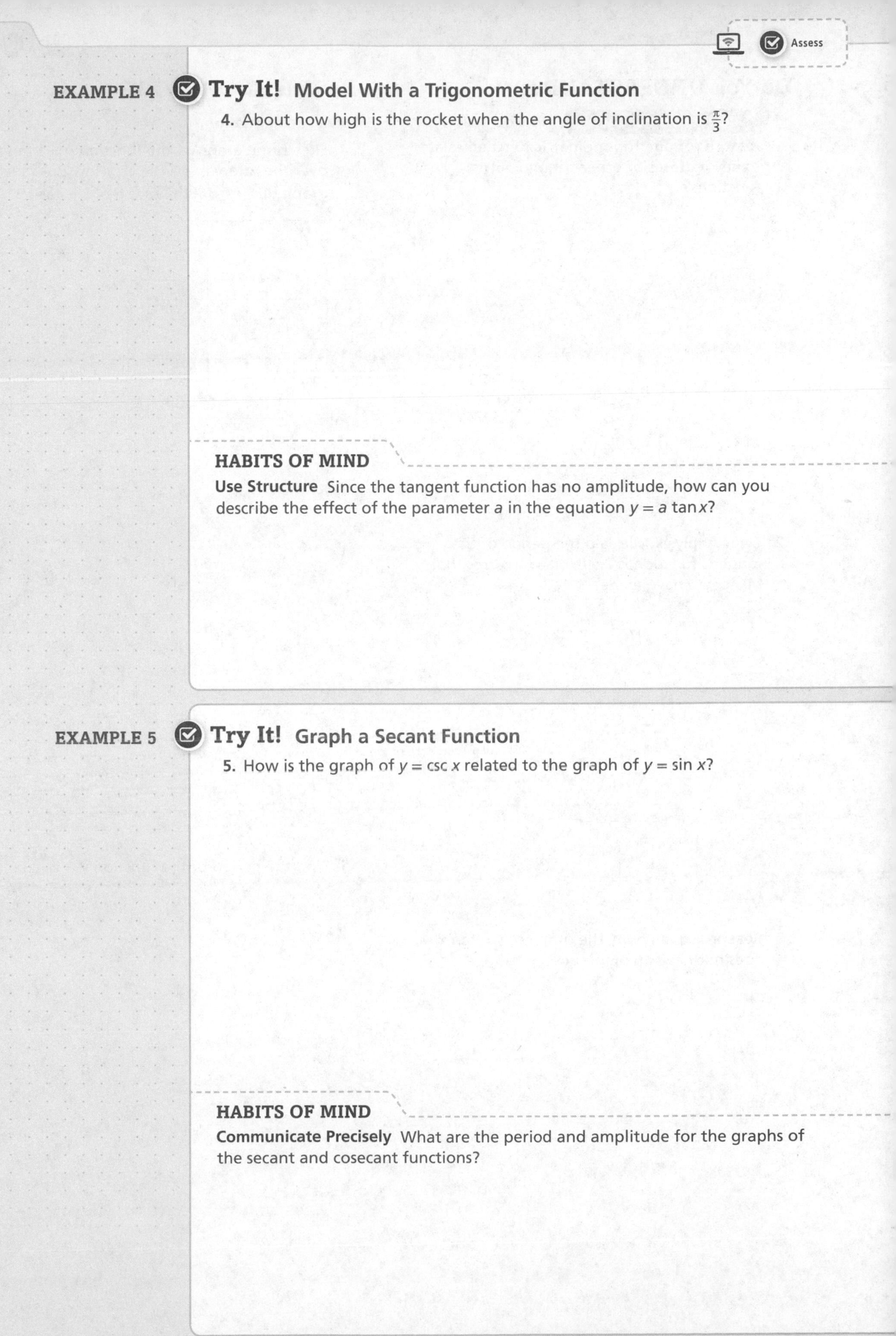

Notes

Assess

EXAMPLE 4

Try It! Model With a Trigonometric Function

4. About how high is the rocket when the angle of inclination is $\frac{\pi}{3}$?

HABITS OF MIND

Use Structure Since the tangent function has no amplitude, how can you describe the effect of the parameter *a* in the equation $y = a \tan x$?

EXAMPLE 5

Try It! Graph a Secant Function

5. How is the graph of $y = \csc x$ related to the graph of $y = \sin x$?

HABITS OF MIND

Communicate Precisely What are the period and amplitude for the graphs of the secant and cosecant functions?

Do You UNDERSTAND?

1. ESSENTIAL QUESTION How do key features of one trigonometric function relate to key features of other trigonometric functions?

2. **Error Analysis** Mia said the period of the tangent function is 2π. Explain an error that Mia could have made.

3. **Reason** Explain why the graph of $y = \tan x$ does not have an amplitude.

Do You KNOW HOW?

Solve each equation.

4. Sketch the graph of the function $y = \frac{1}{2} \tan x$ over the interval $-\frac{\pi}{2} < x < \frac{\pi}{2}$. How does this graph differ from the graph of $y = \tan x$?

5. Find the period of the function $y = \tan 3x$.

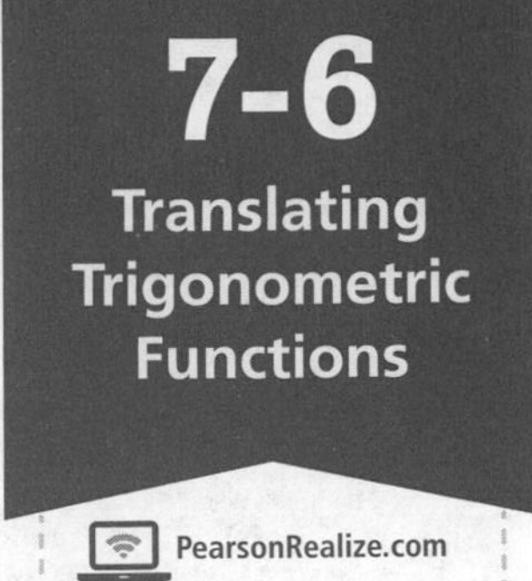

CRITIQUE & EXPLAIN

Sadie and Zhang use translations to relate the graphs of sine and cosine. Sadie claims that $\sin x = \cos\left(x - \frac{\pi}{2}\right)$. Zhang insists that $\cos x = \sin\left(x + \frac{\pi}{2}\right)$.

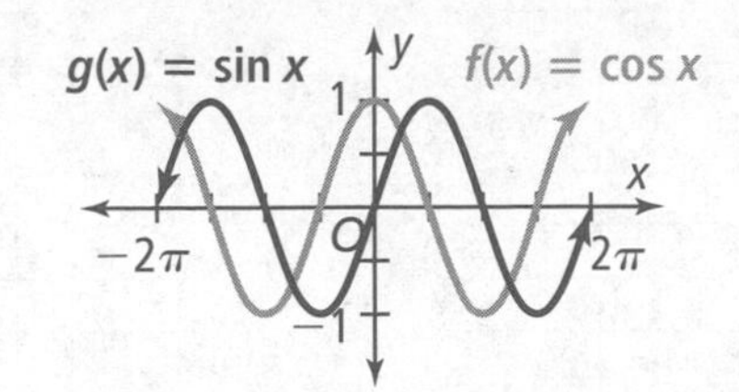

A. Who is correct? How do you know?

B. Communicate Precisely Victor claims that knowing $\sin 0 = \cos \frac{\pi}{2}$ can be used to determine who is correct. Is Victor's suggestion helpful? If so, explain why. If not, explain why not.

HABITS OF MIND

Make Sense and Persevere Do you think there might be a similar relationship between the graphs of tangent and cotangent? Explain.

Notes

Assess

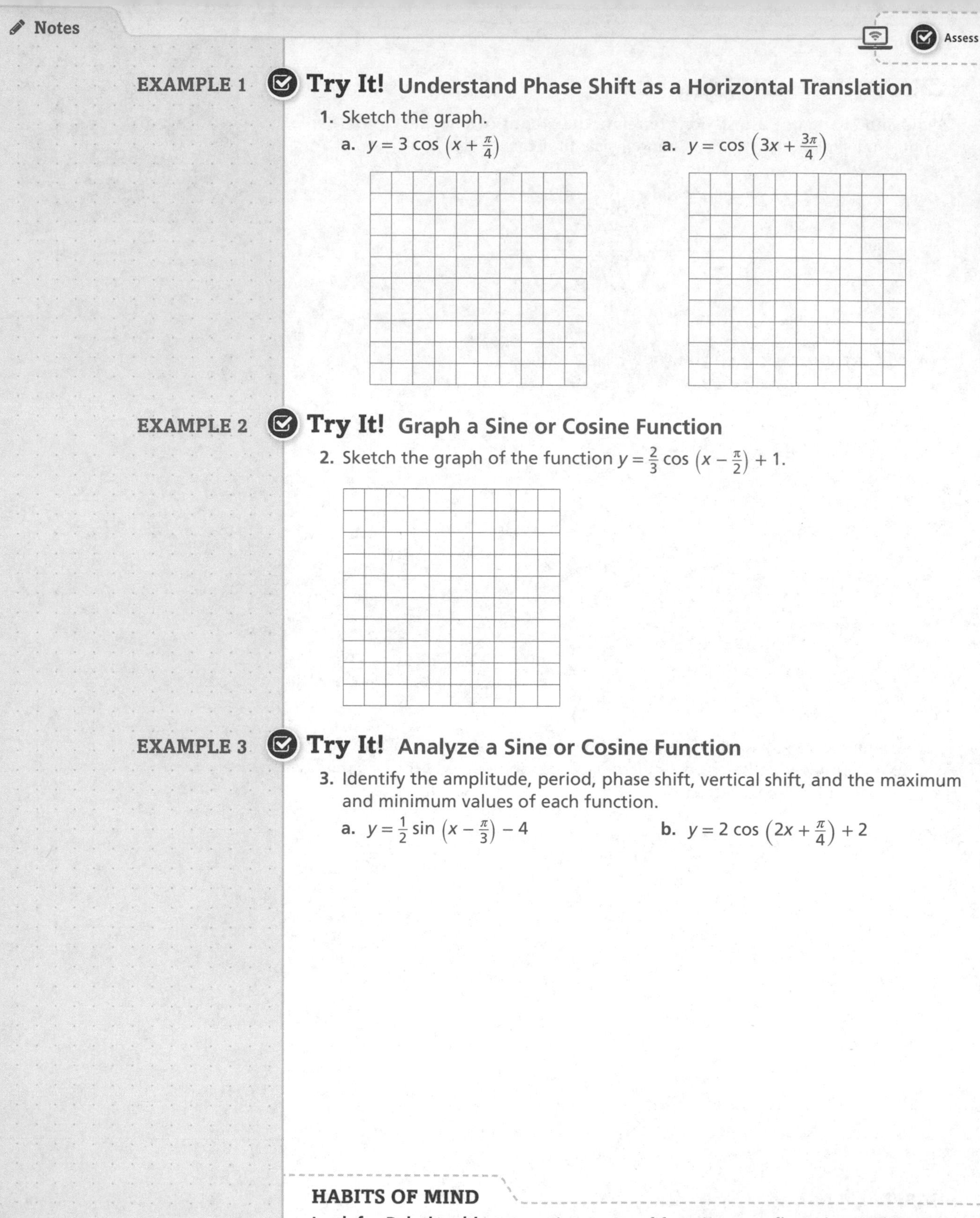

EXAMPLE 1

Try It! Understand Phase Shift as a Horizontal Translation

1. Sketch the graph.

a. $y = 3\cos\left(x + \frac{\pi}{4}\right)$

a. $y = \cos\left(3x + \frac{3\pi}{4}\right)$

EXAMPLE 2

Try It! Graph a Sine or Cosine Function

2. Sketch the graph of the function $y = \frac{2}{3}\cos\left(x - \frac{\pi}{2}\right) + 1$.

EXAMPLE 3

Try It! Analyze a Sine or Cosine Function

3. Identify the amplitude, period, phase shift, vertical shift, and the maximum and minimum values of each function.

a. $y = \frac{1}{2}\sin\left(x - \frac{\pi}{3}\right) - 4$

b. $y = 2\cos\left(2x + \frac{\pi}{4}\right) + 2$

HABITS OF MIND

Look for Relationships For other types of functions $y = f(x - a)$ was always a horizontal translation by a units of the parent function $y = f(x)$. Does that rule hold for trigonometric functions? Explain.

Assess

EXAMPLE 4 Try It! Write the Equation of a Translation

4. Write an equation that models the function represented by the graph.

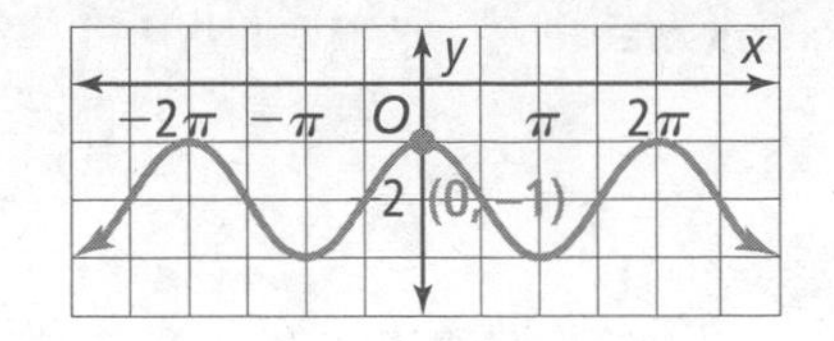

EXAMPLE 5 Try It! Find a Trigonometric Model

5. Write a trigonometric function to model the average high temperatures for Philadelphia, Pennsylvania. How does the midline value compare with the average of the 12 temperatures?

Month	Jan.	Feb.	Mar.	Apr.	May	June	July	Aug.	Sept.	Oct.	Nov.	Dec.
High (°F)	40	44	53	64	74	83	87	85	78	67	56	45

HABITS OF MIND

Model With Mathematics How do you know whether you should use a sine or cosine function to model a periodic graph?

Do You UNDERSTAND?

1. ESSENTIAL QUESTION How can you find and use translations of graphs of trigonometric functions?

2. **Vocabulary** What is a *phase shift*?

3. **Error Analysis** Felipe said the function $y = \frac{1}{2}\cos\left[3\left(x + \frac{\pi}{4}\right)\right] - 3$ has a phase shift $\frac{\pi}{4}$ units to the right and a vertical shift 3 units down. Describe and correct the error Felipe made.

4. **Use Structure** Write a sine function that has an amplitude of $\frac{1}{6}$, a period of $\frac{8\pi}{3}$, a phase shift of 2π units to the right, and a vertical shift of 5 units up.

Do You KNOW HOW?

Identify the amplitude, period, phase shift, and vertical shift of the function.

5. $y = 4\sin\left(x - \frac{\pi}{6}\right) + 2$

6. $y = \frac{1}{3}\cos\left[2\left(x + \frac{\pi}{2}\right)\right] - 1$

7. Write an equation for the function represented by the graph using the cosine function.

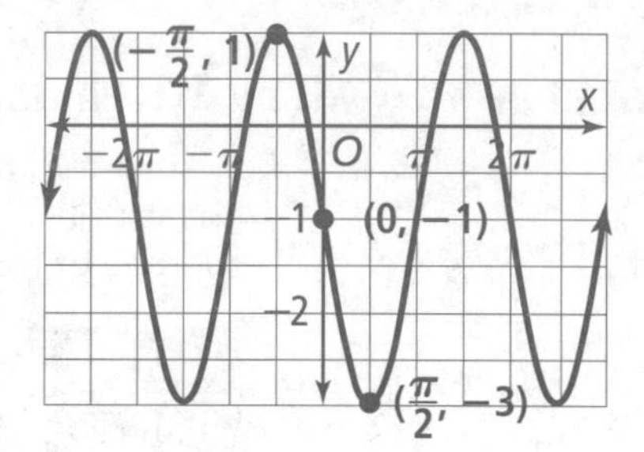

8. Sketch a graph of the function $y = \sin\left[2\left(x + \frac{\pi}{2}\right)\right] + 1$.

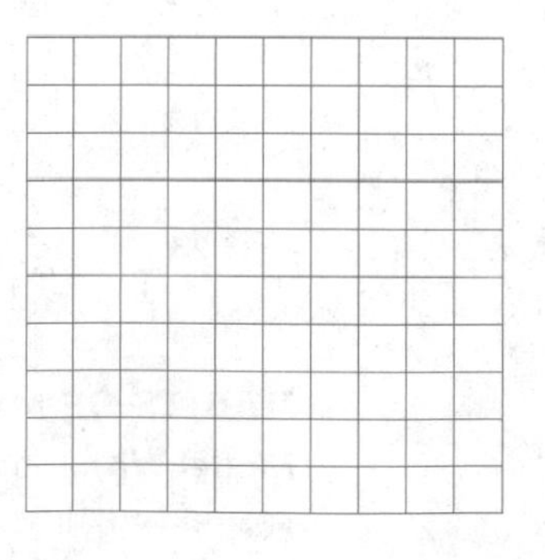

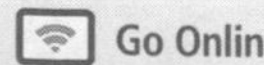

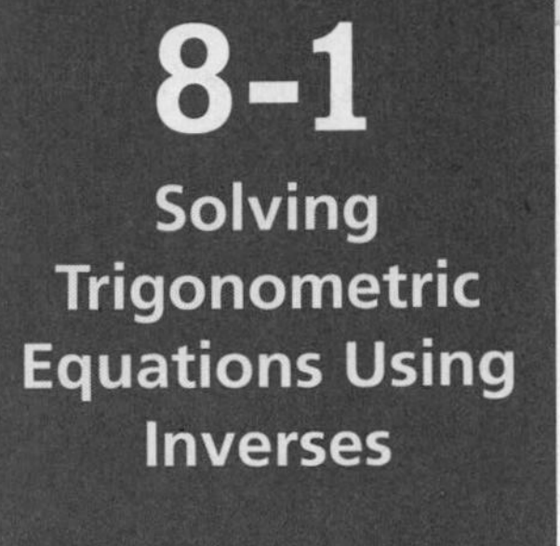

PearsonRealize.com

CRITIQUE & EXPLAIN

Marisol and Nadia are both asked to find θ given $\sin \theta = \frac{\sqrt{3}}{2}$.

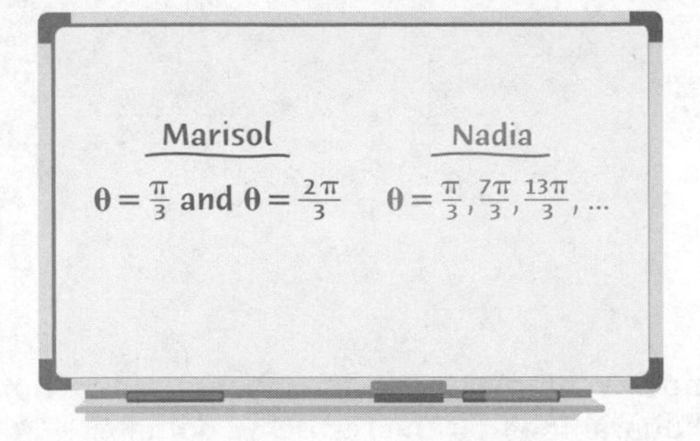

A. Is either student correct? Explain.

B. Make Sense and Persevere What are all of the correct solutions for θ?

HABITS OF MIND

Communicate Precisely Dylan answered the same question by writing $\frac{\pi}{3} + 2k\pi$ and $\frac{2\pi}{3} + 2k\pi$, for integer values of k. Does this show all the possible solutions? Explain.

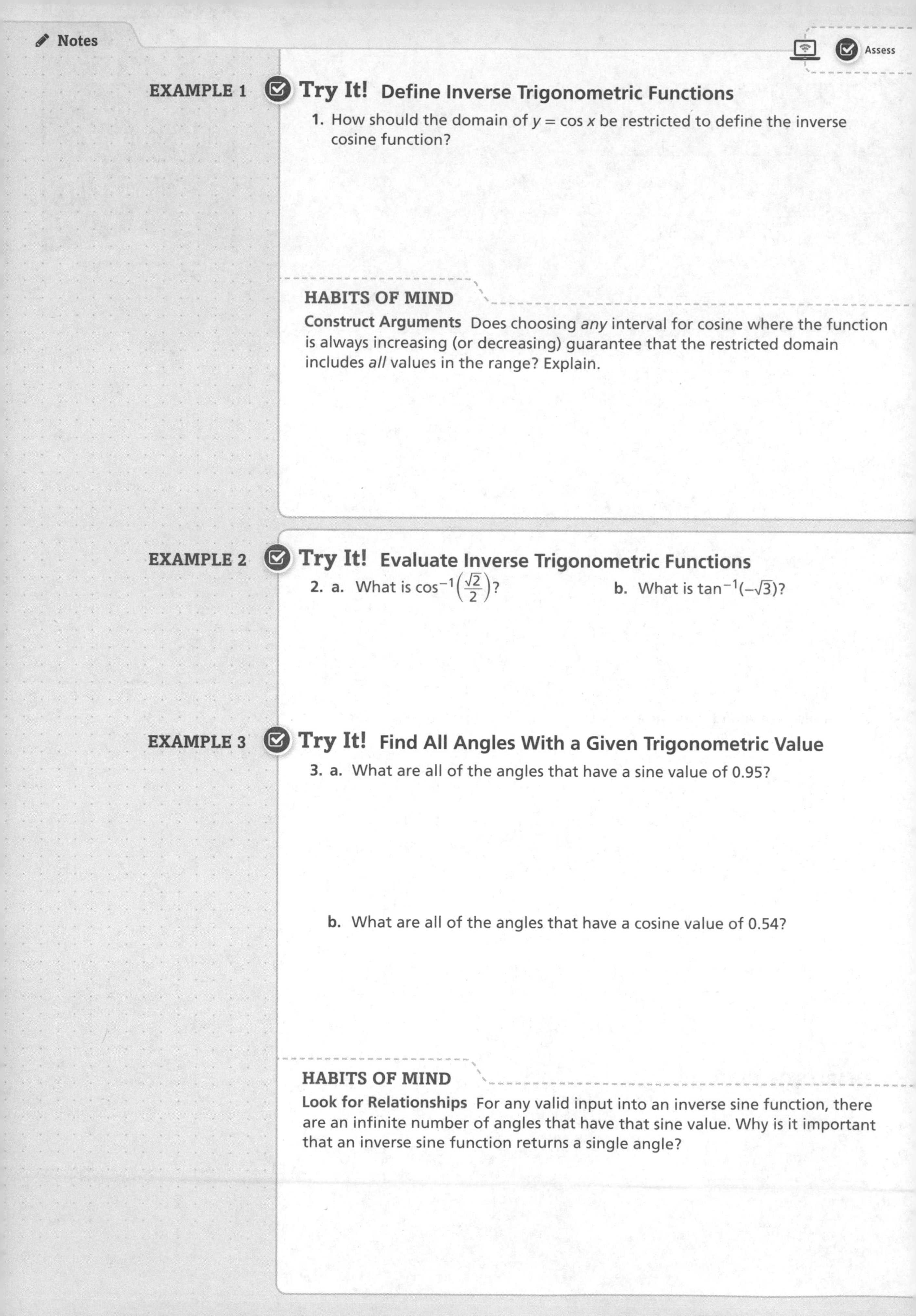

Notes

Assess

EXAMPLE 1

Try It! Define Inverse Trigonometric Functions

1. How should the domain of $y = \cos x$ be restricted to define the inverse cosine function?

HABITS OF MIND

Construct Arguments Does choosing *any* interval for cosine where the function is always increasing (or decreasing) guarantee that the restricted domain includes *all* values in the range? Explain.

EXAMPLE 2

Try It! Evaluate Inverse Trigonometric Functions

2. a. What is $\cos^{-1}\left(\frac{\sqrt{2}}{2}\right)$?

b. What is $\tan^{-1}(-\sqrt{3})$?

EXAMPLE 3

Try It! Find All Angles With a Given Trigonometric Value

3. a. What are all of the angles that have a sine value of 0.95?

b. What are all of the angles that have a cosine value of 0.54?

HABITS OF MIND

Look for Relationships For any valid input into an inverse sine function, there are an infinite number of angles that have that sine value. Why is it important that an inverse sine function returns a single angle?

Notes

Assess

EXAMPLE 4

Try It! Solve a Trigonometric Equation

4. a. What is the value for θ when $0.25\cos\theta + 1 = 1.5\cos\theta$ for values between 0 and 2π?

b. What is the value for θ when $3\tan\theta - 4 = \tan\theta$ for values between 0 and π?

EXAMPLE 5

Try It! Use a Trigonometric Model

5. The average monthly high temperature in a city is modeled by the function $T = 30\sin\left(\frac{\pi}{6}x - 1.8\right) + 61$, where T is the temperature in °F, x is the month, and $x = 1$ corresponds to January. Use this function to determine the months that have a monthly high temperature of 54°.

HABITS OF MIND

Generalize How do the steps for solving the equation $0.25x + 1 = 1.5x$ compare to solving the equation $0.25\cos\theta + 1 = 1.5\cos\theta$?

Do You UNDERSTAND?

1. **ESSENTIAL QUESTION** How can you use an inverse function to find all the solutions of a trigonometric equation?

2. **Error Analysis** Luis said that the inverse of $y = \cos x$ is a function. Explain and correct Luis's error.

3. **Use Structure** What are the radian measures of the angles whose sine is 1?

4. **Error Analysis** Describe and correct the error a student made when asked to find the radian measures of the angles whose sine is 1.

Let n be an integer.
$\sin(0 + 2\pi n) = 1$
✗

Do You KNOW HOW?

5. What is $\sin^{-1}\left(\frac{\sqrt{2}}{2}\right)$?

6. What is $\tan^{-1}(\sqrt{3})$?

7. What are all of the angles (in degrees) that have a cosine value of 0.74?

8. What are all of the angles (in degrees) that have a sine value of 0.83?

9. Solve $4\sin\theta - 1 = 0$ for values between 0 and 2π.

10. Solve $2\tan\theta + 3 = 0$ for values from 0° to 360°. Round angle measures to the nearest degree.

Ramp Up Your Design

Wheelchair users and others with mobility challenges require ramps or elevators to access buildings and other public spaces. Most public buildings are required to have accessible ramps through the Americans with Disabilities Act. However, most homes do not have such ramps. Wheelchair users who move into a home with steps will have to have a new ramp installed.

The construction of accessibility ramps must follow strict guidelines. If ramps are not accurately built to follow these guidelines, they can be dangerous to use. Think about this during the Mathematical Modeling in 3 Acts lesson.

ACT 1 Identify the Problem

1. What is the first question that comes to mind after watching the video?

2. Write down the Main Question you will answer.

3. Make an initial conjecture that answers this Main Question.

4. Explain how you arrived at your conjecture.

5. What information will be useful to know to answer the main question? How can you get it? How will you use that information?

Video

ACT 2 Develop a Model

6. Use the math that you have learned in the topic to refine your conjecture.

ACT 3 Interpret the Results

7. Did your refined conjecture match the actual answer exactly? If not, what might explain the difference?

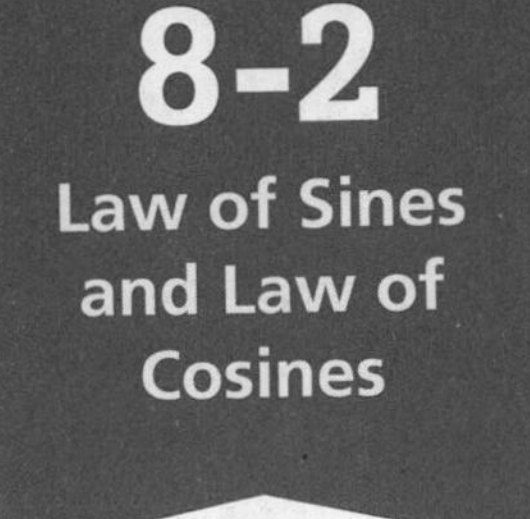

MODEL & DISCUSS

A biologist measures the slant height of a conical termite mound to be about 32 ft. The angle from the ground to the top of the mound is 51°. The base of the mound has a diameter of about 40 ft.

A. Draw a model to help the biologist.

B. **Make Sense and Persevere** What is the height of the mound?

HABITS OF MIND

Reason How did you decide which trigonometric function to use to solve the problem?

Notes

Assess

EXAMPLE 1

Try It! Prove the Law of Sines

1. How can you derive the Law of Sines for angles B and C?

EXAMPLE 2

Try It! Use the Law of Sines

2. In $\triangle NPQ$, $m\angle N = 105°$, $n = 12$, and $p = 10$.
   a. To the nearest degree, what is $m\angle Q$?

   b. What is the length of side q? Round to the nearest tenth of a unit.

EXAMPLE 3

Try It! Understand the Ambiguous Case

3. In $\triangle ABC$, $m\angle A = 30°$, $a = 5$, and $b = 8$. Find $m\angle B$. How many possible triangles are there?

HABITS OF MIND

Use Structure In $\triangle ABC$, $m\angle A = 50°$, $b = 6$, and $c = 3$. Gregory says that the Law of Sines does not allow you to find side length a. Is he correct? If so, what would he need to know in order to be able to find it?

Notes

Assess

EXAMPLE 4 **Try It!** Prove the Law of Cosines

4. a. How can you derive the Law of Cosines for an obtuse angle *C*?

b. How does the equation compare to the equation for an acute angle?

EXAMPLE 5 **Try It!** Use the Law of Cosines

5. a. In $\triangle JKL$, $j = 15$, $k = 13$, and $l = 12$. What is $m\angle J$?

b. In $\triangle ABC$, $a = 11$, $b = 17$, and $m\angle C = 42°$. What is *c*?

EXAMPLE 6 **Try It!** Use the Law of Cosines and the Law of Sines

6. A bike race follows a triangular path, represented by triangle *ABC*. If *A* is the starting point and the measure of the angle at point *B* is 70°, what is the measure of the angle at point *C*?

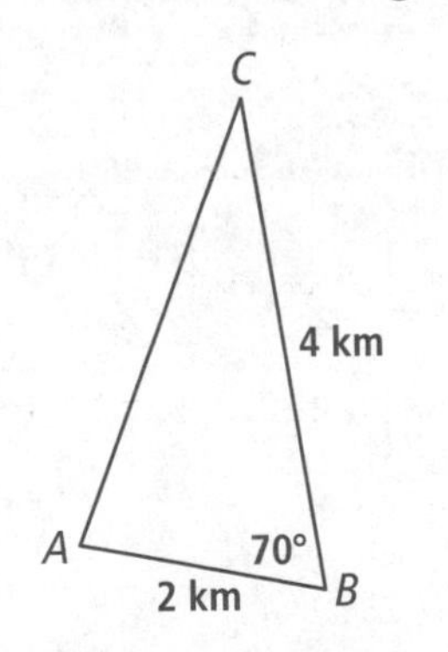

HABITS OF MIND

Use Appropriate Tools Given the lengths of two sides of a triangle, and the measure of one angle, how do you know whether to use the Law of Sines or the Law of Cosines?

Do You UNDERSTAND?

1. ESSENTIAL QUESTION How can you use the sine and cosine functions with non-right triangles?

2. **Error Analysis** Alejandro said the Law of Sines always gives one answer. Explain and correct Alejandro's error.

3. **Construct Arguments** Consider the Law of Cosines as $a^2 = b^2 + c^2 - 2bc(\cos A)$. Explain why the negative square root of a is not a valid solution.

4. **Reason** In what situations do you use the Law of Sines? Law of Cosines?

Do You KNOW HOW?

Use the Law of Sines or the Law of Cosines to find the indicated measure in $\triangle ABC$.

5. $m\angle A = 50°$, $a = 4.5$, $b = 3.8$; find $m\angle B$.

6. $m\angle A = 72°$, $a = 61$, $c = 58$; find $m\angle C$.

7. $m\angle A = 18°$, $m\angle C = 75°$, $c = 101$; find a.

8. $m\angle B = 112°$, $m\angle C = 20°$, $c = 1.6$; find b.

9. $m\angle C = 45°$, $a = 15$, $b = 8$; find c.

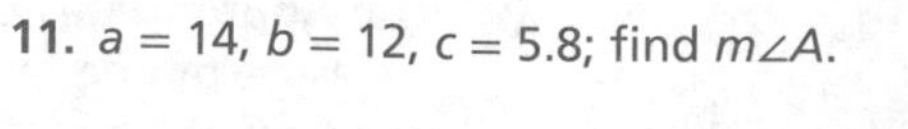

10. $m\angle A = 82°$, $b = 2.5$, $c = 6.8$; find a.

11. $a = 14$, $b = 12$, $c = 5.8$; find $m\angle A$.

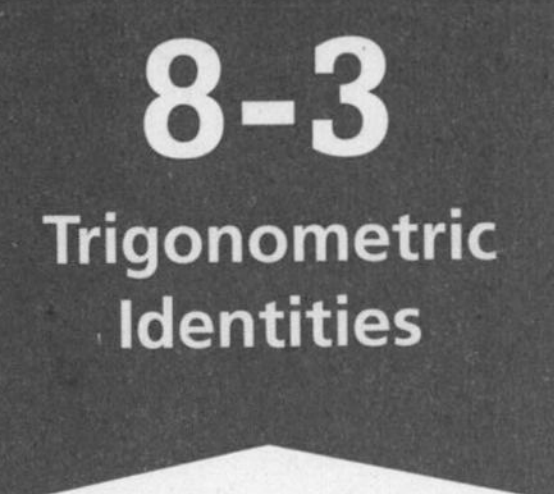

PearsonRealize.com

EXPLORE & REASON

Two right triangles share the same base leg length.

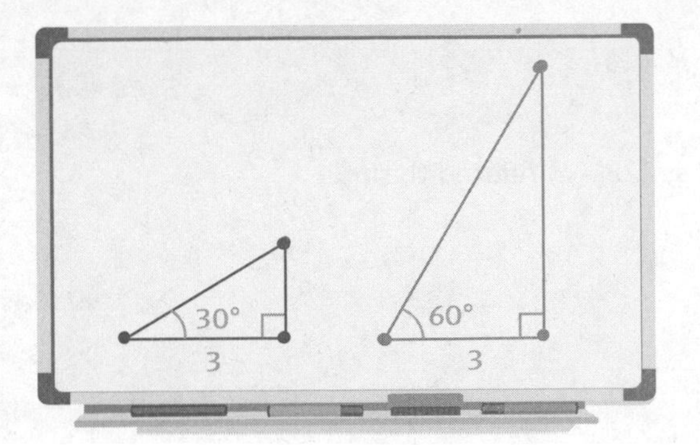

A. Is the ratio between the base angles the same as the ratio between the vertical heights? Explain.

B. How do the values of sin(2(30°)) and 2 sin 30° compare?

C. **Look for Relationships** Graph $y = \sin 2x$ and $y = 2 \sin x$ on the same coordinate plane. How do the two graphs help explain your answer to part (b)?

HABITS OF MIND

Make Sense and Persevere Are there any functions for which $f(2x) = 2f(x)$ for all x? Investigate three different types of functions. Show your work. What do you conclude?

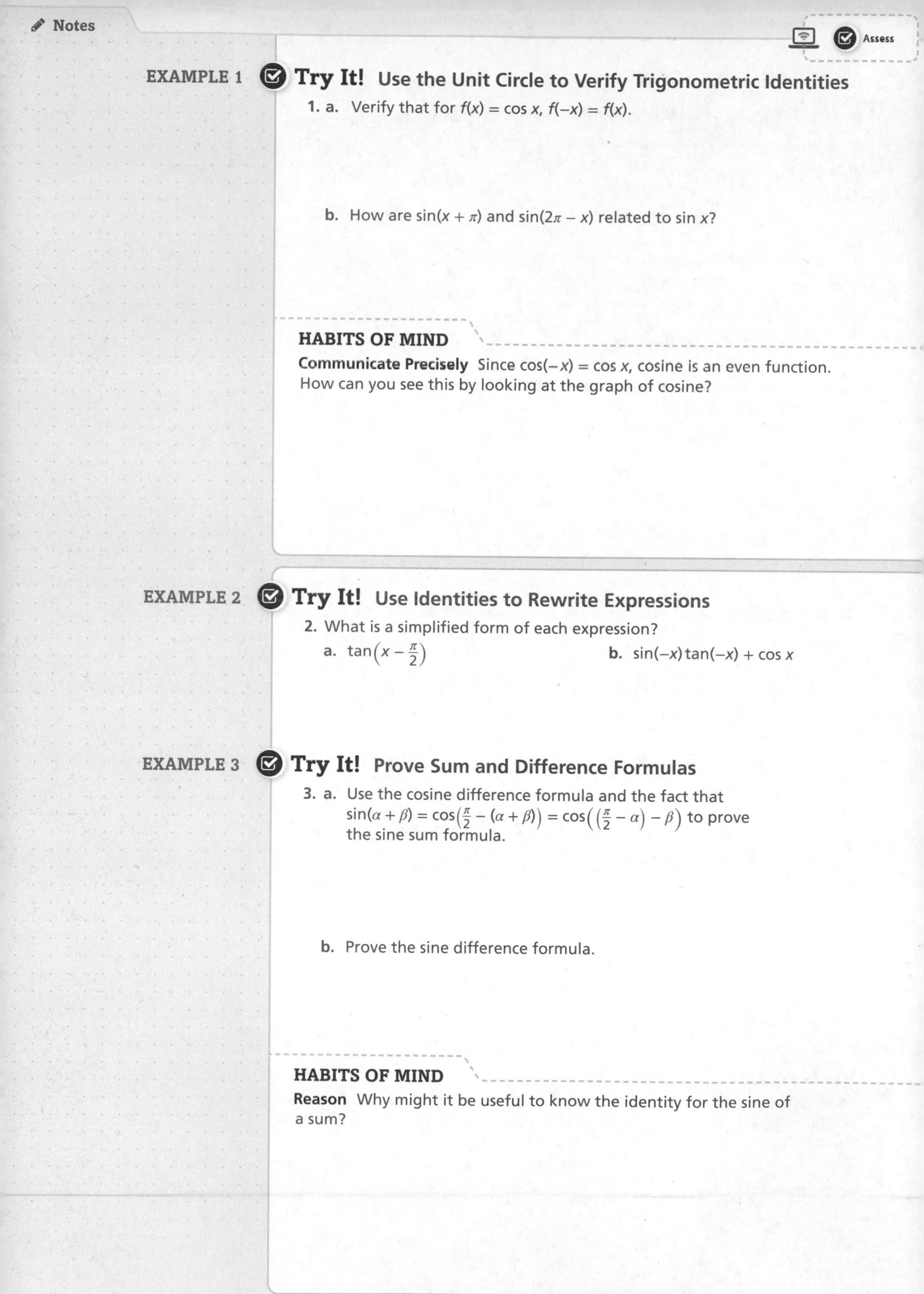

Notes

Assess

EXAMPLE 1

Try It! Use the Unit Circle to Verify Trigonometric Identities

1. a. Verify that for $f(x) = \cos x$, $f(-x) = f(x)$.

   b. How are $\sin(x + \pi)$ and $\sin(2\pi - x)$ related to $\sin x$?

HABITS OF MIND

Communicate Precisely Since $\cos(-x) = \cos x$, cosine is an even function. How can you see this by looking at the graph of cosine?

EXAMPLE 2

Try It! Use Identities to Rewrite Expressions

2. What is a simplified form of each expression?

   a. $\tan\left(x - \frac{\pi}{2}\right)$

   b. $\sin(-x)\tan(-x) + \cos x$

EXAMPLE 3

Try It! Prove Sum and Difference Formulas

3. a. Use the cosine difference formula and the fact that $\sin(\alpha + \beta) = \cos\left(\frac{\pi}{2} - (\alpha + \beta)\right) = \cos\left(\left(\frac{\pi}{2} - \alpha\right) - \beta\right)$ to prove the sine sum formula.

   b. Prove the sine difference formula.

HABITS OF MIND

Reason Why might it be useful to know the identity for the sine of a sum?

Notes

Assess

EXAMPLE 4

Try It! Use a Sum or Difference Formula to Find a Value

4. What is the exact value of each expression?

a. $\tan 15°$

b. $\sin\left(-\frac{\pi}{12}\right)$

EXAMPLE 5

Try It! Model With Sum and Difference Formulas

5. The sound wave for a musical note of A is modeled by $y = \sin(880\pi x)$. The sound wave for a different A note is modeled by $y = \sin\left[880\pi\left(x + \frac{1}{440}\right)\right]$. What is the simplified form of an equation that models the sound wave if the two notes are played at the same time?

HABITS OF MIND

Construct Arguments How do you prove the sum formula for $\tan(\alpha + \beta)$?

Do You UNDERSTAND?

1. ESSENTIAL QUESTION How can you verify and apply relationships between trigonometric functions?

2. **Error Analysis** Sarah said that because of the odd-even identities, both the sine and cosine functions are odd functions. Explain and correct Sarah's error.

3. **Vocabulary** Explain what it means to say that $\cos(-x) = \cos x$ is a trigonometric identity.

4. **Reason** Why do the cofunction identities apply to an angle θ of any size?

5. **Make Sense and Persevere** How can the quotient identity help you to identify angles for which the tangent is undefined?

Do You KNOW HOW?

Verify each identity.

6. $\sin\theta \sec\theta \cot\theta = 1$

7. $\sec\theta \cot\theta = \csc\theta$

Find a simplified form of each expression.

8. $\frac{\tan\theta}{\sin\theta}$

9. $\frac{\sec\theta}{\sin\theta}(1 - \cos^2\theta)$

Use a sum or difference formula to find the exact value of each of the following.

10. $\sin 15°$

11. $\cos 105°$

8-4 The Complex Plane

PearsonRealize.com

CRITIQUE & EXPLAIN

A group of students is asked to simplify the following complex number expressions:

$$6 + 4i - (-3 + 7i)$$
$$(3 + 5i)(3 - 5i)$$

A. How would you simplify $6 + 4i - (-3 + 7i)$? Explain.

B. One student simplified the second expression this way:

$$(3 + 5i)(3 - 5i) = 3^2 - 3(5i) + 3(5i) - 5^2(i)^2$$
$$= 9 - 25i^2$$

Is the student's answer correct? Explain why or why not.

C. Use Structure What is $(a + bi)(a - bi)$?

HABITS OF MIND

Communicate Precisely When Ines calculates with complex numbers, she treats i as a variable until the last step, when she simplifies powers of i. Will her method always work? Explain.

Notes

Assess

EXAMPLE 1

Try It! Represent Numbers in the Complex Plane

1. a. What point in the complex plane represents $-3 + 4i$?

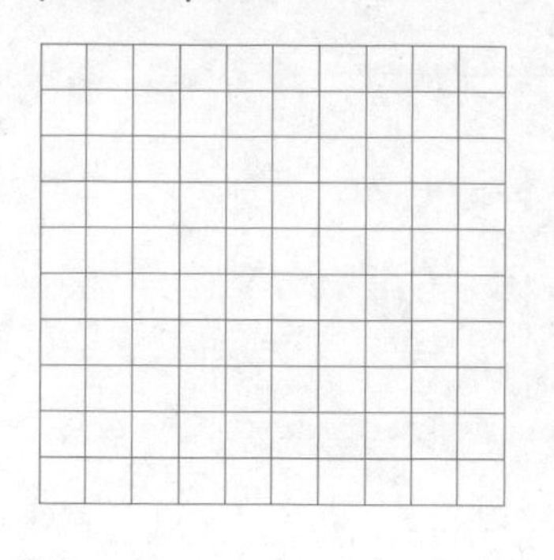

b. Graph $4 + i$ and its complex conjugate.

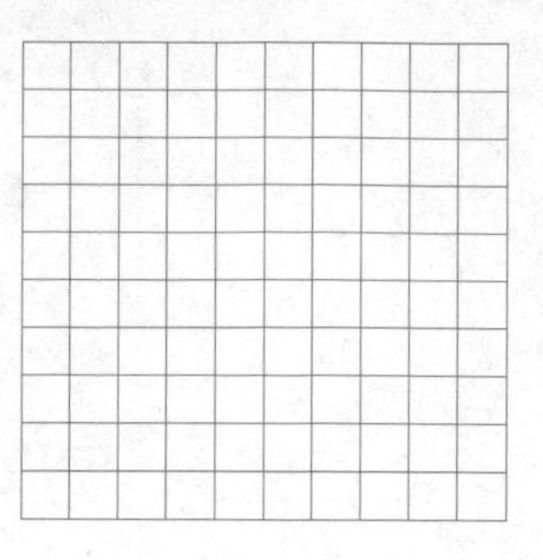

EXAMPLE 2

Try It! Find Midpoint of a Segment in the Complex Plane

2. a. Find the midpoint of the segment that joins the complex numbers $15 - 4i$ and $-11 - 7i$.

b. Find the average of the complex numbers $(-4 + 6i)$ and $(1 - 4i)$. What is the midpoint of the line segment they form when graphed in the complex plane?

HABITS OF MIND

Look for Relationships If the midpoint of a segment joining two complex numbers is the origin, how are the two complex numbers related?

EXAMPLE 3

Try It! Find the Modulus of a Complex Number

3. Find the modulus of each complex number.

a. $-5 - 12i$

b. $\frac{1}{2} - \frac{1}{4}i$

Assess

EXAMPLE 4

Try It! Add and Subtract Complex Numbers Geometrically

4. Use a parallelogram to determine each sum or difference.

a. $(-2 + i) + (-5 - 3i)$

b. $(-8 + 3i) - (-2 - 3i)$

EXAMPLE 5

Try It! Find the Distance Between Two Complex Numbers

5. Find the distance between the complex numbers.

a. $r = 4 - 3i$, $s = 10 + 2i$

b. $r = -3 - i$, $s = -5 - 4i$

HABITS OF MIND

Make Sense and Persevere Two complex numbers determine a parallelogram. How can you use the parallelogram to interpret the modulus of each vector, their sum, and the distance between them?

Do You UNDERSTAND?

1. ESSENTIAL QUESTION How can you represent complex numbers and their relationships on a graph?

2. **Error Analysis** Casey found the complex conjugate of $7 + 3i$ to be $-7 - 3i$. Explain and correct Casey's error.

3. **Vocabulary** Explain how the complex plane is similar to and different from the Cartesian plane.

4. **Use Structure** How does a parallelogram demonstrate that the distance between two points is the same as the modulus of their difference?

Do You KNOW HOW?

Write the ordered pair that corresponds to the complex number.

5. $14 - 7i$

6. $-6 + 2i$

Find the modulus of the complex number.

7. $3 + i$

8. $-5 - 4i$

Find the average of the complex numbers.

9. $8 + i$ and $5 - 6i$

10. $-2 + 3i$ and $-7 - 4i$

11. What point, S, completes the parallelogram $PTSR$ that has points P at (0, 0), R at (−4, −5), and T at (8, −1)?

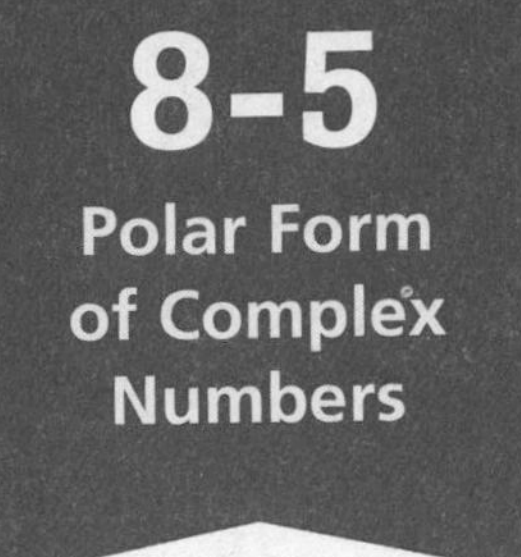

EXPLORE & REASON

Paxton's Pizza delivers via bicycle. Orders are delivered only within a few blocks from the pizzeria. One afternoon, Paxton's receives orders from the places marked on the map. Paxton's is located at point *P*.

A. Paxton's limits its delivery persons to riding five blocks total to get to the delivery spot. Will the riders be able to ride to each location on the map? Explain.

B. Suppose instead that Paxton's limits its riders to delivering only within a five-block *radius* of the pizzeria. Will the riders be able to deliver to each location on the map? Explain.

C. Communicate Precisely Each block on the map is 400 ft long. How can you describe the locations of points 1, 2, and 3, in terms of how far they are from *P* in a straight line?

HABITS OF MIND

Model With Mathematics Rebecca calls into Paxton's to place an order. She says that she is located $800\sqrt{5}$ ft away at an angle of $-\frac{\pi}{3}$ radians south of east. Is Rebecca within the delivery area? If so, what is one possible route to her house?

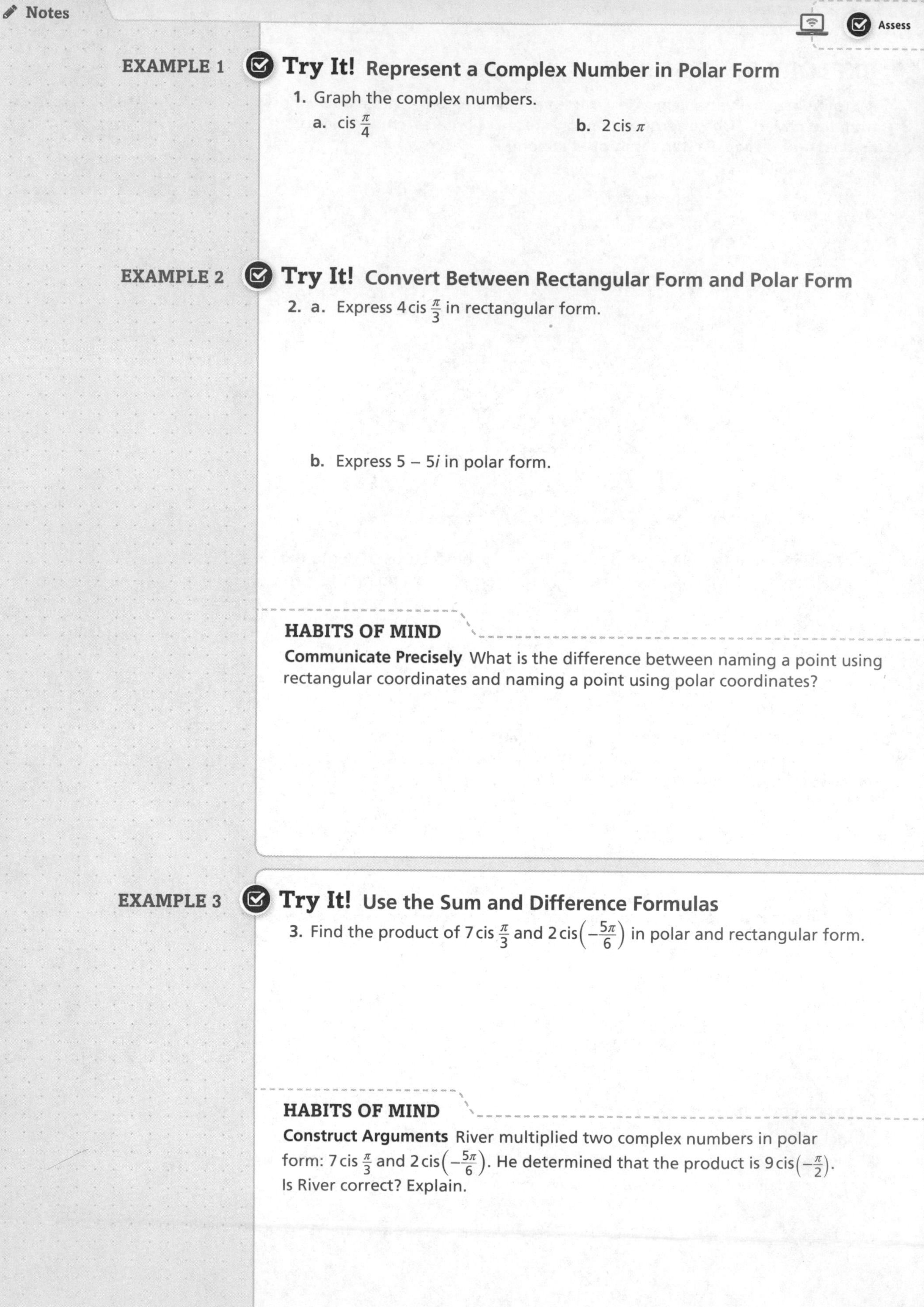

Notes

Assess

EXAMPLE 1

Try It! Represent a Complex Number in Polar Form

1. Graph the complex numbers.

   a. $\text{cis}\,\frac{\pi}{4}$

   b. $2\,\text{cis}\,\pi$

EXAMPLE 2

Try It! Convert Between Rectangular Form and Polar Form

2. a. Express $4\,\text{cis}\,\frac{\pi}{3}$ in rectangular form.

   b. Express $5 - 5i$ in polar form.

HABITS OF MIND

Communicate Precisely What is the difference between naming a point using rectangular coordinates and naming a point using polar coordinates?

EXAMPLE 3

Try It! Use the Sum and Difference Formulas

3. Find the product of $7\,\text{cis}\,\frac{\pi}{3}$ and $2\,\text{cis}\left(-\frac{5\pi}{6}\right)$ in polar and rectangular form.

HABITS OF MIND

Construct Arguments River multiplied two complex numbers in polar form: $7\,\text{cis}\,\frac{\pi}{3}$ and $2\,\text{cis}\left(-\frac{5\pi}{6}\right)$. He determined that the product is $9\,\text{cis}\left(-\frac{\pi}{2}\right)$. Is River correct? Explain.

EXAMPLE 4

Try It! Use Polar Form to Multiply Complex Numbers

4. Use the complex numbers $z_1 = i\sqrt{2}$ and $z_2 = -1 + i$.

   a. Express each number in polar form.

   b. Find the product z_1z_2 in both polar form and rectangular form.

EXAMPLE 5

Try It! Use Polar Form to Raise a Number to a Power

5. Use the polar form to find $(\sqrt{3} - i)^8$.

   a. Write the power in polar form.

   b. Write the power in rectangular form.

HABITS OF MIND

Use Appropriate Tools Shannon used the Binomial Theorem to expand $(\sqrt{3} - i)^8$. Is this the most efficient method for raising a complex number to a power? Explain.

Do You UNDERSTAND?

1. ESSENTIAL QUESTION How can you use trigonometry to represent and multiply complex numbers?

2. **Error Analysis** Lucas said that $\left(2\operatorname{cis}\frac{7\pi}{4}\right)\left(3\operatorname{cis}\frac{3\pi}{4}\right) = 6\operatorname{cis}\pi$. Explain an error Lucas may have made.

3. **Vocabulary** Explain how to find the argument of a complex number.

4. **Communicate Precisely** What information about the graph of a number in the complex plane does the argument of a complex number give you?

Do You KNOW HOW?

Express each complex number in polar form.

5. $2\sqrt{3} + 2i$

6. $-10 + 10i$

Express each complex number in rectangular form.

7. $5\operatorname{cis}\pi$

8. $6\operatorname{cis}\frac{2\pi}{3}$

Find the product of each set of complex numbers in polar form.

9. $2\operatorname{cis}\frac{\pi}{4}$ and $6\operatorname{cis}\frac{3\pi}{4}$

10. $7\operatorname{cis}\frac{\pi}{2}$ and $3\operatorname{cis}\frac{\pi}{4}$

11. $2\operatorname{cis}-\frac{\pi}{3}$ and $3\operatorname{cis}\frac{5\pi}{6}$

12. $3\operatorname{cis}\frac{4\pi}{3}$ and $7\operatorname{cis}\frac{\pi}{3}$

Use the polar form to find each power. Write the power in rectangular form.

13. $(\sqrt{2} + i\sqrt{2})^4$

14. $(\sqrt{3} - i)^3$

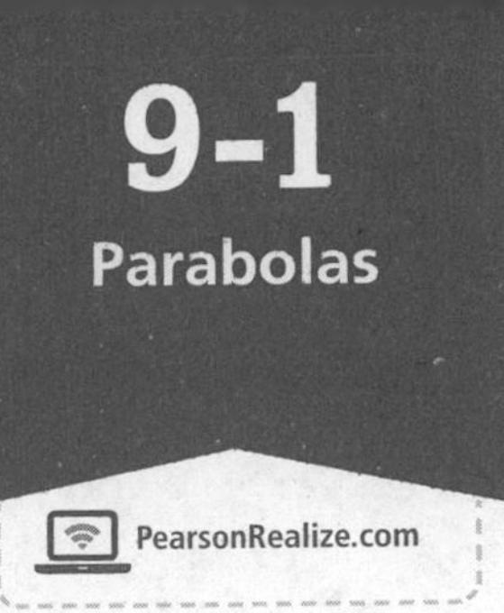

EXPLORE & REASON

Consider the square pyramid and the cylinder shown.

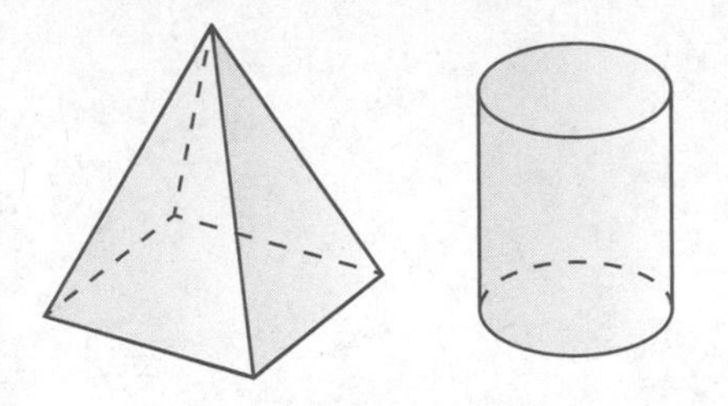

A. What shapes can be created by intersecting a vertical plane with each figure? What shapes can be created by intersecting a horizontal plane with each figure?

B. Make Sense and Persevere What shapes can be created by intersecting a diagonal plane with each figure?

HABITS OF MIND

Look for Relationships What are other three-dimensional figures that have a cross section that is the same as either the cylinder or the pyramid? Give two examples.

Assess

EXAMPLE 1 **Try It!** **Derive an Equation of a Parabola**

1. What is an equation for the parabola with the given focus and directrix?
   a. focus (0, −3) and directrix $y = 3$

   b. focus (−2, 0) and directrix $x = 2$

EXAMPLE 2 **Try It!** **Relate the Focal Length of a Parabola to Its Equation**

2. A parabola has a focus of (4, 0) and a directrix at $x = -4$.
   a. What is the vertex of the parabola?
   b. Is the equation in the form $y = ax^2$ or $x = ay^2$?
   c. What is the focal length?
   d. What is the equation of the parabola?

EXAMPLE 3 **Try It!** **Write an Equation of a Parabola**

3. a. What is the equation of a parabola with focus (0, 6) and directrix $y = -6$?
   b. What is the equation of a parabola with focus $\left(\frac{1}{5}, 0\right)$ and vertex (0, 0)?

HABITS OF MIND

Communicate Precisely What is the formal geometric definition of a parabola?

Assess

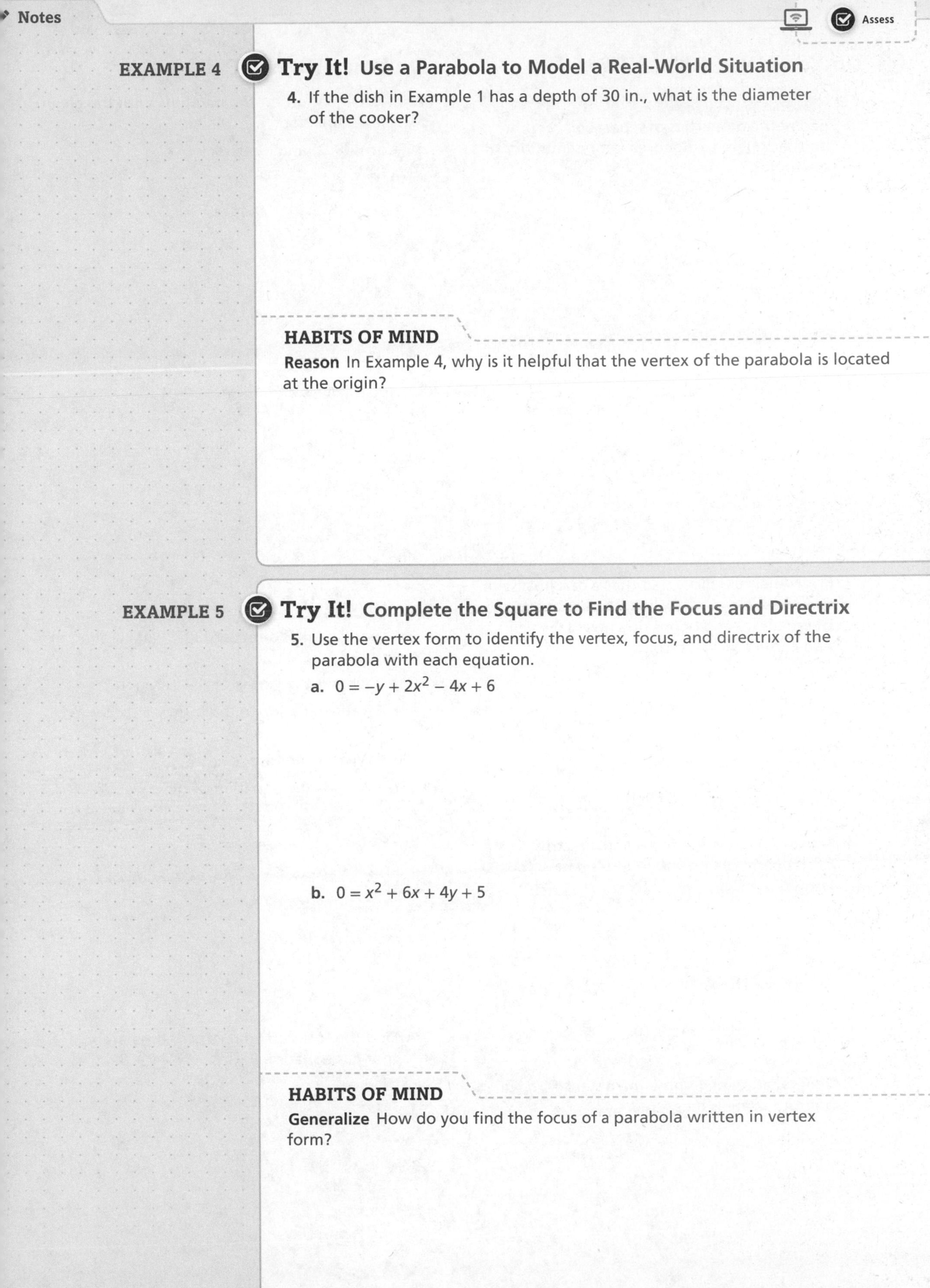

EXAMPLE 4

Try It! Use a Parabola to Model a Real-World Situation

4. If the dish in Example 1 has a depth of 30 in., what is the diameter of the cooker?

HABITS OF MIND

Reason In Example 4, why is it helpful that the vertex of the parabola is located at the origin?

EXAMPLE 5

Try It! Complete the Square to Find the Focus and Directrix

5. Use the vertex form to identify the vertex, focus, and directrix of the parabola with each equation.

   a. $0 = -y + 2x^2 - 4x + 6$

   b. $0 = x^2 + 6x + 4y + 5$

HABITS OF MIND

Generalize How do you find the focus of a parabola written in vertex form?

Do You UNDERSTAND?

1. ESSENTIAL QUESTION What are the geometric properties of a parabola, and how do they relate to algebraic representations of a parabola?

2. **Vocabulary** Explain what is meant by a *conic section.*

3. **Error Analysis** Nicky said that a parabola with the equation $y^2 = -9x$ has the y-axis as its line of symmetry and opens downward. Explain and correct Nicky's error.

4. **Reason** What is the focus and directrix of the parabola $y = -4x^2$? Explain how you know.

5. **Generalize** Explain how the distance from a point to a line is measured.

Do You KNOW HOW?

Write an equation for the parabola with the given focus and directrix.

6. focus (0, 2) and directrix $y = -2$

7. focus (−1, 0) and directrix $x = 1$

8. A parabola has a focus of (0, 3) and a directrix at $y = -3$.
   a. What is the vertex of the parabola?
   b. Is the equation in the form $y = ax^2$ or $x = ay^2$?
   c. What is the focal length?
   d. What is the equation of the parabola?

9. Find the focus and directrix of the parabola that has equation $0 = x^2 - 6x - y + 8$.

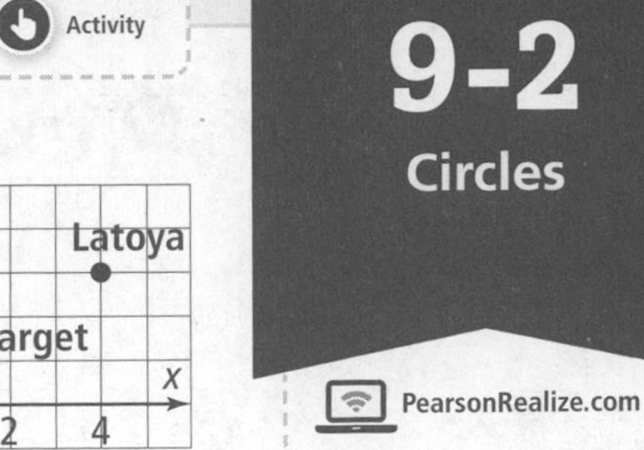

CRITIQUE & EXPLAIN

Latoya and Jason are lawn bowling. Each player tries to toss his or her ball closer to the target ball than his or her opponent's ball.

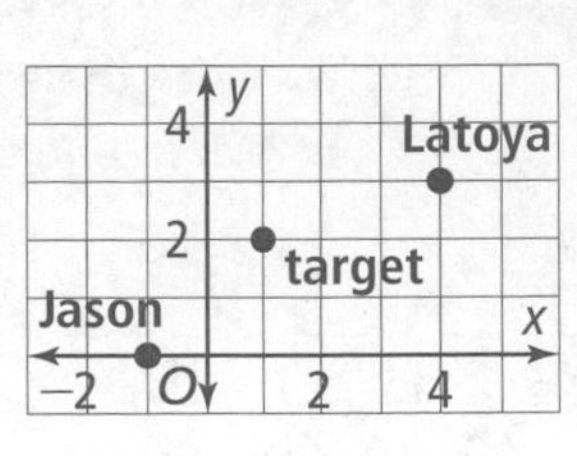

The graph shows the locations of their first attempts.

Latoya calculates the distance her ball is from the target ball:

$d^2 = (4 - 1)^2 + (3 - 2)^2 = 10$**, so** $d \approx 3.2$ **ft.**

Jason calculates the distance his ball is from the target ball:

$\sqrt{(1 - (-1))^2} + \sqrt{(2 - 0)^2} = 2 + 2 = 4.$

A. Did both players calculate the distances correctly? If not, who is in error and what is the correct distance?

B. Make Sense and Persevere Latoya's next ball stops at a position described by (−2, 1). Is she now ahead? Explain.

HABITS OF MIND

Use Structure How might the grid help you to determine distances?

Notes

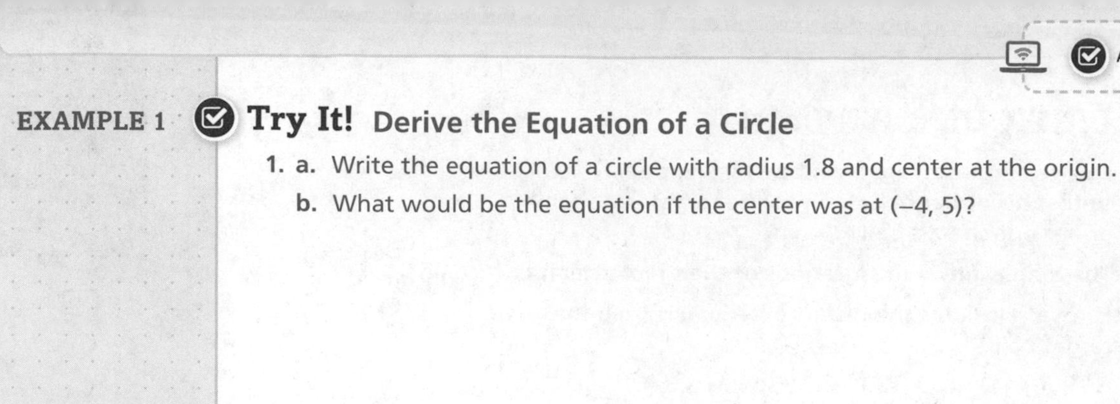

EXAMPLE 1

Try It! Derive the Equation of a Circle

1. a. Write the equation of a circle with radius 1.8 and center at the origin.
   b. What would be the equation if the center was at (−4, 5)?

EXAMPLE 2

Try It! Write and Graph an Equation of a Circle

2. Find an equation of each circle described. Sketch the graph.
   a. center (0, 0) and radius 4
   b. center (8, −3) and radius 1

HABITS OF MIND

Construct Arguments Sadie wrote the equation of a circle with center (3, −5) and radius 4 as $(x + 3)^2 + (y - 5)^2 = 16$. Is Sadie correct? Explain.

EXAMPLE 3

Try It! Use a Circle to Model a Real-World Situation

3. A second information kiosk is planned for the location represented by the point (3, 9). Should the kiosk be moved so as to not interfere with the fence?

Notes

Assess

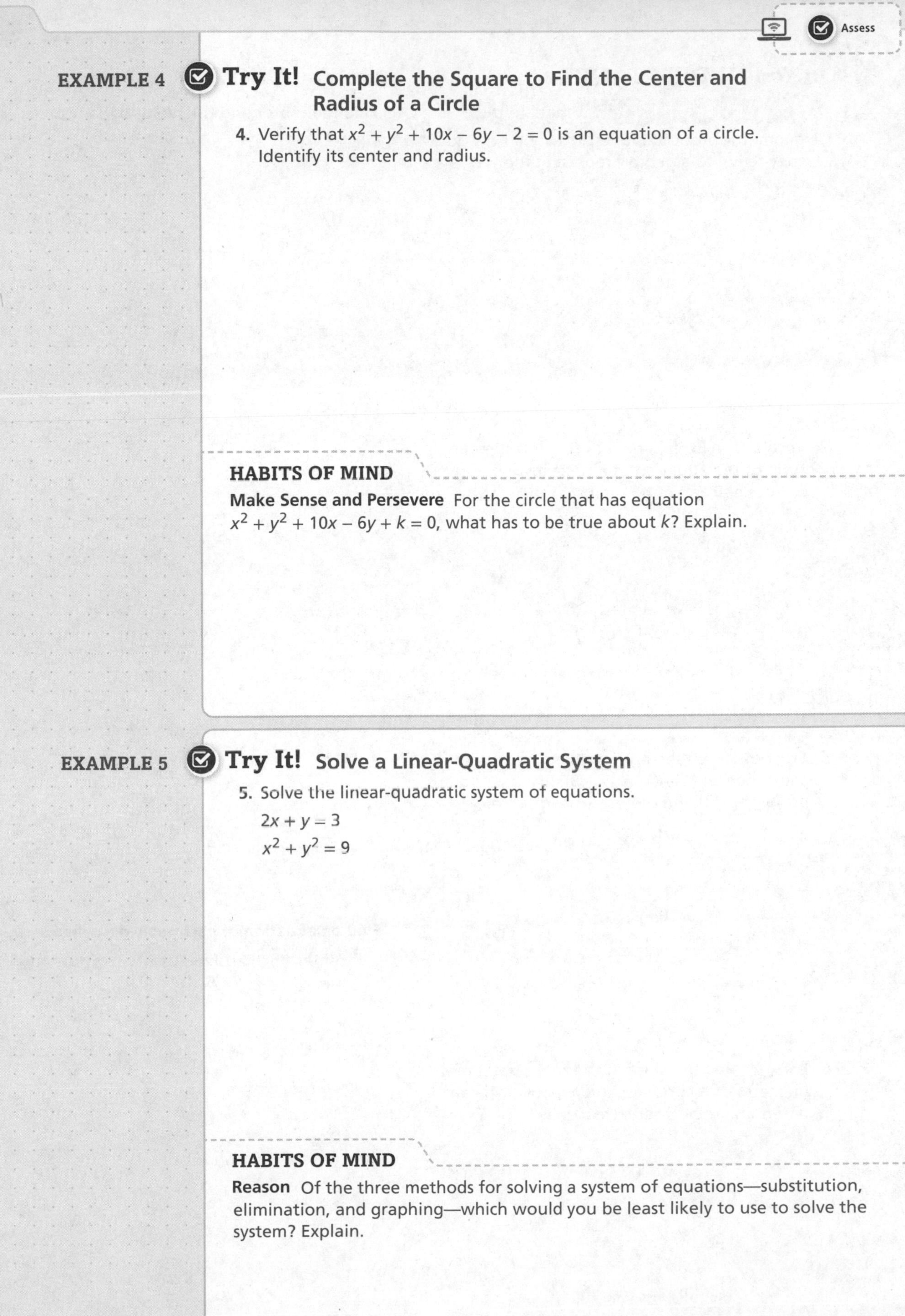

EXAMPLE 4

Try It! Complete the Square to Find the Center and Radius of a Circle

4. Verify that $x^2 + y^2 + 10x - 6y - 2 = 0$ is an equation of a circle. Identify its center and radius.

HABITS OF MIND

Make Sense and Persevere For the circle that has equation $x^2 + y^2 + 10x - 6y + k = 0$, what has to be true about k? Explain.

EXAMPLE 5

Try It! Solve a Linear-Quadratic System

5. Solve the linear-quadratic system of equations.

$2x + y = 3$
$x^2 + y^2 = 9$

HABITS OF MIND

Reason Of the three methods for solving a system of equations—substitution, elimination, and graphing—which would you be least likely to use to solve the system? Explain.

Do You UNDERSTAND?

1. ESSENTIAL QUESTION What are the geometric properties of a circle, and how do they relate to algebraic representations of a circle?

2. **Vocabulary** Explain how to find the standard form of the equation of a circle if you know the circle's center and radius.

3. **Error Analysis** Chiang said that a circle with the equation $(x + 2)^2 + (y - 5)^2 = 6$ has a radius of 36. Explain and correct Chiang's error.

4. **Look for Relationships** If the coordinates of a diameter of a circle are known, how can you determine the center of the circle?

Do You KNOW HOW?

Find the center and the radius of each circle.

5. $x^2 + y^2 = 25$

6. $(x + 3)^2 + (y + 7)^2 = 49$

7. $(x - 1)^2 + (y + 6)^2 = 5$

8. $(x - 9)^2 + (y - 4)^2 = 11$

Find an equation of each circle described.

9. center (0, 0) and radius 8

10. center (−3, 9) and radius 4

MATHEMATICAL MODELING IN 3 ACTS

PearsonRealize.com

Watering the Lawn

Like all plants, grass must receive water regularly to survive. When local rainfall is not enough to keep the grass healthy, it needs to be watered. To make the watering process easier, some property owners have sprinkler systems designed and installed to automate the watering process.

What should be considered while designing a sprinkler system? Think about this during the Mathematical Modeling in 3 Acts lesson.

Identify the Problem

1. What is the first question that comes to mind after watching the video?

2. Write down the Main Question you will answer.

3. Make an initial conjecture that answers this Main Question.

4. Explain how you arrived at your conjecture.

5. What information will be useful to know to answer the main question? How can you get it? How will you use that information?

Video

ACT 2 Develop a Model

6. Use the math that you have learned in the topic to refine your conjecture.

ACT 3 Interpret the Results

7. Did your refined conjecture match the actual answer exactly? If not, what might explain the difference?

9-3
Ellipses

PearsonRealize.com

MODEL & DISCUSS

A dog's harness can be attached to a 40 ft tether. The tether runs freely through the harness. The dog has an area to run that is related to the length of the tether. The ends of the tether can be anchored at the same point or different points.

A. Sketch a graph of the area a dog can run if the two ends of the tether are attached at the same point. What is the relationship between the length of the tether and the shape you graphed?

B. Sketch a graph of the area a dog can run if the two ends are attached at different points. How is the shape similar to and different from the first shape you graphed?

C. **Reason** What is the relationship between the length of the tether and the distances of the dogs to their anchors?

HABITS OF MIND

Look for Relationships How would the shape be different if the two anchor points were moved closer together? Farther apart?

Notes

Assess

EXAMPLE 1

Try It! Derive the Equation of an Ellipse

1. What is the equation of the ellipse in standard form which has foci at (−2, 0) and (2, 0) and for which the sum of the distances from the foci to any point on the ellipse is 8?

EXAMPLE 2

Try It! Graph an Ellipse

2. Graph the ellipse represented by each equation. Then find the coordinates of the foci.

   a. $\frac{x^2}{64} + \frac{y^2}{100} = 1$

   b. $\frac{x^2}{16} + \frac{y^2}{8} = 1$

HABITS OF MIND

Generalize From the equation of an ellipse, how can you tell which axis is the major axis?

EXAMPLE 3

Try It! Write the Equation of an Ellipse

3. a. What is the equation of an ellipse with foci at (0, −12) and (0, 12) and that passes through the points (−5, 0) and (5, 0)?

   b. What is the equation of an ellipse centered at the origin if the sum of the distances to the foci from any point is 30 units and the vertical minor axis is 24 units long?

Assess

EXAMPLE 4

Try It! Use an Ellipse to Model a Real-World Situation

4. Consider a whispering gallery like the one above, but 30 m east to west and 34 m north to south. Find the equation of the ellipse representing the shape of the room. How far are the whispering points from the center of the room?

HABITS OF MIND

Make Sense and Persevere The foci of an ellipse are located at (4, 0) and (–4, 0). Is this enough information to write the equation of the ellipse? If not, what else would you need to know?

EXAMPLE 5

Try It! Graph a Translated Ellipse

5. a. Graph the ellipse represented by $10x^2 + 40x + 2y^2 + 30 = 0$. Label the coordinates of the center, vertices, co-vertices, and foci.

b. Graph the ellipse represented by $x^2 + 3y^2 - 8x + 6y + 10 = 0$. Label the coordinates of the center, vertices, co-vertices, and foci.

HABITS OF MIND

Generalize After graphing the ellipses in the Try It!, make a conjecture about how the coefficients of the x^2- and y^2-terms can be used to predict whether the major axis is horizontal or vertical.

Do You UNDERSTAND?

1. ESSENTIAL QUESTION How does the equation of an ellipse relate to the features of its graph?

2. **Vocabulary** What are the co-vertices of an ellipse?

3. **Error Analysis** Darren said that an ellipse with the equation $\frac{(x-4)^2}{25} + \frac{(y+1)^2}{9} = 1$ has vertices at (4, 2) and (4, −4). Explain and correct Darren's error.

4. **Generalize** For any ellipse, which measure is greatest, *a*, *b*, or *c*? Explain.

Do You KNOW HOW?

Find the vertices and co-vertices of each ellipse.

5. $\frac{x^2}{49} + \frac{y^2}{64} = 1$

6. $\frac{(x-1)^2}{16} + \frac{(y+5)^2}{4} = 1$

Find the foci of each ellipse.

7. $\frac{x^2}{2} + \frac{y^2}{8} = 1$

8. $\frac{(x+5)^2}{16} + \frac{(y-9)^2}{4} = 1$

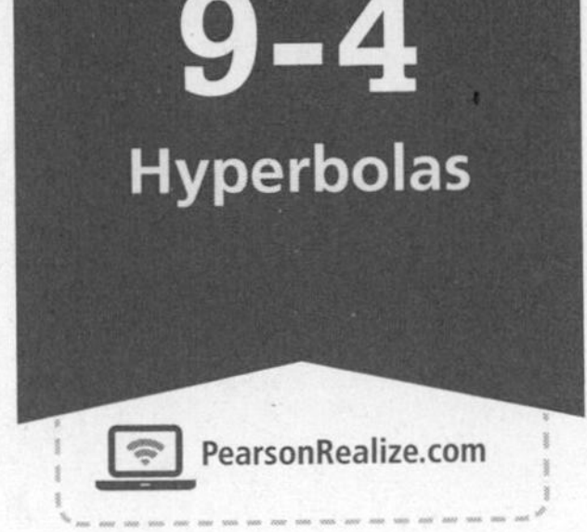

EXPLORE & REASON

An ellipse is the set of all points where the sum of the distance of any point to two set points called foci is a constant.

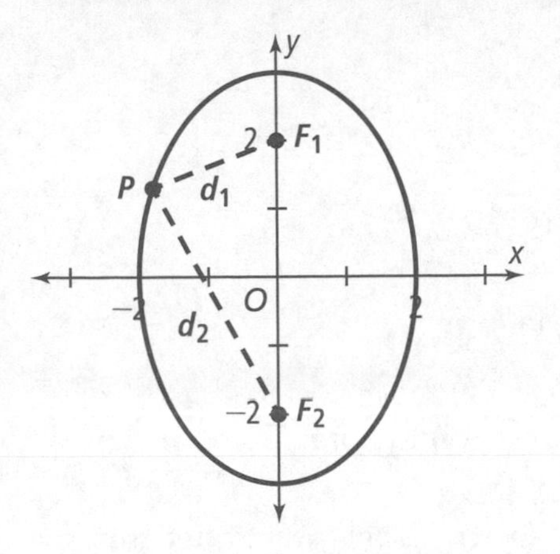

A. Describe how the length of d_1 and d_2 in the ellipse relate to each other. What happens to d_2 as d_1 gets larger?

B. Imagine that instead of the *sum* of the distances being a constant, the *difference* of the distances was a constant. What would happen to d_2 as d_1 gets larger?

C. Make Sense and Persevere Imagine what the graph of those points would look like. Where would the points lie in relation to the foci? How would it compare to the graph of an ellipse?

HABITS OF MIND

Reason Do you think that the graph of the figure in Part C is symmetric across the *y*-axis? Explain.

Notes

Assess

EXAMPLE 1

Try It! Derive an Equation of a Hyperbola

1. What is the equation for the hyperbola with foci at (10, 0) and (−10, 0) and a constant difference of 16?

EXAMPLE 2

Try It! Understand the Graph of a Hyperbola

2. Graph the hyperbola $\frac{y^2}{64} - \frac{x^2}{36} = 1$.
(*Hint:* Notice that in this equation the *x*-term is being subtracted from the *y*-term, so this hyperbola will open vertically rather than horizontally.)

HABITS OF MIND

Use Structure In an ellipse, the magnitude of denominators in the equation determines the orientation of the graph of the ellipse. Is the same true for a hyperbola? Explain.

EXAMPLE 3

Try It! Write an Equation of a Hyperbola

3. What is the equation of a hyperbola with foci $(-\sqrt{5}, 0)$ and $(\sqrt{5}, 0)$ and constant difference 2?
(*Hint:* What is the relationship between the constant difference and the vertices?)

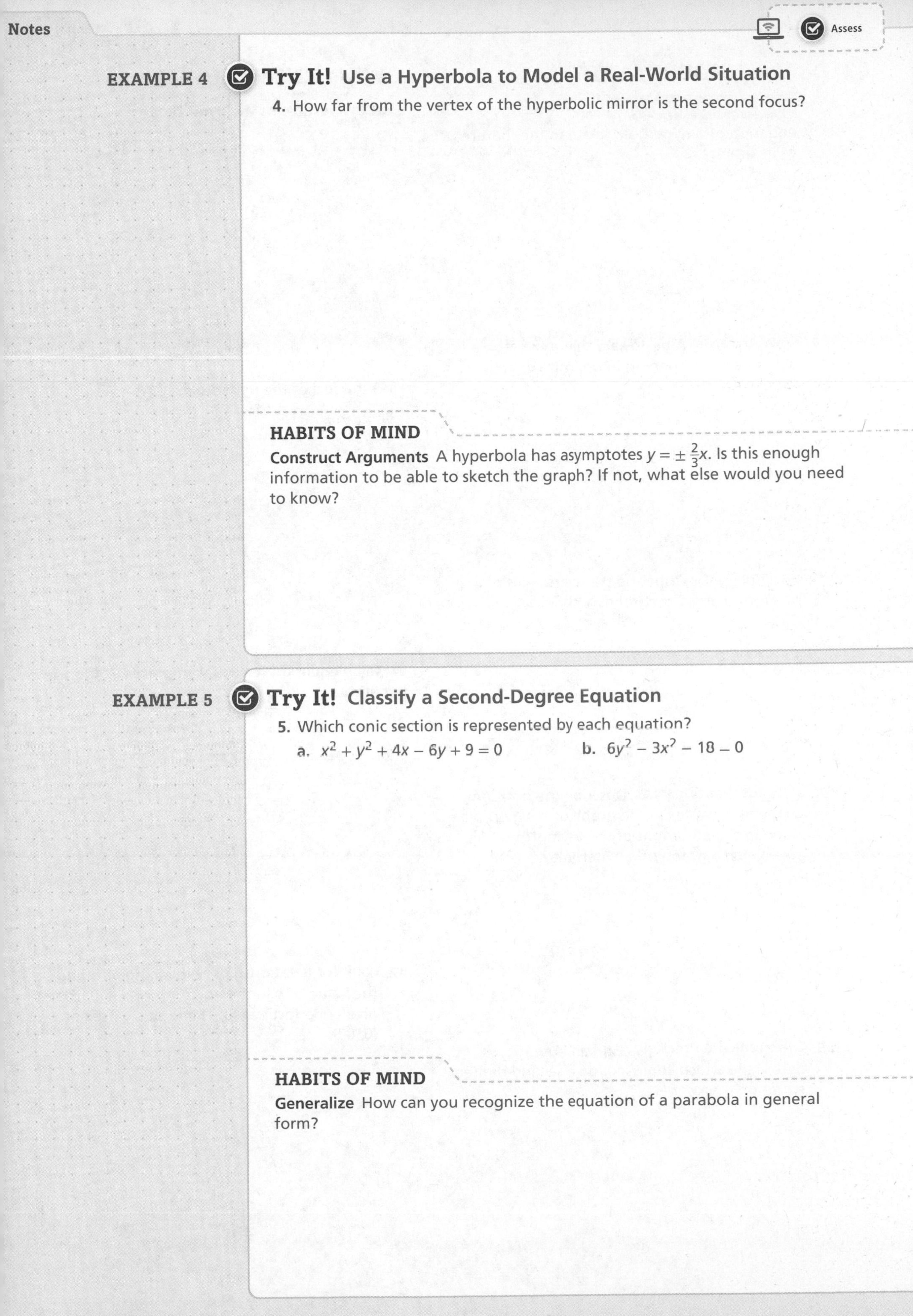

EXAMPLE 4

Try It! Use a Hyperbola to Model a Real-World Situation

4. How far from the vertex of the hyperbolic mirror is the second focus?

HABITS OF MIND

Construct Arguments A hyperbola has asymptotes $y = \pm \frac{2}{3}x$. Is this enough information to be able to sketch the graph? If not, what else would you need to know?

EXAMPLE 5

Try It! Classify a Second-Degree Equation

5. Which conic section is represented by each equation?

a. $x^2 + y^2 + 4x - 6y + 9 = 0$

b. $6y^2 - 3x^2 - 18 = 0$

HABITS OF MIND

Generalize How can you recognize the equation of a parabola in general form?

Do You UNDERSTAND?

1. ESSENTIAL QUESTION How does the equation of a hyperbola relate to the features of its graph?

2. **Error Analysis** Alberto said that a hyperbola is two parabolas opening in opposite directions. Explain his error.

3. **Vocabulary** Describe the transverse axis of a horizontal and a vertical hyperbola.

4. **Look for Relationships** Describe the position of the asymptotes in the graph of a hyperbola. How do the equations of the asymptotes help you sketch a graph of a hyperbola?

5. **Communicate Precisely** Explain how to determine which conic section a second-degree equation represents.

Do You KNOW HOW?

Find the vertices of the hyperbola.

6. $\frac{y^2}{144} - \frac{x^2}{56} = 1$

7. $\frac{x^2}{121} - \frac{y^2}{12} = 1$

Find the foci of the hyperbola.

8. $\frac{x^2}{64} - \frac{y^2}{36} = 1$

9. $\frac{y^2}{9} - \frac{x^2}{16} = 1$

Write an equation for the asymptotes of the hyperbola.

10. $\frac{x^2}{9} - \frac{y^2}{100} = 1$

11. $\frac{y^2}{4} - \frac{x^2}{36} = 1$

12. **Look for Relationships** Explain how to find the value of b in the equation of a hyperbola, given one focus at (0, 1) and one vertex at (0, 0.5).

Activity

10-1 Operations With Matrices

PearsonRealize.com

MODEL & DISCUSS

This screen shows the number of Small, Medium, Large, and Extra Large limited-edition silkscreen shirts on sale at an online boutique.

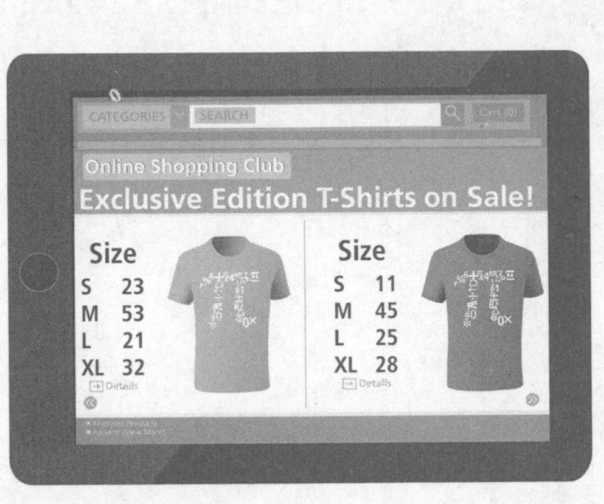

A. Construct a table to summarize the inventory that is on sale.

B. At the end of the day, the boutique has sold this many of each T-shirt from the sale items: red: 4 S, 6 M, 3 L, 5 XL; blue: 2 S, 8 M, 4 L, 0 XL. Make two new tables, one showing the merchandise sold and one showing the inventory that is left.

C. Look for Relationships What relationships did you use in creating the two tables in Part B?

HABITS OF MIND

Make Sense and Persevere Edwin summarized the information given in the problem in 2 rows and 4 columns. In Part B, he summarized the information about the number of shirts sold in a table that had 4 rows and 2 columns. Was this organizational strategy helpful? Explain.

Notes

Assess

EXAMPLE 1

Try It! Represent Data With a Matrix

1. In matrix C, the entries are the numbers of students on a committee. Column 1 lists girls, column 2 lists boys, row 1 lists sophomores, and row 2 lists juniors. Find a_{12}, a_{21}, and a_{22}, and tell what each number represents.

$$C = \begin{bmatrix} 7 & 5 \\ 8 & 10 \end{bmatrix}$$

EXAMPLE 2

Try It! Apply Scalar Multiplication

2. In this matrix C, the rows represent prices for shirts and khakis. The columns have the same meaning as in Example 2. If the sales tax rate is 6%, use scalar multiplication to find the sales tax for each item.

$$C = \begin{bmatrix} 75 & 40 & 25 \\ 100 & 60 & 30 \end{bmatrix}$$

HABITS OF MIND

Generalize Let the dimensions of matrix Z be 3×4. After multiplying this matrix by a scalar, what are the dimensions of the product matrix? Explain.

Notes

Assess

EXAMPLE 3

Try It! Add and Subtract Matrices

3. Consider matrices M and N.

$M = \begin{bmatrix} -3 & 5 \\ 2 & 0 \end{bmatrix}$, $N = \begin{bmatrix} 6 & 5 \\ -8 & 0.2 \end{bmatrix}$

a. What are matrices $M + N$ and $N + M$?

b. What are matrices $M - N$ and $N - M$?

EXAMPLE 4

Try It! Understand Matrix Addition and Subtraction

4. Consider the matrices below.

$P = \begin{bmatrix} 5 & 2 & -3 \\ 7 & 0 & -5 \end{bmatrix}$, $Q = \begin{bmatrix} 2 & -2 \\ 5 & -5 \\ -7 & 7 \end{bmatrix}$, $R = \begin{bmatrix} 6 & 0.5 \\ -3 & 0 \\ -2 & -2 \end{bmatrix}$

a. Find $R - Q$. What other matrix sums or differences can be calculated?

b. Find the additive inverses of P, Q, and R.

HABITS OF MIND

Communicate Precisely What must be true about two matrices for their sum or difference to exist?

EXAMPLE 5

Try It! Use Matrices to Translate and Dilate Figures

5. A segment has endpoints $M(8, -7)$ and $N(1, 2)$.

a. Use matrices to represent a translation of $\overline{MN}$ to $\overline{RS}$ by 6 units left and 3 units down. What are the coordinates of R and S?

b. Use matrices to represent a dilation of $\overline{MN}$ to $\overline{DE}$ by a scale factor of 3, centered at the origin. What are the coordinates of D and E?

HABITS OF MIND

Model With Mathematics The matrix $T = \begin{bmatrix} 1 & 1 & 4 \\ 2 & 3 & 2 \end{bmatrix}$ represents a triangle. Use matrices to determine whether dilating by a factor of 2 and then translating 5 units right is the same as translating the triangle 5 units right and then dilating by a factor of 2. Does the order of the transformations matter? Explain.

Do You UNDERSTAND?

1. ESSENTIAL QUESTION How can you interpret matrices and operate with matrices?

2. **Error Analysis** Tonya says $\begin{bmatrix} 3 & 2 \\ -4 & 1 \end{bmatrix} - \begin{bmatrix} 3 & 2 \\ 4 & 1 \end{bmatrix}$ would produce a zero matrix. Explain her error.

3. **Communicate Precisely** Explain how you know if two matrices can be added. Then explain how to add them.

4. **Vocabulary** What are equal matrices? Give an example of equal matrices.

Do You KNOW HOW?

Identify the element for each matrix.

5. $\begin{bmatrix} 4 & 1 & 0 \\ 7 & 3 & 5 \end{bmatrix}$; a_{23}

6. $\begin{bmatrix} -6 \\ 2 \end{bmatrix}$; a_{11}

Given $A = \begin{bmatrix} 3 & -2 \\ 7 & 1 \end{bmatrix}$ and $B = \begin{bmatrix} 0 & 7 \\ -4 & 12 \end{bmatrix}$, calculate each of the following.

7. $A + B$

8. $B - A$

9. $4A$

10. $A - B$

11. The endpoints of $\overline{AB}$ are represented by the matrix $\begin{bmatrix} 3 & 7 \\ 1 & 5 \end{bmatrix}$.
Find the image of the segment after a dilation, centered at the origin, by a scale factor of 2.

10-2 Matrix Multiplication

EXPLORE & REASON

Two stores, Quick Repair and TechRite, buy and sell pre-owned phones, tablets, and computers. The matrices below represent their average revenue *R*, purchase costs *C*, and repair expenses *E* for each item:

		Phone	Tablet	Computer
R	Quick Repair	$150	$100	$400
	TechRite	$200	$250	$500
C	Quick Repair	$100	$50	$200
	TechRite	$125	$75	$300
E	Quick Repair	$25	$20	$50
	TechRite	$10	$50	$50

A. Would it make sense to find the sum and/or difference of any two of the three matrices? Explain.

B. Make Sense and Persevere Quick Repair and TechRite both need to estimate their total purchase and repair costs. They each predict that they will need to purchase 100 phones, 100 tablets, and 100 computers, and that they will need to repair 50% of them. Explain what you would do to find the total costs.

HABITS OF MIND

Reason Which store makes a greater profit from the sale of a repaired phone? Explain.

Notes

Assess

EXAMPLE 1

Try It! Understand Matrix Multiplication

1. How could you organize the weighting and grade information differently so that Oscar's and Reagan's final grades are given by GW?

EXAMPLE 2

Try It! Examine Multiplication of Square Matrices

2. Determine whether each equation may be true for the following matrices.

$A = \begin{bmatrix} 3 & 0 \\ -1 & -2 \end{bmatrix}$, $B = \begin{bmatrix} -2 & 1 \\ 3 & -4 \end{bmatrix}$, $C = \begin{bmatrix} 6 & 2 \\ 4 & 8 \end{bmatrix}$

a. $(AB)C = A(BC)$

b. $(A + B)C = AC + BC$

HABITS OF MIND

Construct Arguments Let $M = \begin{pmatrix} 1 & 2 \\ 3 & 4 \end{pmatrix}$ and $N = \begin{pmatrix} -2 & 1 \\ 1.5 & -0.5 \end{pmatrix}$. Is $MN = NM$? If so, can you conclude that matrix multiplication is commutative?

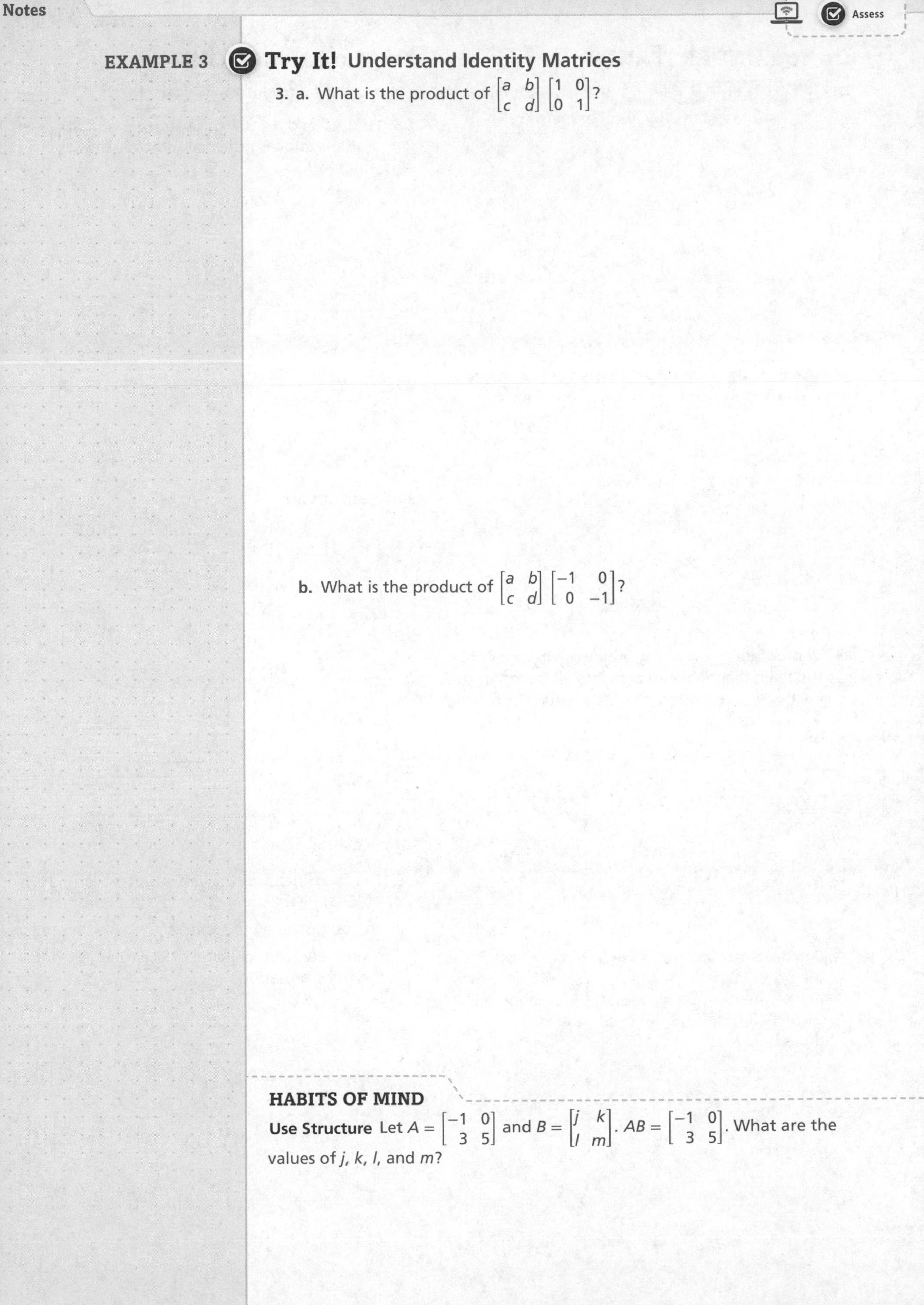

Assess

EXAMPLE 3 **Try It! Understand Identity Matrices**

3. a. What is the product of $\begin{bmatrix} a & b \\ c & d \end{bmatrix} \begin{bmatrix} 1 & 0 \\ 0 & 1 \end{bmatrix}$?

b. What is the product of $\begin{bmatrix} a & b \\ c & d \end{bmatrix} \begin{bmatrix} -1 & 0 \\ 0 & -1 \end{bmatrix}$?

HABITS OF MIND

Use Structure Let $A = \begin{bmatrix} -1 & 0 \\ 3 & 5 \end{bmatrix}$ and $B = \begin{bmatrix} j & k \\ l & m \end{bmatrix}$. $AB = \begin{bmatrix} -1 & 0 \\ 3 & 5 \end{bmatrix}$. What are the values of j, k, l, and m?

Do You UNDERSTAND?

1. ESSENTIAL QUESTION What does it mean to multiply a matrix by another matrix?

2. **Use Structure** Would it be possible to multiply $A_{3 \times 5}$ and $B_{4 \times 5}$? Explain your reasoning.

3. **Vocabulary** Explain why a matrix with ones on the main diagonal and zeros for all the other elements is called the *identity matrix*.

4. **Construct Arguments** A student thought that the product of $A_{1 \times 5}$ and $B_{5 \times 1}$ should have five elements in the answer. Is the student correct? If not, how many elements will there be?

Do You KNOW HOW?

Let $A = \begin{bmatrix} 3 & 0 \\ -1 & -2 \end{bmatrix}$ and $B = \begin{bmatrix} -2 & 1 \\ 3 & -4 \end{bmatrix}$.

5. Find *AB* and *BA* to demonstrate that matrix multiplication is not commutative. Show your work.

Find each product.

6. $\begin{bmatrix} 4 & 7 \\ 1 & -2 \end{bmatrix} \begin{bmatrix} 1 & 0 \\ 0 & 1 \end{bmatrix}$

7. $\begin{bmatrix} 1 & 0 \\ 0 & 1 \end{bmatrix} \begin{bmatrix} 5 & 0 \\ 8 & 2 \end{bmatrix}$

8. The coordinates of the vertices of a triangle are *A*(−2, 3), *B*(1, 1), and *C*(2, −1). The coordinate are multiplied by the matrix $\begin{bmatrix} 1 & 0 \\ 0 & -1 \end{bmatrix}$. Find the coordinates of the image of the triangle after the transformation.

Activity

10-3 Vectors

PearsonRealize.com

CRITIQUE & EXPLAIN

Olivia and Benito are taking part in a scavenger hunt. They are given a map that shows the start and finish line. They are also given a list of directions to the finish line. They get to choose how they want to follow the directions, so they took different paths.

Start

Finish

Olivia's path:	Benito's path:
5 blocks south	7 blocks west
7 blocks west	3 blocks north
3 blocks north	4 blocks west
4 blocks west	5 blocks south

A. Will both Olivia and Benito reach the finish line? Explain.

B. Create a different set of directions that would get someone to the finish line.

C. **Communicate Precisely** Does the order of the instructions that pair distance and direction affect the outcome? Explain.

HABITS OF MIND

Look for Relationships Russel looked at his list of four directions and decided that he could reach the finish line in fewer blocks. What is a possible set of directions for a path he could take?

Notes

Assess

EXAMPLE 1 **Try It!** **Represent Vector Quantities**

1. A vector has an initial point at (8, 2) and a terminal point at (5, 6). What is the vector in component form, and what are its magnitude and direction?

EXAMPLE 2 **Try It!** **Understand Vector Addition**

2. a. If $\overrightarrow{MN} = \langle 9, 12\rangle$ and $\overrightarrow{NO} = \langle 2, 7\rangle$, what is $\overrightarrow{MN} + \overrightarrow{NO}$?

b. If $\vec{v} = \langle -3, 4\rangle$ and $\vec{w} = \langle 5, -8\rangle$, what is $\vec{v} + \vec{w}$?

EXAMPLE 3 **Try It!** **Find the Magnitude and Direction of a Sum**

3. If the engine speed was 9 mph northwest at 135° with the same current, what would be the magnitude and direction of the boat's speed? Round the magnitude and angle of direction to the nearest tenth.

HABITS OF MIND

Reason Let $\vec{v} = \langle -4, 12\rangle$ and $\vec{w} = \langle -3, 9\rangle$. Find $|\vec{v}| + |\vec{w}|$ and $|\vec{v} + \vec{w}|$. Does this mean that the sum of the magnitudes of two vectors is equal to the magnitude of their sum? Explain.

Assess

EXAMPLE 4

Try It! Understand Vector Subtraction

4. a. What are the components, magnitude, and direction of $\vec{s} - \vec{t}$, where $\vec{s} = \langle 6, -3 \rangle$ and $\vec{t} = \langle 3, 2 \rangle$?

b. For $\overrightarrow{m} = \langle 1, -3 \rangle$ and $\overrightarrow{n} = \langle -2, 7 \rangle$, what is $\overrightarrow{m} - \overrightarrow{n}$?

EXAMPLE 5

Try It! Multiply a Vector by a Scalar

5. a. If $\vec{t} = \langle -5, -7 \rangle$, what are the components, magnitude, and direction of $-4(\vec{t})$?

b. What are the components, magnitude, and direction of $2t$?

HABITS OF MIND

Make Sense and Persevere Suppose you were to multiply a vector by the scalar $\frac{1}{3}$. Subtract this result from the original vector. How would the magnitude and direction of the difference relate to the original magnitude and direction?

EXAMPLE 6

Try It! Use Matrices to Transform a Vector

6. a. $\overrightarrow{EF} = \langle 5, 10 \rangle$. How is $\overrightarrow{EF}$ transformed when it is multiplied by the matrix $\begin{bmatrix} -1 & 0 \\ 0 & 1 \end{bmatrix}$?

b. How is $\overrightarrow{EF}$ transformed when it is multiplied by the matrix $\begin{bmatrix} 0 & -1 \\ 1 & 0 \end{bmatrix}$?

HABITS OF MIND

Communicate Precisely How can a matrix and a vector be multiplied?

Do You UNDERSTAND?

1. ESSENTIAL QUESTION How does including a direction with a quantity affect how you carry out operations on quantities?

2. **Error Analysis** Drew says the sum of the vectors $\overrightarrow{AB} = \langle 5, 11 \rangle$ and $\overrightarrow{BC} = \langle 2, -4 \rangle$ is $\overrightarrow{AC} = \langle 7, 13 \rangle$. Explain and correct Drew's error.

3. **Communicate Precisely** Explain the process for vector subtraction.

4. **Look for Relationships** Explain why you can use matrix multiplication to perform transformations on vectors.

5. **Reason** A boat is at the origin and is headed 60° north of west. In which quadrant is the vector representing the boat's movement?

Do You KNOW HOW?

Write the component form of the vector, given its initial and terminal points.

6. initial point (6, 2);
   terminal point (3, –5)

7. initial point (4, –1);
   terminal point (–8, 0)

8. A vector has an initial point at (6, 13) and a terminal point at (3, 2). What is the vector in component form, and what are its magnitude and direction?

9. A vector has a direction of 235° and a magnitude of 6. What is the component form of the vector? Express your answer to the nearest tenth of a unit.

10. Find $\overrightarrow{MN} + \overrightarrow{NO}$ and $\overrightarrow{MN} - \overrightarrow{NO}$ if $\overrightarrow{MN} = \langle 6, 10 \rangle$ and $\overrightarrow{NO} = \langle -3, 0 \rangle$.

Activity

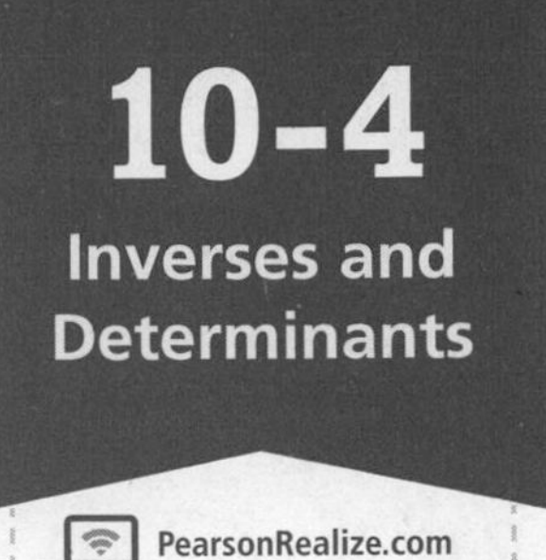

EXPLORE & REASON

A teacher writes these three equations on the board.

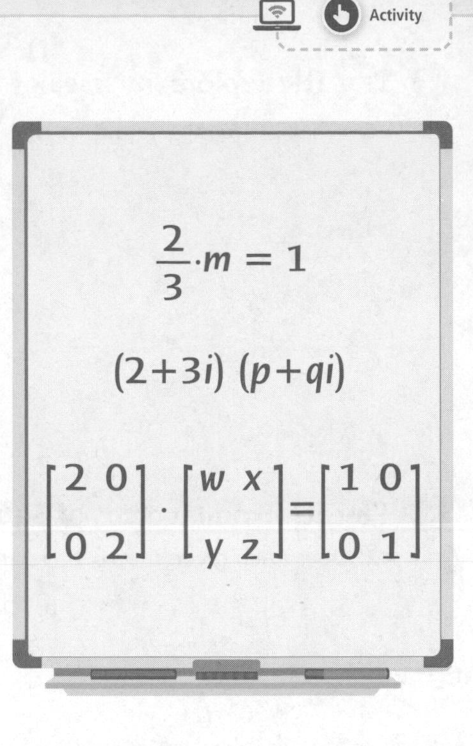

A. Carolina notices that the solution to the first equation is given by $\frac{3}{2}$, and she hypothesizes that

$p + qi = \frac{1}{2 + 3i}$ and $\begin{bmatrix} w & x \\ y & z \end{bmatrix} = \frac{\begin{bmatrix} 1 & 0 \\ 0 & 1 \end{bmatrix}}{\begin{bmatrix} 2 & 0 \\ 0 & 2 \end{bmatrix}}$.

Is Carolina correct?

B. Look for Relationships What do the methods for solving these equations have in common?

HABITS OF MIND

Communicate Precisely What does the term *multiplicative inverse* mean?

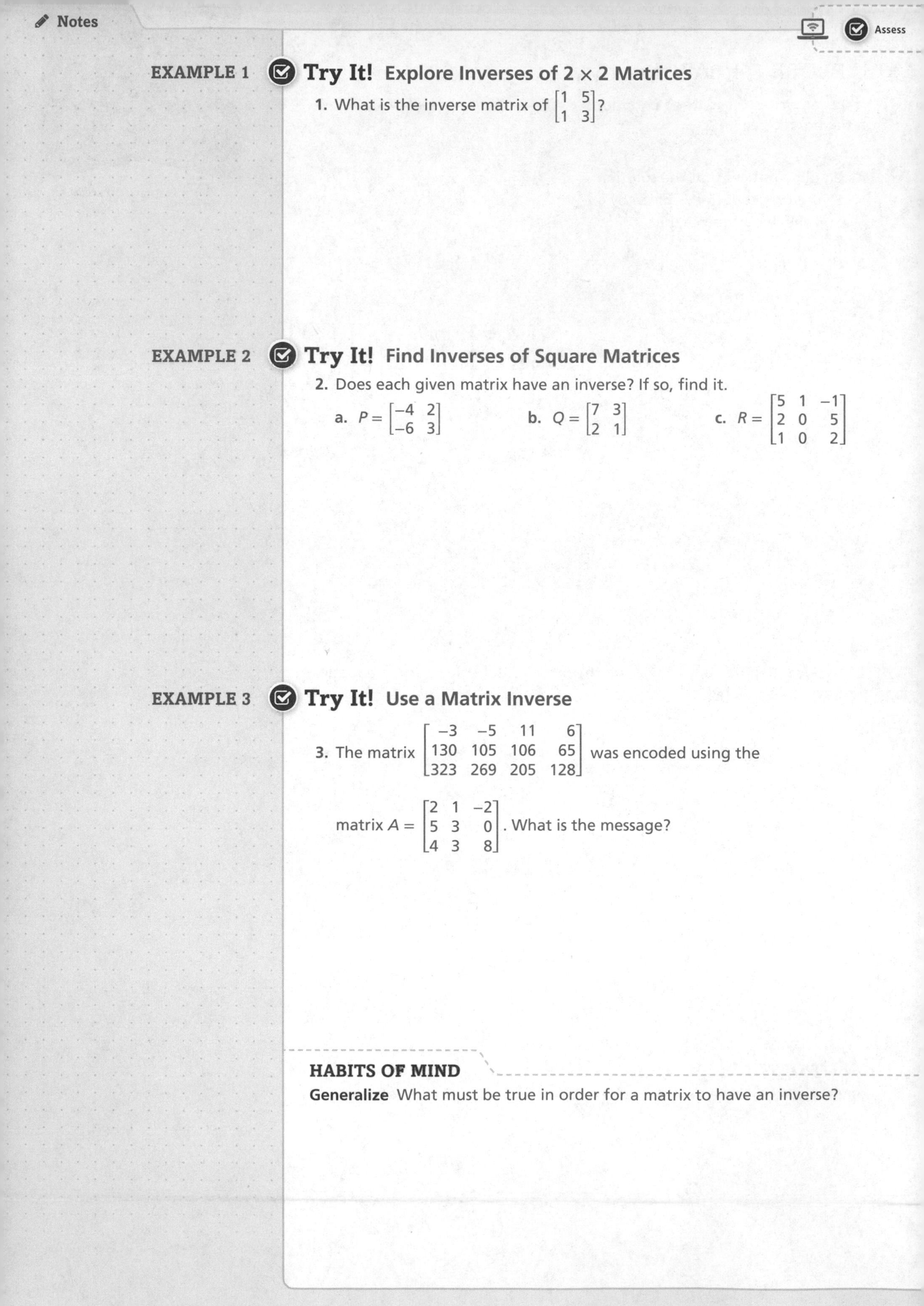

Notes

Assess

EXAMPLE 1

Try It! Explore Inverses of 2 × 2 Matrices

1. What is the inverse matrix of $\begin{bmatrix} 1 & 5 \\ 1 & 3 \end{bmatrix}$?

EXAMPLE 2

Try It! Find Inverses of Square Matrices

2. Does each given matrix have an inverse? If so, find it.

a. $P = \begin{bmatrix} -4 & 2 \\ -6 & 3 \end{bmatrix}$

b. $Q = \begin{bmatrix} 7 & 3 \\ 2 & 1 \end{bmatrix}$

c. $R = \begin{bmatrix} 5 & 1 & -1 \\ 2 & 0 & 5 \\ 1 & 0 & 2 \end{bmatrix}$

EXAMPLE 3

Try It! Use a Matrix Inverse

3. The matrix $\begin{bmatrix} -3 & -5 & 11 & 6 \\ 130 & 105 & 106 & 65 \\ 323 & 269 & 205 & 128 \end{bmatrix}$ was encoded using the matrix $A = \begin{bmatrix} 2 & 1 & -2 \\ 5 & 3 & 0 \\ 4 & 3 & 8 \end{bmatrix}$. What is the message?

HABITS OF MIND

Generalize What must be true in order for a matrix to have an inverse?

Assess

EXAMPLE 4

Try It! Use Determinants to Find the Area of a Triangle

4. a. Find the area of the triangle determined by the vectors $\langle -2, 10\rangle$ and $\langle -1, -5\rangle$.

b. Find the area of the triangle determined by the vectors $\langle 8, 4\rangle$ and $\langle 7, -3\rangle$.

EXAMPLE 5

Try It! Use a Determinant to Find the Area of a Parallelogram

5. Find the area of the parallelogram defined by the vectors $\langle 3, 8\rangle$ and $\langle 1, 4\rangle$.

HABITS OF MIND

Look for Relationships Find the area of the triangle defined by the vectors $\langle 2, 6\rangle$ and $\langle -1, -3\rangle$. How do you explain the result?

Do You UNDERSTAND?

1. ESSENTIAL QUESTION How do you find and use an inverse matrix?

2. **Vocabulary** What is the determinant of a 2×2 matrix?

3. **Error Analysis** Enrique says the matrix $\begin{bmatrix} 3 & 4 \\ 6 & 8 \end{bmatrix}$ has an inverse. Explain his error.

4. **Communicate Precisely** Explain how to use the determinant of a matrix to find the area of a triangle.

Do You KNOW HOW?

Find the inverse of each matrix, if it exists.

5. $\begin{bmatrix} -2 & -4 \\ 2 & 3 \end{bmatrix}$

6. $\begin{bmatrix} -1 & 3 \\ -3 & 9 \end{bmatrix}$

7. $\begin{bmatrix} -3 & -2 & 1 \\ 5 & 4 & -3 \\ 6 & -4 & 2 \end{bmatrix}$

8. $\begin{bmatrix} 2 & 0 & -4 \\ 0 & 6 & 3 \\ -1 & 1 & 3 \end{bmatrix}$

9. **Make Sense and Persevere** What is the area of a triangle determined by the vectors $\langle 2, 3 \rangle$ and $\langle 6, -1 \rangle$?

10. What is the area of a parallelogram determined by the vectors $\langle 5, 2 \rangle$ and $\langle -1, -10 \rangle$?

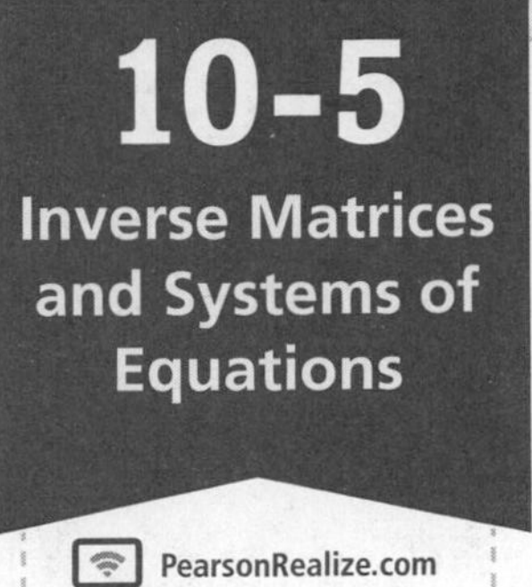

Activity

CRITIQUE & EXPLAIN

This augmented matrix represents a system of linear equations in three variables. Students are asked to identify possible values of *a* and *b* for which the system has an infinite number of solutions.

$$\left[\begin{array}{ccc|c} 1 & 1 & 2 & -1 \\ 0 & 2 & 0 & 8 \\ 0 & 0 & a & b \end{array}\right]$$

Recall that an augmented matrix for a system of equations has a row for each equation showing its coefficients and constants.

Here are the answers that three students wrote:

Deshawn: $a = 0$, $b = 1$; Jacy: $a = 0$, $b = 0$; Avery: $a = 1$, $b = 0$

A. Which student, if any, is correct? Explain your reasoning.

B. For each student you think has an incorrect response, explain how many solutions their suggested values generate.

C. **Look for Relationships** Which of the coefficient matrices that the three students wrote has an inverse? Is the number of solutions related to the existence of an inverse?

HABITS OF MIND

Reason Why were you asked in part (c) to find the inverse of the coefficient matrices and not the augmented matrices?

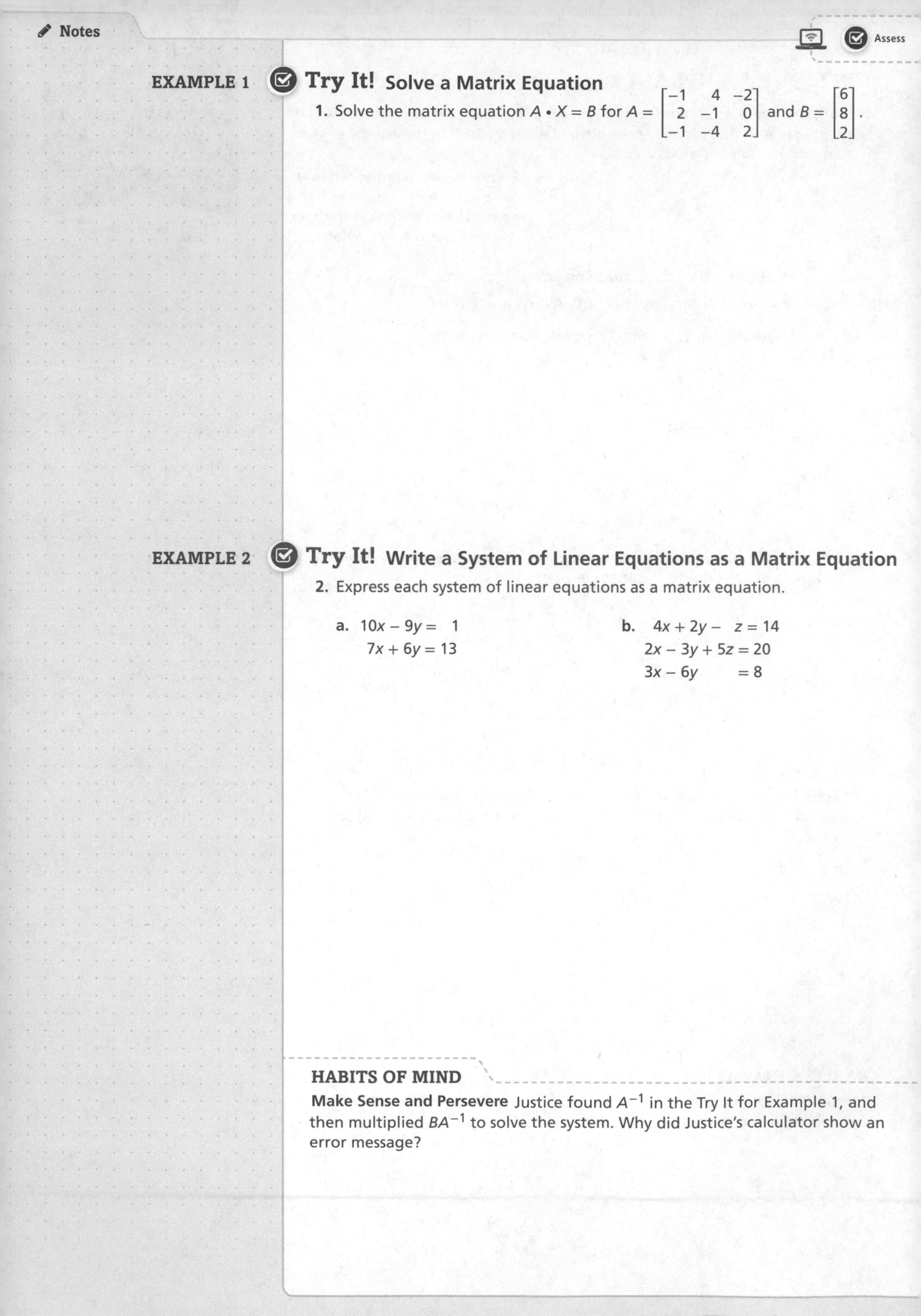

Notes

Assess

EXAMPLE 1

Try It! Solve a Matrix Equation

1. Solve the matrix equation $A \cdot X = B$ for $A = \begin{bmatrix} -1 & 4 & -2 \\ 2 & -1 & 0 \\ -1 & -4 & 2 \end{bmatrix}$ and $B = \begin{bmatrix} 6 \\ 8 \\ 2 \end{bmatrix}$.

EXAMPLE 2

Try It! Write a System of Linear Equations as a Matrix Equation

2. Express each system of linear equations as a matrix equation.

a. $10x - 9y = 1$
$7x + 6y = 13$

b. $4x + 2y - z = 14$
$2x - 3y + 5z = 20$
$3x - 6y = 8$

HABITS OF MIND

Make Sense and Persevere Justice found A^{-1} in the Try It for Example 1, and then multiplied BA^{-1} to solve the system. Why did Justice's calculator show an error message?

Notes

Assess

EXAMPLE 3

Try It! Solve a System of Linear Equations Using an Inverse Matrix

3. Solve the following systems of linear equations using inverse matrices, if possible.

a. $\begin{cases} 3x + 4y = 8 \\ \frac{3}{2}x + 2y = 5 \end{cases}$

b. $\begin{cases} x + 2y - 4z = 4 \\ x - 2y + 2z = -10 \\ -x - y + z = 4 \end{cases}$

EXAMPLE 4

Try It! Solve a Real-World System With an Inverse

4. For a three-week period, the same company budgets \$860 for labor and \$1,080 for materials. How many pairs of men's and women's sneakers can they make in three weeks?

HABITS OF MIND

Generalize If the coefficient matrix for a system of equations does not have an inverse, does that mean that the system of equations has no solution? Explain.

Do You UNDERSTAND?

1. **ESSENTIAL QUESTION** How can matrix inverses be used to simplify the process of solving a system of linear equations?

2. **Error Analysis** Corey says the matrix equation $\begin{bmatrix} 3 & 2 \\ -1 & 4 \\ 2 & 6 \end{bmatrix}\begin{bmatrix} x \\ y \\ z \end{bmatrix} = \begin{bmatrix} 8 \\ 13 \\ 22 \end{bmatrix}$ represents the system of linear equations $\begin{cases} 3x + 2y = 8 \\ -y + 4z = 13. \\ 2x + 6z = 22 \end{cases}$ Explain Corey's error.

3. **Vocabulary** How do you determine the coefficient matrix for a particular system of linear equations?

4. **Communicate Precisely** Explain how to solve a system of linear equations using an inverse matrix.

Do You KNOW HOW?

Express the system of linear equations as a matrix equation.

5. $\begin{cases} 5x + 3y = -21 \\ 2x - 4y = -24 \end{cases}$

6. $\begin{cases} 6x - 8y + 2z = -46 \\ -x + 5y + 3z = 29 \\ 9x - 4z = -35 \end{cases}$

7. Given the matrix equation $A \cdot X = B$ for $A = \begin{bmatrix} 1 & 3 & -4 \\ 2 & -2 & 3 \\ -4 & -6 & -1 \end{bmatrix}$ and $B = \begin{bmatrix} 0 \\ -5 \\ -5 \end{bmatrix}$, find A^{-1}. Then use A^{-1} to solve the matrix equation for X.

8. Write an equation that shows what your next step would be in solving this matrix equation for x, y, and z. $\begin{bmatrix} -1 & 2 & -3 \\ 2 & -13 & 9 \\ -4 & 12 & -6 \end{bmatrix} \cdot \begin{bmatrix} x \\ y \\ z \end{bmatrix} = \begin{bmatrix} 2 \\ -7 \\ 2 \end{bmatrix}$

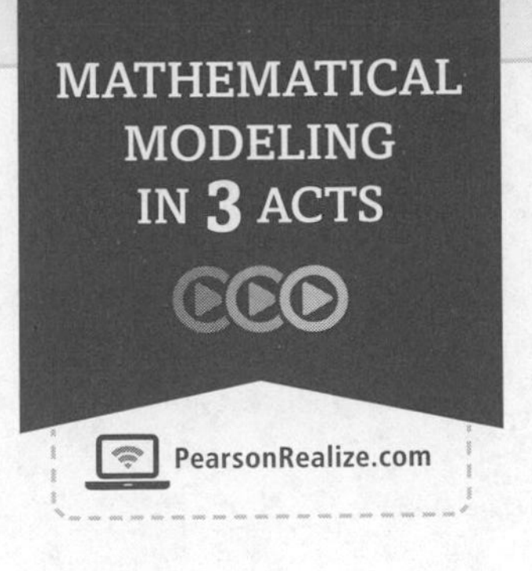

The Big Burger

For many people, hamburgers are a hallmark of American food. Nearly every restaurant, from fast food chains, to diners, to fine dining establishments, offers some kind of hamburger on their menu.

Some restaurants offer various types of burgers: beef, turkey, and veggie burgers are all quite popular. You can also often choose extras to add to your burger: double patties of beef, cheese, pickles, onions, lettuce, tomatoes . . . The options are endless! Think about this during the Mathematical Modeling in 3 Acts lesson.

ACT 1 Identify the Problem

1. What is the first question that comes to mind after watching the video?

2. Write down the Main Question you will answer.

3. Make an initial conjecture that answers this Main Question.

4. Explain how you arrived at your conjecture.

5. What information will be useful to know to answer the main question? How can you get it? How will you use that information?

Video

ACT 2 Develop a Model

6. Use the math that you have learned in the topic to refine your conjecture.

ACT 3 Interpret the Results

7. Did your refined conjecture match the actual answer exactly? If not, what might explain the difference?

Activity

11-1 Statistical Questions and Variables

PearsonRealize.com

EXPLORE & REASON

A state questioned some of its high schools about the price they were charging for prom tickets. The results are summarized in the histogram.

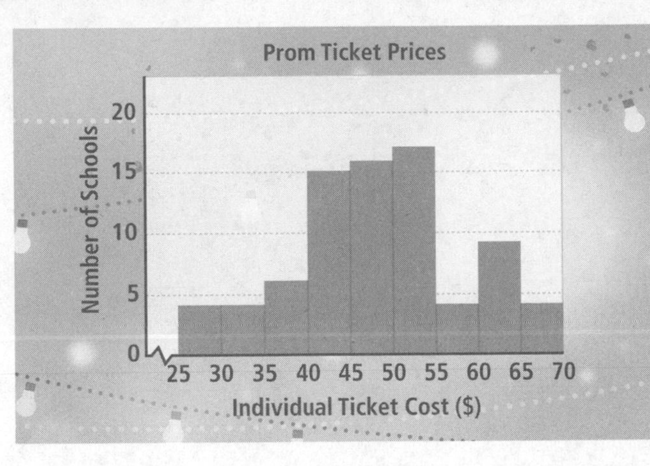

A. What questions can be answered using the data in this histogram?

B. Who might be interested in the answers to these questions? Explain.

C. Construct Arguments Anastasia is surprised that the median cost of a prom ticket is not higher, given that her school is charging $60 per ticket. What are some possible reasons for the data not conforming to her expectations?

HABITS OF MIND

Make Sense and Persevere How many high schools were surveyed? How many charged between $40 and $44 for a ticket to prom?

Notes

Assess

EXAMPLE 1

Try It! Understand Statistical Questions

1. Is the given question a statistical question?

   a. *"Which is the most popular visual art form: photography, painting, sculpting, or drawing?"*

   b. *"How many lithographs were created by the artist M.C. Escher?"*

EXAMPLE 2

Try It! Understand Statistical Variables

2. What is the statistical variable represented by each of the following questions, and is it categorical or quantitative?

   a. *"What breed of dog is most likely to be adopted from an animal shelter?"*

   b. *"What is the average number of students per activity participating in after-school activities at Jefferson High School?"*

HABITS OF MIND

Look for Relationships Consider the sentence, "There are 3 birthdays in our class in the 3rd month." What are the differences in how the 3 is used?

EXAMPLE 3

Try It! Distinguish Between Populations and Samples

3. A city worker collects five vials of water from each of ten randomly selected locations all over the city to test the levels of bacteria in the city water supply.
   a. What is the sample in this experiment?

   b. What is the population?

HABITS OF MIND

Construct Arguments Can a sample be the same as the population? Explain.

EXAMPLE 4

Try It! Distinguish Between Parameters and Statistics

4. Is the given data summary a parameter or statistic?
   a. 53.2% of a district's eligible voters voted for the sitting U.S. House Representative.

   b. The median age of a car in 20 randomly selected spaces in the school parking lot is 7 years.

HABITS OF MIND

Communicate Precisely Describe the difference between a parameter and a statistic.

Do You UNDERSTAND?

1. ESSENTIAL QUESTION What kinds of questions about quantities and relationships among quantities can be answered with statistics?

2. **Error Analysis** Dyani says she identified a quantitative variable and conducted a survey when she asked her fellow classmates in her homeroom about their favorite style of sweatshirt from the categories: hoodie, pullover, or zip-up. Explain her error.

3. **Vocabulary** Explain the difference between a categorical variable and a quantitative variable.

4. **Communicate Precisely** Suppose Hana wants to find out the most commonly driven type of vehicle among the students at her high school. Since 1,560 students attend her high school, she asks every tenth student who enters the building one morning what kind of vehicle he or she drives. What is the population in this scenario?

Do You KNOW HOW?

5. Is the following question a statistical question?

   "During which month did your family take a vacation?"

6. What is the statistical variable represented by the following question, and is it categorical or quantitative?

   "How many TV sets are owned by families?"

7. Forty randomly-selected members of a high school music program were asked to report the number of hours they spend practicing each week. If you were to compute the mean number of hours, would your answer be a parameter or a statistic? Explain.

Activity

CRITIQUE & EXPLAIN

Jacinta and Felix were each asked to design a study to answer the question: "What proportion of students at this school listen to music while studying?"

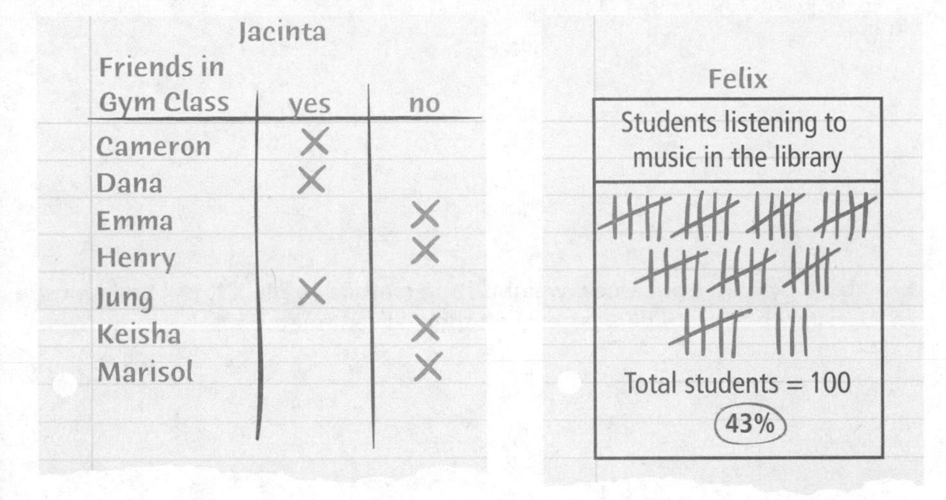

Jacinta
Friends in Gym Class
yes
no
Cameron
Dana
Emma
Henry
Jung
Keisha
Marisol
Felix
Students listening to music in the library
Total students = 100
43%

A. What group did Jacinta select from to conduct her study? What group did Felix select from?

B. How did Jacinta choose which members of her group to question? How did Felix choose which members from his group to observe?

C. Look for Relationships Who designed a better study, Jacinta or Felix? Explain.

HABITS OF MIND

Communicate Precisely Did either Jacinta or Felix use randomness? Explain.

Notes

Assess

EXAMPLE 1

Try It! Choose a Type of Study

1. What type of study is described?

   a. A gym asks its customers if they would prefer the gym to open earlier in the morning.

   b. A gym tries out a new weightlifting method to see if it will build muscle for their customers faster than their current method.

   c. A gym counts the customers who come before 8 A.M.

HABITS OF MIND

Model With Mathematics The gym wants to know whether or not they should buy more elliptical machines. What kind of statistical study could they use to answer their question? Describe the study you propose.

EXAMPLE 2

Try It! Determine Sources of Bias

2. A soft drink company calls 500 people at random and asks, "Is our product or our rival's product the best soft drink on the market?" Why is this question a potential source of bias?

Go Online | PearsonRealize.com

EXAMPLE 3

Try It! Identify a Sampling Method

3. What sampling method is used in the following examples? Is the method likely to be biased or not?

   a. The population is grouped according to age, and a random sample is chosen from each group.

   b. A number of hospitals around the country were randomly chosen. Within each hospital, all of the nurses were chosen.

HABITS OF MIND

Make Sense and Persevere Of the five sampling methods, which two are most likely to introduce bias? Explain.

EXAMPLE 4

Try It! Randomize Experiments

4. Design an experiment to test whether drinking coffee improves memory. How will you choose the experimental and control groups?

HABITS OF MIND

Construct Arguments Why is it important to have the memory test administered by someone who was not aware of which subjects were in the experimental group?

Do You UNDERSTAND?

1. ESSENTIAL QUESTION How can you choose the best type of study to answer a given statistical question and choose a reasonable sample?

2. **Vocabulary** A city is weighing whether to increase fares for public transit, or to provide more funding to public transit through the city's general fund, which is primarily funded by local property taxes. A survey of public transit riders was conducted to determine popular opinion. What is this sampling method an example of?

3. **Error Analysis** When Lila conducted an experiment on citywide pond water, all of her samples came from the pond in her uncle's backyard. Explain her error.

Do You KNOW HOW?

4. An ice cream shop asks its customers if they would like the shop to offer containers of ice cream to take home. What type of study does this describe?

5. A television news program asks its viewers to call in to give their opinions on an upcoming ballot question. What type of sampling method does this represent?

6. A doctor assigns people to treatment groups based on data from their medical records. Is this method of selecting treatment groups biased or unbiased? Explain.

11-3
Data Distributions

PearsonRealize.com

CRITIQUE & EXPLAIN

Chen and Dakota were asked to estimate the mean and median of the following data set.

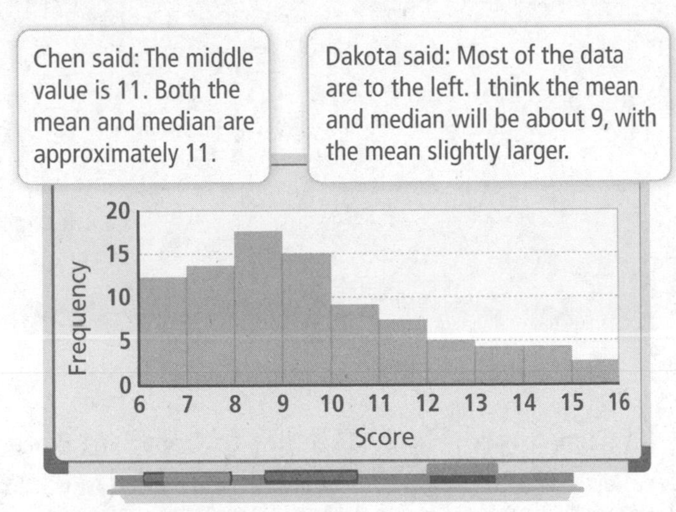

Chen said: The middle value is 11. Both the mean and median are approximately 11.
Dakota said: Most of the data are to the left. I think the mean and median will be about 9, with the mean slightly larger.
Frequency
20
15
10
5
0
6 7 8 9 10 11 12 13 14 15 16
Score

A. Is either Chen or Dakota correct? Explain.

B. What strategies could you use to approximate the exact mean and median?

C. Reason Which measure of center is more representative in this case, the mean or the median? Explain.

HABITS OF MIND

Construct Arguments Kyle thinks that the mode is the most representative measure of center for this set of data. Do you agree? Explain.

Notes

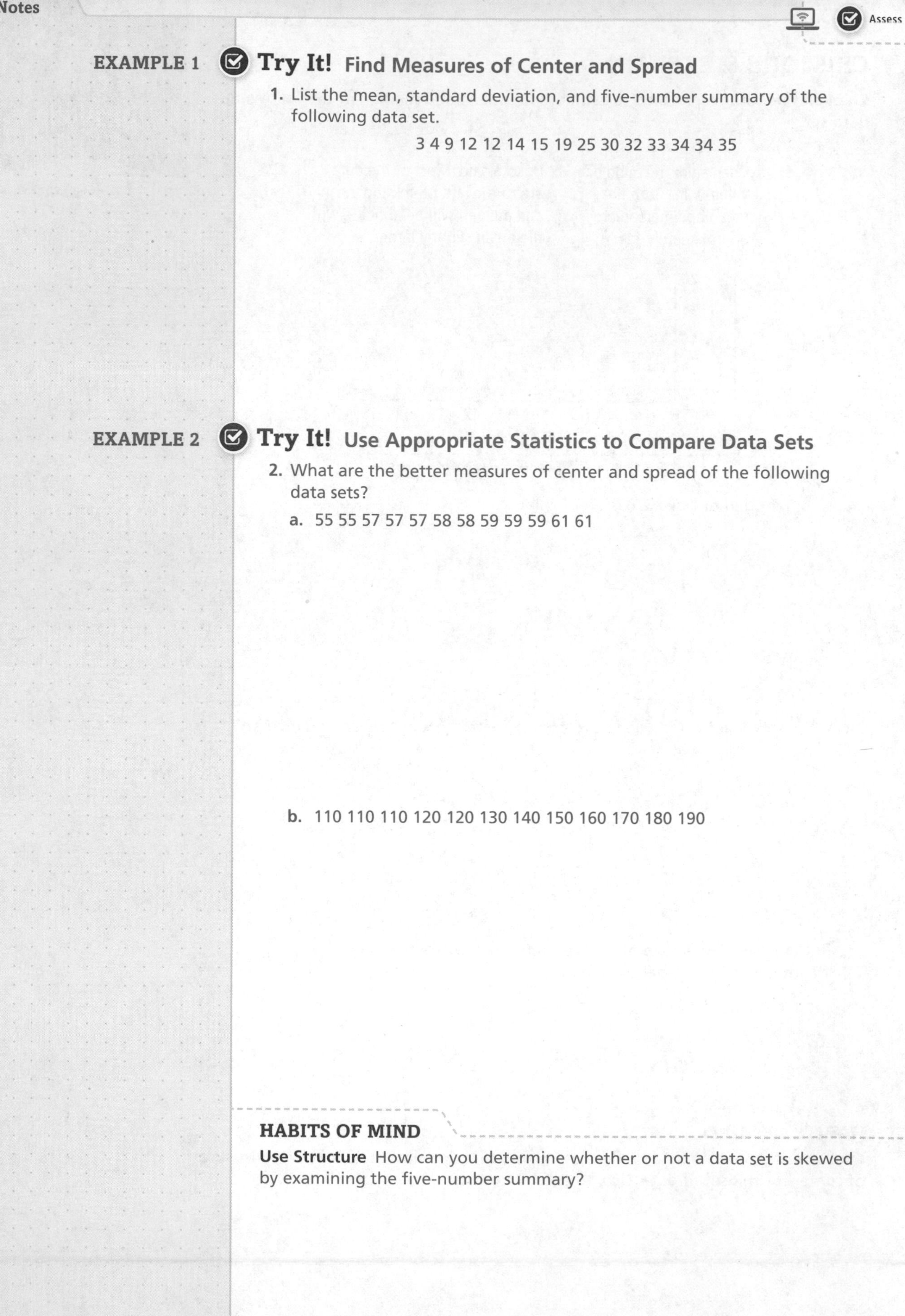

Assess

EXAMPLE 1

Try It! Find Measures of Center and Spread

1. List the mean, standard deviation, and five-number summary of the following data set.

3 4 9 12 12 14 15 19 25 30 32 33 34 34 35

EXAMPLE 2

Try It! Use Appropriate Statistics to Compare Data Sets

2. What are the better measures of center and spread of the following data sets?

   a. 55 55 57 57 57 58 58 59 59 59 61 61

   b. 110 110 110 120 120 130 140 150 160 170 180 190

HABITS OF MIND

Use Structure How can you determine whether or not a data set is skewed by examining the five-number summary?

Go Online | PearsonRealize.com

Assess

EXAMPLE 3

Try It! Recognize a Normal Distribution

3. Is each situation likely to be normally distributed? Explain.

   a. weight of individuals in a population

   b. the scores on a difficult test

EXAMPLE 4

Try It! Classify a Data Distribution

4. What is the type of distribution and the center and spread of the data?
   20 17 17 12 18 21 19 18 13 14 17 23 25

HABITS OF MIND

Look for Relationships How are the mean and median of a normally distributed data set related?

Do You UNDERSTAND?

1. ESSENTIAL QUESTION How can you interpret the distribution of data in a data set?

2. **Vocabulary** Write a definition for *normally distributed* and *normal curve* in your own words.

3. **Error Analysis** A data set has a mean that is approximately equal to the median. Ralph says the median should be used to describe the measure of center, and the quartiles should be used to describe the measure of spread. Explain his error.

4. **Communicate Precisely** Explain how to determine if the data distribution shown is skewed left, right, or is symmetric.

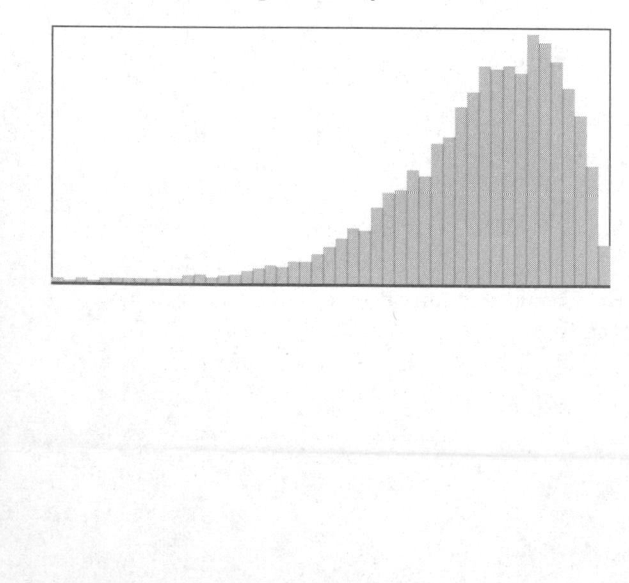

Do You KNOW HOW?

Determine the mean, standard deviation, and five-number summary of each data set. Round to the nearest hundredth, if necessary.

5. 5, 8, 5, 9, 6, 14, 9, 3, 8, 7, 10, 12

6. 10.5, 2.25, 7.75, 8.8, 3.4, 9.2, 6.5, 4.3, 3.9, 6.4

Describe the shape of the data summarized in the histograms.

7.

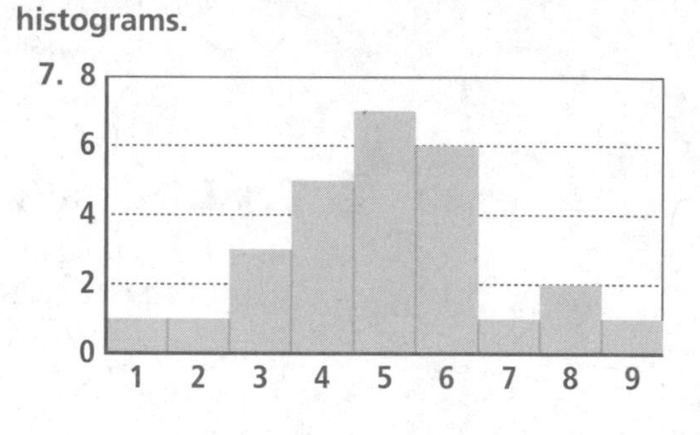

8.

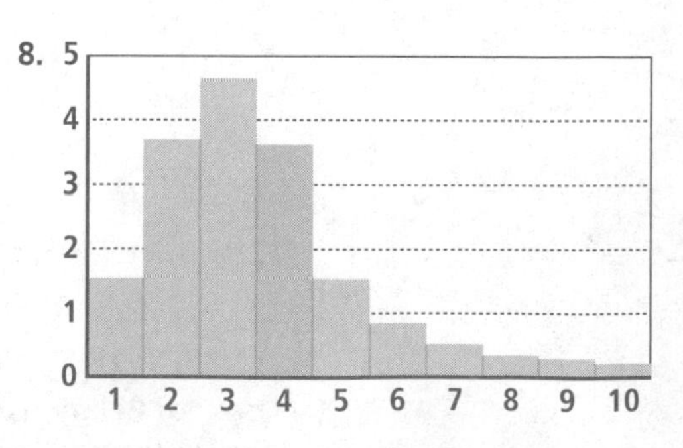

11-4 Normal Distributions

PearsonRealize.com

EXPLORE & REASON

The owner of an apple orchard and the owner of an orange grove create histograms to display fruit production data.

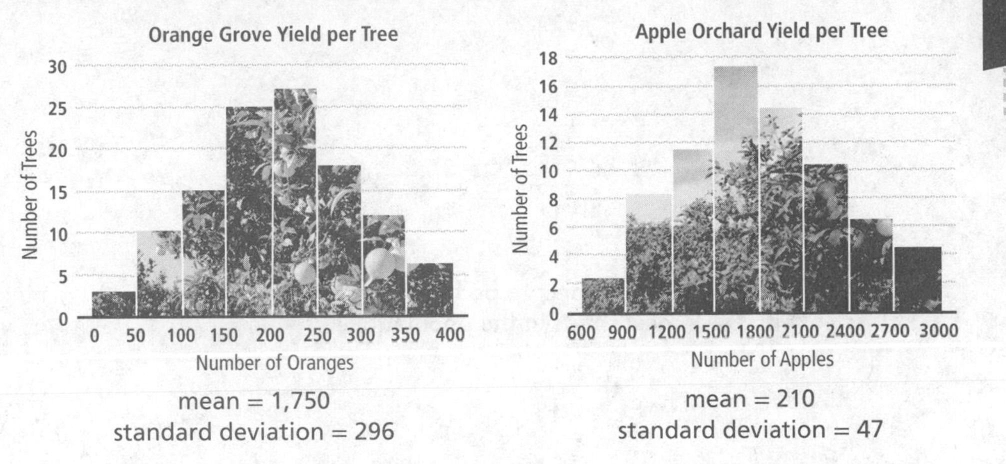

mean = 1,750
standard deviation = 296

mean = 210
standard deviation = 47

A. Describe the shape of each distribution. Discuss how the distributions are alike and how they are different.

B. Use Structure Explain how you could estimate the mean from the graphs. The standard deviation measures spread from the mean. Which data values are within a standard deviation of the mean on each graph?

HABITS OF MIND

Reason Could you calculate an exact value for the mean and standard deviation for either of the distributions? Explain.

Notes

Assess

EXAMPLE 1

Try It! Find Population Intervals

1. a. What would you expect to be the smallest and largest chest measurements of the "middle" 95% of the men?

   b. What would you expect to be the measurements of the 16% of the men with the largest chests in the population?

EXAMPLE 2

Try It! Use The Empirical Rule

2. Find the proportion of students who earned SAT Math scores in the following ranges.

   a. between 266 and 750

   b. between 266 and 629

HABITS OF MIND

Use Structure A set of data is normally distributed with a mean of 80 and a standard deviation of 10. How do you use the symmetry of the distribution to find the percentage of the values that lie between 80 and 90? Explain.

EXAMPLE 3

Try It! Compare Values Using *z*-Scores

3. How does an SAT score of 1120 compare to an ACT score of 23?

EXAMPLE 4

Try It! Use a *z*-Score to Compute Percentage

4. Find the percentage of all values in a normal distribution with $z \leq 1.85$.

HABITS OF MIND

Communicate Precisely Why is the *z*-score a good measure to use to compare data values from two different normally distributed data sets?

Do You UNDERSTAND?

1. ESSENTIAL QUESTION How can you use the normal distribution to explain where data values fall within a population?

2. **Vocabulary** Write a definition for *z-score* using your own words.

3. **Look for Relationships** Why is it useful to compare a normal distribution to the standard normal distribution?

Do You KNOW HOW?

A data set with a mean of 75 and a standard deviation of 3.8 is normally distributed.

4. What value is three standard deviations above the mean?

5. What percent of the data is from 67.4 to 82.6?

6. What is the *z*-score for a data value of 69.3?

PearsonRealize.com

MODEL & DISCUSS

With a partner or a group, toss a number cube 30 times and record the number showing on each toss.

A. Compute the means of the numbers in the first five tosses, the first ten tosses, and all thirty tosses.

B. Use Appropriate Tools Compile the results for your entire class in three sets of data: the means of the first five tosses, the means of the first ten tosses, and the means of all thirty tosses. Create a histogram for each data set.

C. Compare the histograms. Describe how the distribution of the mean changes as the number of tosses increases.

HABITS OF MIND

Generalize One group, on the first set of ten trials, got the same number five times. What does their distribution look like? How do you think their results will affect the overall distribution of the class' results?

Notes

EXAMPLE 1

Try It! Estimate a Population Parameter

1. Use the sample data to estimate the mean distance from home. Estimate the proportion of seniors to the total population at the college.

EXAMPLE 2

Try It! Make an Inference Using Multiple Samples

2. Each classmate calculates the mean distance from home in miles reported by participants. Seth and Tia create this histogram to investigate the sample statistics. How many samples reported an average distance from home between 101 and 125 mi? Use the histogram to suggest a reasonable interval to estimate the population parameter.

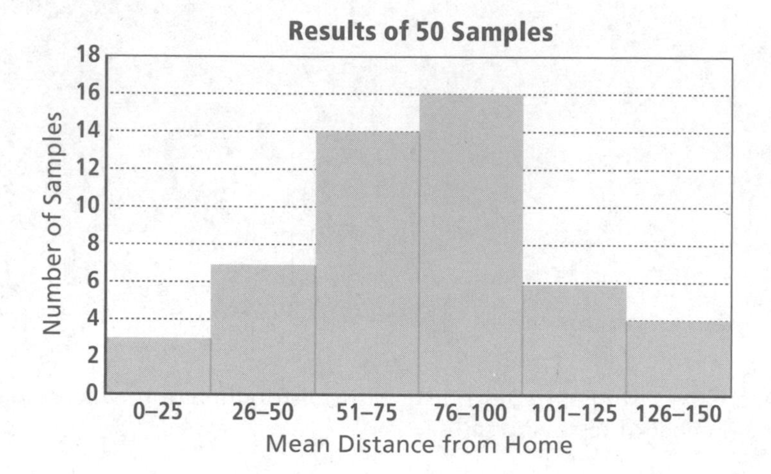

HABITS OF MIND

Look for Relationships As the number of samples increases, what is the relationship between the statistic you calculate and the population parameter?

Assess

EXAMPLE 3

Try It! Use a Simulation to Evaluate a Claim

3. How would your conclusion in Example 3 differ if you did 100 simulations of 10 shots each? How would it differ if you did 100 simulations of 1,000 shots each?

EXAMPLE 4

Try It! Use a Margin of Error for a Mean

4. A random sample of 100 Washington High seniors reveals that 40% plan to take the SAT this year. Use the margin of error to predict the actual proportion of seniors planning to take the exam.

HABITS OF MIND

Reason As the number of samples increases, what happens to the margin of error? Explain.

Do You UNDERSTAND?

1. ESSENTIAL QUESTION How can you determine how far a statistic is likely to be from a parameter?

2. **Error Analysis** In a sample of 16 students from a teacher's physical education classes, students attempted to do as many sit-ups as possible in one minute. The mean was 10 with a standard deviation of 2. The teacher said that the margin of error was $\frac{1}{4}$. What is the teacher's error?

3. **Vocabulary** Explain what a sampling distribution is in your own words.

4. **Communicate Precisely** Suppose you want to find the margin of error for a certain sample. Explain when to use the formula Margin of Error $\frac{2\sigma}{\sqrt{n}}$ and when to use the formula Margin of Error $= \frac{1}{\sqrt{n}}$.

Do You KNOW HOW?

Suppose an event occurs *x* times in a sample size of *n*. Find the sample proportion and the margin of error to the nearest percent.

5. $x = 80$ and $n = 700$

6. $x = 45$ and $n = 1{,}200$

Suppose a sample has a standard deviation of σ and a sample size of *n*. Find the margin of error to the nearest tenth.

7. $\sigma = 21.26$ and $n = 500$

8. $\sigma = 122.18$ and $n = 850$

9. **Model with Mathematics** In a sample of 400 adults, 348 have never been to Australia. Find the sample proportion for those who have never been to Australia. Write the answer as a percent.

Activity

11-6 Introduction to Hypothesis Testing

PearsonRealize.com

EXPLORE & REASON

The tables below each show the results of flipping a coin 30 times.

Coin 1					
H	H	H	H	H	T
H	T	T	H	H	T
T	T	H	H	T	H
H	H	T	T	T	H
H	T	T	H	T	H

Coin 2					
T	T	H	T	H	H
H	T	T	T	H	T
T	T	H	T	T	T
H	T	T	T	T	T
T	T	T	H	T	T

A. How many heads and how many tails resulted from flipping each coin 30 times?

B. How many heads and how many tails would you expect from flipping a fair coin 30 times? Are either of these coins close to what you would expect?

C. **Construct Arguments** Can you conclude with certainty that either of the coins is fair? Can you conclude that either of the coins is unfair?

HABITS OF MIND

Reason If you got exactly 15 heads and 15 tails, could you say for certain that the coin was fair? Explain.

Notes

Assess

EXAMPLE 1

Try It! Write Hypotheses

1. A soccer goalie saved 46.4% of her opponents' tiebreaker attempts. After her coach adjusted her position in the goal, she saved 47.3% of the attempts. Write the null hypothesis and alternative hypothesis for a statistical study to evaluate the population parameter *P*, the proportion of tiebreaker goals she saves after working with her coach.

HABITS OF MIND

Make Sense and Persevere In the Try It! problem, what are the quantities of interest? How do you know?

EXAMPLE 2

Try It! Examine Data from an Experiment

2. In one particular randomization one group has these data values:

34.1, 36.7, 35.1, 36.1, 36.8

 a. Identify the data values for the other group.

 b. Calculate the difference of the means for the two groups.

HABITS OF MIND

Look for Relationships If you perform a random resampling of the data and get a greater difference between the two new sample means, what conjecture could you make?

Notes

Assess

EXAMPLE 3 ## Try It! Use Simulation Results to Test Hypotheses

3. The fuel additive was tested again, resulting in the data displayed below. Use a simulation to randomly assign the data into two new groups. Find the difference of the means of the original sample and the new groups you just created. How do they differ? Explain what additional information you need to be able to test the hypotheses from Example 2.

Without Additive	34.1	32.8	33.8	30.9	36.7
	33.4	35.1	32.1	30.4	33.1
With Additive	34.8	35.1	32.9	35.3	36.1
	36.9	36.0	37.2	36.3	36.8

EXAMPLE 4 ## Try It! Evaluate a Report Based on Data

4. Best Bet revises their claim and now reports an average retail price of \$1.60. A second marketing study sampled 300 prices for Best Bet Mac & Cheese finding a mean price of \$1.64.

   a. What is the margin of error for the new sample?

   b. Is Best Bet's revised claim supported by this new study? Explain why or why not.

HABITS OF MIND

Make Sense and Persevere You want to determine whether the difference between sample means is due to the treatment or to natural variation. How do you do this through resampling? Through margin of error?

Assess

Do You UNDERSTAND?

1. ESSENTIAL QUESTION How do you formulate and test a hypothesis using statistics?

2. **Error Analysis** When presented with an experiment about teeth whitening strips claiming to deliver visibly whiter teeth within two weeks, Mercedes said the null hypothesis of the experiment was that the teeth would become significantly whiter after two weeks of using the whitening strips. Explain Mercedes' error.

3. **Vocabulary** Explain the difference between a *null hypothesis* and an *alternative hypothesis*.

4. **Communicate Precisely** If the null hypothesis of an experiment is H_0: $\mu \leq 10.8$, then what is the alternative hypothesis, H_a?

Do You KNOW HOW?

5. A baseball player's career batting average was .278. After working with a new coach, the player batted .315. Write the null hypothesis and alternative hypothesis for a study of the effect of the change.

6. A a lumber company claims that at least 80% of its plywood is made from recycled materials. It tests 25 pieces of the plywood and finds that the mean of the percentage of recycled material in the sample is 78%. The standard deviation of the population is 3%. Give an interval of reasonable values for the percentage of recycled material in the plywood. Is the company's claim likely true?

7. Terrence grows two varieties of tomatoes, TomTom and Hugemato. Hugemato claims to grow 10% heavier tomatoes. Find the difference of the sample means for the samples shown. Resample randomly and find the new difference of sample means. How do they compare?

TomTom	10.1	10.5	9.9	10.4	11.2
Hugemato	13.1	11	12.1	11.4	12.9

Mark and Recapture

It wouldn't take very long for you to count the number of people who live in your home or the number of socks in your drawer. How about the number of deer in Yellowstone National Park or the number of sharks in the waters around Hawaii?

The mark and recapture method is a popular way researchers can estimate an animal population. You will see an example of this method in the Mathematical Modeling in 3 Acts lesson.

ACT 1 Identify the Problem

1. What is the first question that comes to mind after watching the video?

2. Write down the Main Question you will answer.

3. Make an initial conjecture that answers this Main Question.

4. Explain how you arrived at your conjecture.

5. What information will be useful to know to answer the main question? How can you get it? How will you use that information?

Video

ACT 2 Develop a Model

6. Use the math that you have learned in the topic to refine your conjecture.

ACT 3 Interpret the Results

7. Did your refined conjecture match the actual answer exactly? If not, what might explain the difference?

EXPLORE & REASON

Allie spins the spinner and draws one card without looking. She gets a 3 on the spinner and the 3 card. Then she sets the card aside, spins again, and draws another card.

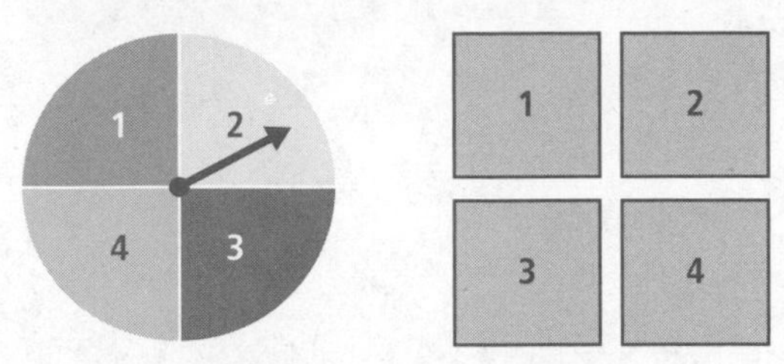

A. Is it possible for Allie to get a 3 on her second spin? On her second card? Explain.

B. **Construct Arguments** How does getting the 3 card on her first draw affect the probability of getting the 2 card on her second draw? Explain.

HABITS OF MIND

Look for Relationships How are the results from the spinner related to the results from the cards? Explain.

Notes

Assess

EXAMPLE 1

Try It! Find Probabilities of Mutually Exclusive Events

1. A box contains 100 balls. Thirty of the balls are purple and 10 are orange. If you select one of the balls at random, what is the probability of each of the following events?

   a. The ball is purple or orange.

   b. The ball is not purple and not orange.

EXAMPLE 2

Try It! Find the Probabilities of Non-Mutually Exclusive Events

2. A video game is played on a 34 cm by 20 cm rectangular computer screen. A starship is represented by two overlapping circles of radius 6 cm whose area of overlap is 20 cm^2. A black hole is equally likely to appear at any point on the screen. To the nearest whole percent, what is the probability that the point will appear within the starship?

HABITS OF MIND

Generalize Explain in your own words the meaning of mutually exclusive events. Include examples.

EXAMPLE 3

Try It! Identify Independent Events

3. There are 10 cards in a box, 5 black and 5 red. Two cards are selected from the box, one at a time.

   a. A card is chosen at random and then replaced. Another card is chosen. Does the color of the first card chosen affect the possibilities of the second card chosen? Explain.

   b. A card is chosen at random and *not* replaced. Another card is chosen. Does the color of the first card chosen affect the possibilities of the second card chosen? Explain

EXAMPLE 4

Try It! Find Probabilities of Independent Events

4. You spin the spinner two times. Assume that the probability of Blue each spin is $\frac{1}{3}$ and the probability of Orange each spin is $\frac{2}{3}$. What is the probability of getting the same color both times? Explain.

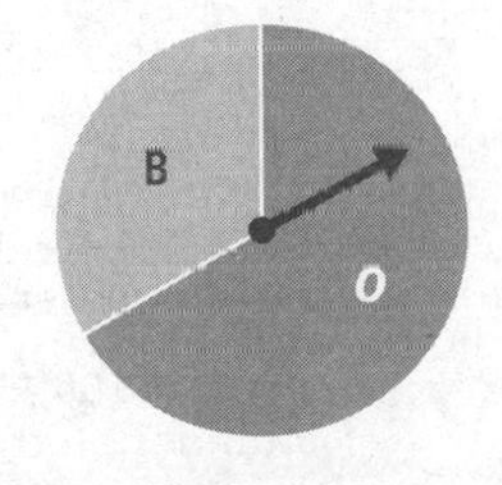

HABITS OF MIND

Make Sense and Persevere Explain the difference between mutually exclusive events and independent events.

Do You UNDERSTAND?

1. **ESSENTIAL QUESTION** How does describing events as independent or mutually exclusive affect how you find probabilities?

2. **Reason** Two marbles are chosen, one at a time, from a bag containing 6 marbles, 4 red marbles and 2 green marbles. Suppose the first marble chosen is green. Is the probability that the second marble will be red greater if the first marble is returned to the bag or if it is not returned to the bag? Explain.

3. **Error Analysis** The probability that Deshawn plays basketball (event *B*) after school is 20%. The probability that he talks to friends (event *T*) after school is 45%. He says that *P*(*B* or *T*) is 65%. Explain Deshawn's error.

4. **Vocabulary** What is the difference between mutually exclusive events and independent events?

Do You KNOW HOW?

5. A bag contains 40 marbles. Eight are green and 2 are blue. You select one marble at random. What is the probability of each event?
   a. The marble is green or blue.
   b. The marble is not green and not blue.

6. A robot at a carnival booth randomly tosses a dart at a square target with 8 inch sides and a circle with a 3 inch radius in the middle. To the nearest whole percent, what is the probability that the dart will land in the circle?

For Exercises 7 and 8, assume that you roll a standard number cube two times.

7. What is the probability of rolling an even number on the first roll and a number less than 3 on the second roll?

8. What is the probability of rolling an odd number on the first roll and a number greater than 3 on the second roll?

EXPLORE & REASON

At Central High School, 85% of all senior girls attended and 65% of all senior boys attended the Spring Dance. Of all attendees, 20% won a prize.

A. Assuming that the number of senior girls is about equal to the number of senior boys, estimate the probability that a randomly selected senior won a prize at the dance. Explain.

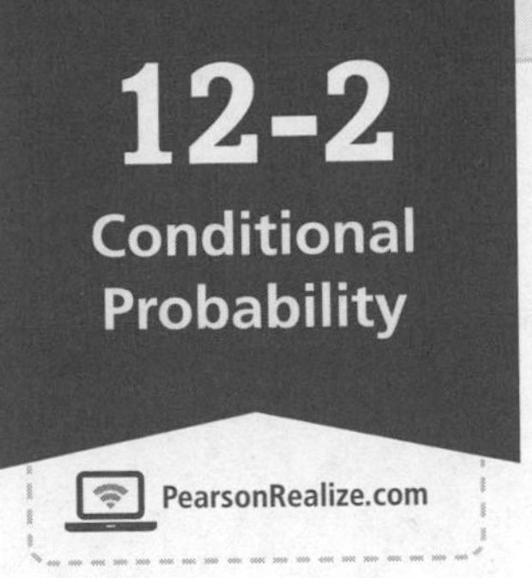

B. Construct Arguments If you knew whether the selected student was a boy or a girl, would your estimate change? Explain.

HABITS OF MIND

Look for Relationships How would the probability that a senior selected at random won a prize be different if only 60% of senior girls and 50% of senior boys attended the dance? Explain.

Assess

EXAMPLE 1

Try It! Understand Conditional Probability

1. a. What is the probability that a member of the drama club is a sophomore, $P(\text{sophomore} \mid \text{drama})$?

   b. What is the probability that a sophomore is a member of the drama club, $P(\text{drama} \mid \text{sophomore})$? Is $P(\text{sophomore} \mid \text{drama})$ the same as $P(\text{drama} \mid \text{sophomore})$? Explain

EXAMPLE 2

Try It! Use the Test for Independence

2. Let R represent "selecting a red vehicle" and C represent "selecting a car." Are the events R and C independent or dependent? Explain.

HABITS OF MIND

Make Sense and Persevere Suppose you know that events A and B are independent, and you find that $P(B \mid A) = P(A \mid B)$. What else do you know?

EXAMPLE 3

Try It! Apply the Conditional Probability Formula

3. What is the probability that a surveyed student plans to attend but is not a fan of the group?

EXAMPLE 4

Try It! Use Conditional Probability to Make a Decision

4. The marketer also has data from desktop computers. Which product is most likely to be purchased after a related search?

Computer Search and Buying Behavior (% of computer-based site visitors)

Product	Search	Search & Buy
J	35%	10%
K	28%	9%
L	26%	8%
M	24%	5%

HABITS OF MIND

Communicate Precisely Compare the formula used in Example 3, $P(A \text{ and } B) = P(A) \cdot P(B \mid A)$, to the formula used in Example 4, $P(B \mid A) = \frac{P(A \text{ and } B)}{P(A)}$. How are they related? When would you use each formula?

Do You UNDERSTAND?

1. ESSENTIAL QUESTION How are conditional probability and independence related in real-world experiments?

2. **Vocabulary** How is the sample space for $P(B \mid A)$ different from the sample space for $P(B)$?

3. **Vocabulary** Why does the definition of $P(B \mid A)$ have the condition that $P(A) \neq 0$?

4. **Use Structure** Why is $P(A) \bullet P(B \mid A) = P(B) \bullet P(A \mid B)$?

5. **Error Analysis** Taylor knows that $P(\text{red}) = 0.8$, $P(\text{blue}) = 0.2$, and $P(\text{red and blue}) = 0.05$. Explain Taylor's error.

$$P(\text{blue} \mid \text{red}) = \frac{0.05}{0.2} = 0.25$$ ✗

6. **Reason** At a sports camp, a coach wants to find the probability that a soccer player is a local camper. Because 40% of the students in the camp are local, the coach reasons that the probability is 0.4. Is his conclusion justified? Explain.

Do You KNOW HOW?

7. Let $P(A) = \frac{3}{4}$, $P(B) = \frac{2}{3}$, and $P(A \text{ and } B) = \frac{1}{6}$. Find each probability.
   a. What is $P(B \mid A)$?
   b. What is $P(A \mid B)$?

8. Students randomly generate two digits from 0 to 9 to create a number between 0 and 99. Are the events "first digit 5" and "second digit 6" independent or dependent in each case? What is $P(56)$ in each experiment?
   a. The digits may not be repeated.
   b. The digits may be repeated.

9. Suppose that you select one card at random from the set of 6 cards below.

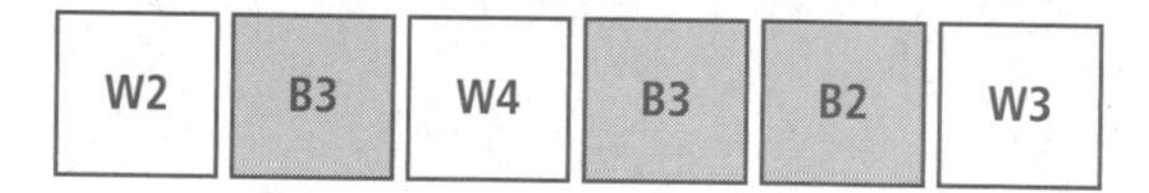

Let B represent the event "select a blue card" and T represent the event "select a card with a 3." Are B and T independent events? Explain your reasoning.

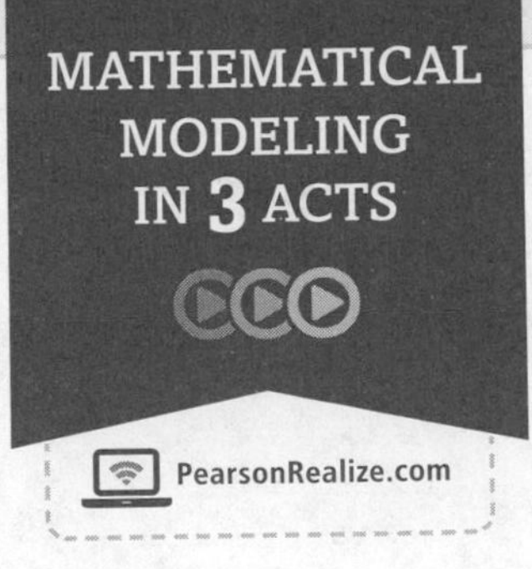

Place Your Guess

A coin toss is a popular way to decide between two options or settle a dispute. The coin toss is popular because it is a simple and unbiased way of deciding. Assuming the coin being tossed is a fair coin, both parties have an equally likely chance of winning.

What other methods could you use to decide between two choices fairly? Think about this during the Mathematical Modeling in 3 Acts lesson.

ACT 1 Identify the Problem

1. What is the first question that comes to mind after watching the video?

2. Write down the main question you will answer about what you saw in the video.

3. Make an initial conjecture that answers this main question.

4. Explain how you arrived at your conjecture.

5. What information will be useful to know to answer the main question? How can you get it? How will you use that information?

Video

ACT 2 Develop a Model

6. Use the math that you have learned in this Topic to refine your conjecture.

ACT 3 Interpret the Results

7. Did your refined conjecture match the actual answer exactly? If not, what might explain the difference?

12-3 Permutations and Combinations

PearsonRealize.com

EXPLORE & REASON

Holly, Tia, Kenji, and Nate are eligible to be officers of the Honor Society. Two of the four students will be chosen at random as president and vice-president. The table summarizes the possible outcomes.

Honor Society Officers

		Vice-President			
		Holly	Tia	Kenji	Nate
President	Holly	–	HT	HK	HN
	Tia	TH	–	TK	TN
	Kenji	KH	KT	–	KN
	Nate	NH	NT	NK	–

A. Holly wants to be an officer with her best friend Tia. How many outcomes make up this event?

B. How many outcomes show Holly as president and Tia as vice-president?

C. **Generalize** How many outcomes have only one of them as an officer? Explain.

HABITS OF MIND

Make Sense and Persevere How could you use the table to calculate the probability that both Holly and Tia will be officers?

Notes

Assess

EXAMPLE 1

Try It! Use the Fundamental Counting Principle

1. The car that Ms. Garcia is buying comes with a choice of 3 trim lines (standard, sport, or luxury), 2 types of transmission (automatic or manual), and 8 colors. How many different option packages does Ms. Garcia have to choose from? Explain.

EXAMPLE 2

Try It! Find the Number of Permutations

2. How many possible playlists are there for each situation?

   a. Gabriela's 4 favorite songs

   b. 5 of the 10 most popular songs

HABITS OF MIND

Communicate Precisely Explain how the Fundamental Counting principle can be used to find the number of ways to arrange 5 different colored beads on a string.

Notes

Assess

EXAMPLE 3

Try It! Find the Number of Combinations

3. How many ways can a camper choose 5 activities from the 10 available activities at the summer camp?

EXAMPLE 4

Try It! Use Permutations and Combinations to Find Probabilities

4. Using the data from Example 4, what is the probability that the 5 students' names end with a vowel?

HABITS OF MIND

Look for Relationships What is the relationship between ${}_{10}P_5$ and ${}_{10}C_5$? Is the number of permutations always greater than the number of combinations?

Do You UNDERSTAND?

1. ESSENTIAL QUESTION How are permutations and combinations useful when finding probabilities?

2. **Use Structure** How is the formula for a combination related to the formula for a permutation?

3. **Vocabulary** Why is it important to distinguish between a *permutation* and a *combination* when counting items?

4. **Look for Relationships** How is ${}_9C_2$ related to ${}_9C_7$? Explain. How can you generalize this observation for any values of *n* and *r*?

5. **Error Analysis** Explain Beth's error.

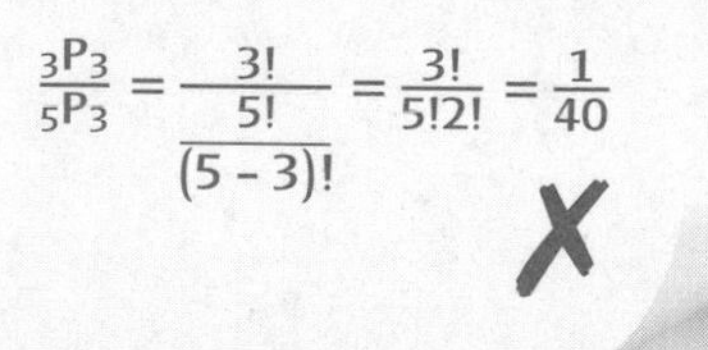

$\frac{{}_3P_3}{{}_5P_3} = \frac{3!}{\frac{5!}{(5-3)!}} = \frac{3!}{5!2!} = \frac{1}{40}$
X

6. **Construct Arguments** A company wants to form a committee of 4 people from its 12 employees. How can you use a combination to find the probability that the 4 people newest to the company will be selected?

Do You KNOW HOW?

Do the possible arrangements represent permutations or combinations?

7. Jennifer will invite 3 of her 10 friends to a concert.

8. Jennifer must decide how she and her 3 friends will sit at the concert.

Find the number of permutations.

9. How many ways can 12 runners in a race finish first, second, and third?

Find the number of combinations.

10. In how many ways can 11 contestants for an award be narrowed down to 3 finalists?

11. How many different teams of 4 people can be chosen from a group of 8 people?

Students will be chosen at random for school spirit awards. There are 6 athletes and 8 non-athletes who are eligible for 2 possible prizes. What is each probability?

12. *P*(both prizes are awarded to athletes)

13. *P*(both prizes are awarded to non-athletes)

14. *P*(no prize is awarded to an athlete)

15. *P*(no prize is awarded to a non-athlete)

16. Explain how Exercises 12 and 13 are similar to Exercises 14 and 15.

12-4 Probability Distributions

PearsonRealize.com

EXPLORE & REASON

Mr. and Mrs. Mason have three children. Assume that the probability of having a baby girl is 0.5 and the probability of having a baby boy is also 0.5.

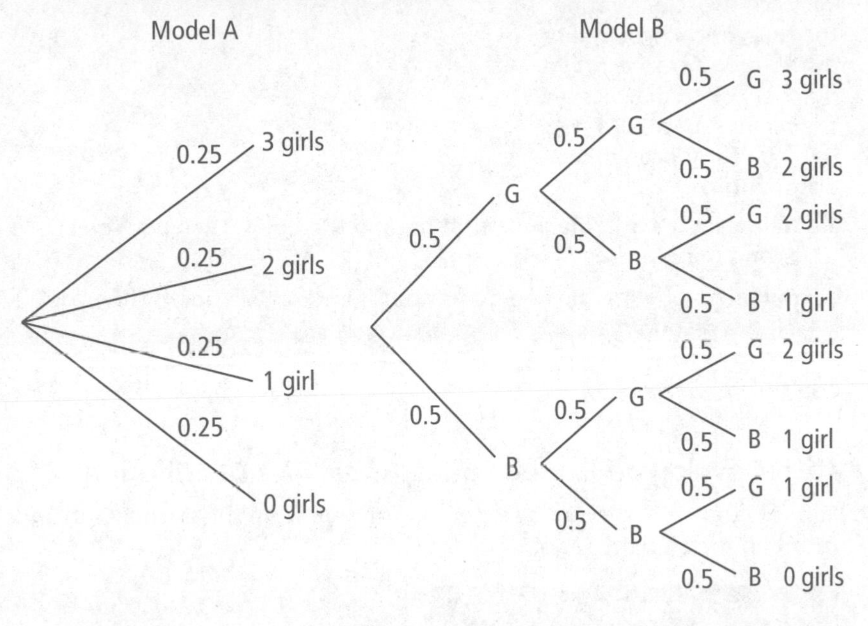

A. **Reason** Which model represents the situation correctly, Model A or Model B? Explain.

B. What is the probability that Mr. and Mrs. Mason have 3 girls?

C. Compare the probability that the Masons' first child was a boy and they then had two girls to the probability that their first two children were girls and they then had a boy. Does the order affect the probabilities? Explain.

HABITS OF MIND

Look for Relationships Which combinations of children are most common? Is one order of this combination more likely? Explain.

Assess

EXAMPLE 1

Try It! Develop a Theoretical Probability Distribution

1. You select two marbles at random from the bowl. For each situation, define the theoretical probability distribution for selecting a number of red marbles on the sample space {0, 1, 2}. Is it a uniform probability distribution?

   a. You select one marble and put it back in the bowl. Then you select a second marble.

   b. You select one marble and do not put it back in the bowl. Then you select a second marble.

EXAMPLE 2

Try It! Develop an Experimental Probability Distribution

2. Suppose that you selected a student at random from the Drama Club and recorded the student's age.

Ages of Students in Drama Club					
Age	14	15	16	17	18
Number	4	7	10	7	9

   a. Define an experimental probability distribution on the sample space {14, 15, 16, 17, 18}.

   b. Graph the probability distribution you defined.

HABITS OF MIND

Look for Relationships Compare the graph of a uniform probability distribution with the graph of a non-uniform distribution.

Notes

Assess

EXAMPLE 3

Try It! Binomial Experiments

3. Is the experiment a binomial experiment? If so, find the probability of success. Explain.

a. You select one card at random from a set of 7 cards, 4 labeled A and 3 labeled B. Then you select another card at random from the cards that remain. Success is getting a card labeled A each time.

b. You roll a standard number cube 4 times. Assume that each time you roll the number cube, each number is equally likely to come up. For each trial, success is getting an even number.

EXAMPLE 4

Try It! Probabilities in a Binomial Experiment

4. To the nearest tenth of a percent, what is the probability that Terrell has more than 3 winning cards? Explain.

HABITS OF MIND

Use Structure Explain why ${}_nC_r$ appears in the formula for the probability of a binomial experiment.

Do You UNDERSTAND?

1. ESSENTIAL QUESTION What does a probability distribution tell you about an experiment?

2. **Vocabulary** What is the difference between a binomial experiment and one that is not binomial?

3. **Error Analysis** A regular tetrahedron has four triangular sides, with one of the letters A, B, C, and D on each side. Assume that if you roll the tetrahedron, each of the letters is equally likely to end up on the bottom. {A, B, C, D} is a sample space for the experiment. Rochelle was asked to find the theoretical probability distribution for the experiment. Explain and correct the error.

$P(A) = 0.3$
$P(B) = 0.3$
$P(C) = 0.3$
$P(D) = 0.3$

✗

Do You KNOW HOW?

Graph the probability distribution *P*.

4. Theoretical probability of selecting a student at random from a group of 3 students Jack, Alani, and Seth

5. Experimental probability of flipping a fair coin 3 times and counting the number of heads. The sample space is the set of numbers 0, 1, 2, 3. $P(0) = 0.125$, $P(1) = 0.375$, $P(2) = 0.375$, $P(3) = 0.125$

A bag contains 5 balls: 3 green, 1 red, and 1 yellow. You select a ball at random 4 times, replacing the ball after each selection. Calculate the theoretical probability of each event to the nearest whole percent.

6. getting a green ball exactly 3 times

7. getting a green ball exactly 4 times

8. getting a green ball at least 3 times

9. getting a yellow ball twice

10. getting only red and green balls

Activity

12-5 Expected Value

PearsonRealize.com

EXPLORE & REASON

A company has 20 employees whose hourly wages are shown in the bar graph.

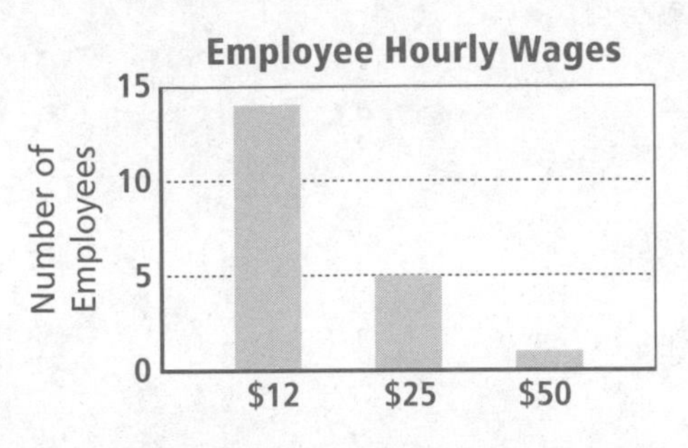

A. An employee is chosen at random. What is the probability that his or her hourly wage is \$12? \$25? \$50?

B. What is the mean hourly wage? Explain your method.

C. Construct Arguments Is the mean a good description of the typical hourly wage at this company? Explain.

HABITS OF MIND

Reasoning Compare the mean hourly wage to the median hourly wage. Which would be a more useful value to know if you want to estimate the total amount the company pays its employees? Explain.

Assess

EXAMPLE 1

Try It! Evaluate and Apply Expected Value

1. a. What would happen to the expected value if fewer people ordered chili and more people ordered stew? Explain.

b. Suppose the owner of the restaurant increased the cost of an order of stew by \$.05 and decreased the cost of an order of chili by \$.05. How would these changes affect the average value per meal?

EXAMPLE 2

Try It! Find Expected Payoffs

2. What is the expected payoff for the person making the donation?

HABITS OF MIND

Construct Arguments What happens to expected value when the value of an outcome increases while its probability decreases?

EXAMPLE 3

Try It! Use Expected Values to Evaluate Strategies

3. Latoya is considering two options for a homeowner policy. She estimates there is a 5% chance she will need home repairs costing more than $500 in any given year. Which policy has the lesser expected total cost?

Homeowner Policy Options

Option	Annual Cost ($)	Deductible ($)
A+	1400	0
Economy	1250	500

EXAMPLE 4

Try It! Use Binomial Probability to Find Expected Value

4. A carnival game has 4 orange lights and 1 green light that flash rapidly one at a time in a random order. When a player pushes a button, the game stops, leaving one light on. If the light is green, the player wins a prize. Copy and complete the table, then determine the number of prizes that a player can expect to win if the game is played 4 times.

Number of Green Lights (wins)	Probability
0	${}_4C_0(0.2)^0(0.8)^4 = ■$
1	${}_4C_{■}(0.2)^{■}(0.8)^{■} = ■$
2	${}_{■}C_{■}(0.2)^{■}(0.8)^{■} = ■$
3	${}_{■}C_{■}(0.2)^{■}(0.8)^{■} = ■$
4	${}_{■}C_{■}(0.2)^{■}(0.8)^{■} = ■$

HABITS OF MIND

Generalize When do you add expected values and when do you compare individual expected values? Explain.

Do You UNDERSTAND?

1. ESSENTIAL QUESTION What does expected value tell about situations involving probability?

2. **Error Analysis** What is Benjamin's error?

Toss a coin 10 times ✗
$E(\text{heads}) = 50\%$

3. **Construct Arguments** A carnival game costs \$1 to play. The expected payout for each play of this game is \$1.12. Should the carnival operators modify the game in way? Explain.

4. **Reason** The students in Ms. Kahn's class are raising money to help earthquake victims. They expect to raise \$0.52 for each raffle ticket they sell. If each raffle ticket is sold for \$2, what can you conclude?

5. **Vocabulary** When is the expected value of a set of items equal to the average of the items?

Do You KNOW HOW?

6. What is the expected value when rolling a standard number cube?

7. What is the expected value when rolling two standard number cubes?

8. A travel website reports that in a particular European city, the probability of rain on any day in April is 40%. What is the expected number of rainy days in this city during the month of April?

9. You buy an airplane ticket for \$900. You discover that if you cancel or rebook your vacation flight to Europe, you will be charged an extra \$300. There is a 20% chance that you will not be able to travel on that flight.

   a. What is the expected value of the ticket?

   b. Does the expected value help you make a decision to buy the ticket? Explain.

10. A child-care service charges families an hourly rate based upon the age of the child. Their hourly rate per child is \$20 per hour for infants less than 1 year old, \$18 for toddlers 1 to 3 years old, \$15 per hour children 3 or more years old. The ratio of infants : toddlers : 3+ years is 2 : 3 : 5. What is the expected charge per child per hour?

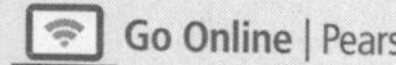

12-6 Probability and Decision Making

PearsonRealize.com

CRITIQUE & EXPLAIN

Your friend offers to play the following game with you. "If the product of the rolls of two number cubes is 10 or less, I win. If not, you win!"

A. If you were to play the game many times, what percent of games would you expect to win?

B. Is the game fair? Should you take the offer? Explain.

C. **Make Sense and Persevere** Suggest a way to change the game from fair to unfair, or vice versa, while still using the product of the two number cubes. Explain.

HABITS OF MIND

Use Structure Change the game from using products to using a different mathematical number operation. Can you make the game fair? Explain your reasoning.

EXAMPLE 1

Try It! Use Probability to Make Fair Decisions

1. Your trainer creates training programs for you. How can you use index cards to randomly choose the following: Strength training 1 day per week; Cardio training 2 days per week, with no consecutive days; Swimming 1 day per week.

EXAMPLE 2

Try It! Determine Whether a Decision Is Fair or Unfair

2. Justice and Tamika use the same 3 cards, but change the game. In each round, a player draws a card and replaces it, and then the other player draws. The differences between the two cards are used to score each round. Order matters, so the difference can be negative. Is each game fair? Explain.

   a. If the difference between the first and second cards is 2, Justice gets a point. Otherwise Tamika gets a point.

   b. Each player subtracts the other person's number from her own to find the score. They take turns drawing first, and the first person who draws keeps the score for that turn.

Assess

EXAMPLE 3

Try It! Make a Decision Based on Expected Value

3. Additional data is collected for the TAB5000 and TAB5001. The manufacturing cost and the replacement cost for the TAB5001 remain unchanged.
   a. The manufacturing cost for the TAB5000 increased by $10. What would the expected profit be for the TAB5000?
   b. The failure rate for the TAB5001 increased by 1%. What would the expected profit be for the TAB5001?
   c. As a consultant for the company, what would you recommend they do to maximize their profit?

HABITS OF MIND

Construct Arguments When do you need to compute and compare expected values instead of just comparing probabilities? Explain.

EXAMPLE 4

Try It! Use a Binomial Distribution to Make Decisions

4. A play calls for a crowd of 12 extras with non-speaking parts. Because 10% of the extras have not shown up in the past, the director selects 15 students as extras. Find the probabilities that 12 extras show up to the performance, 15 extras show up to the performance, and more than 12 extras show up to the performance.

HABITS OF MIND

Use Structure What three expressions are multiplied to find the binomial probability and what do they represent?

Do You UNDERSTAND?

1. ESSENTIAL QUESTION How can you use probability to make decisions?

2. **Reason** How can you use random numbers to simulate rolling a 6-sided number cube?

3. **Error Analysis** Explain the error in Diego's reasoning.

> If a game uses random numbers, it is always fair. ✗

4. **Use Structure** Describe what conditions are needed for a fair game.

5. **Use Appropriate Tools** Explain how you can visualize probability distributions to help you make decisions.

6. **Reason** Why must the expected value of a fair game equal zero?

Do You KNOW HOW?

7. A teacher assigns 30 students a number from 1 to 30. The teacher uses the random numbers shown to select students for presentations. Which student was selected first? second?

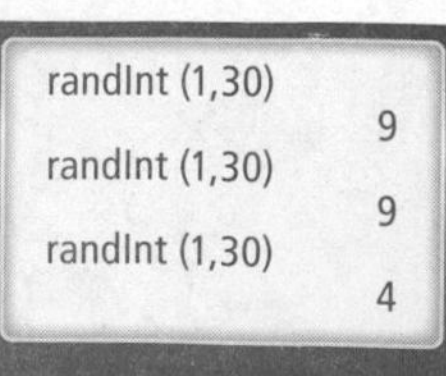

8. Three friends are at a restaurant and they all want the last slice of pizza. Identify three methods involving probability that they can use to determine who gets the last slice. Explain mathematically why each method will guarantee a fair decision.

9. Edgar rolls one number cube and Micah rolls two. If Edgar rolls a 6, he wins a prize. If Micah rolls a sum of 7, she gets a prize. Is this game fair? Explain.

10. The 10 parking spaces in the first row of the parking lot are reserved for the 12 members of the Student Council. Ten percent of Student Council members usually do not drive to school dances. What is the probability that more members of the Student Council will drive to a dance than there are reserved parking spaces?